Praise for this book

Essential contribution to understanding the cultural diversity in our cosmopolitan world

Jorge Enrique Gonzalez, Ph.D, the UNESCO Chair on Intercultural Dialogue of the National University of Colombia

This carefully curated edited volume by Darla K. Deardorff and Mizuho Tatebayashi offers a timely and invaluable exploration of evolving intercultural and global competence in our complex, tension-ridden world. By bringing together captivating case studies from Algeria and Latin America, as well as pioneering frameworks for transcultural education and innovative practices in virtual and healthcare realms, this book is an absolute must-read for scholars, practitioners, and students hungry for transformative insights to help them reframe their own points of contact and exchange into valuable world-making practices.

Jieyoung Kong, Ph.D., Associate Professor, Graduate Program Coordinator, School of Media & Communication, Western Kentucky University, USA

Intercultural competence is the need of the global village, STILL (!) embroiled in wars and posturing by nation states, and this volume sets the research agenda for the next decade, and more.

Dharm P S Bhawuk, University of Hawai'i at Mānoa, USA

In an area dominated by Eurocentric perspectives, this collection offers an excellent set of studies and essays on intercultural communication competence originating from many corners of the global context. Deardorff and Tatebayashi bring their considerable expertise to bear with highly accessible curated contributions by scholar-members of the World Council on Intercultural and Global Competence. Their investigations span the important intersections of intercultural communication competence, education, health care, human resources, and assessment. It provides a useful resource for those who want to see where we've been, where we are, and where we can be going.

Brian H. Spitzberg, Ph.D., Senate Distinguished Professor Emeritus, School of Communication, San Diego State University

A must read for anyone interested in improving communication across cultures and a timely addition to our understanding of the complex nature of identity, culture, and human interactions in a constantly changing global knowledge economy.

Peter O. Nwosu, Professor of Communication Studies & President, State University of New York at Oswego, USA

I fully support the book's global perspectives on transformative journeys and reflective cultural explorations to help overcome challenges in intercultural communication, to promote resilience and to celebrate diversity.

Ildikó Lázár, Associate professor, Department of English Language Pedagogy, Eötvös Loránd University, Budapest

Current Perspectives on Intercultural and Global Competence

Darla K. Deardorff, Mizuho Tatebayashi

STAR SCHOLARS PRESS

First Published 2024
by
STAR SCHOLARS PRESS
Baltimore, Maryland (US)

Category
Education/Higher Education

Series Editor: Krishna Bista
Comparative and International Education

Volume Editors
Darla K. Deardorff
Mizuho Tatebayashi

ISBN: 978-1-957480-39-8

President: Dr Uttam Gaulee, STAR Scholars Network, US
Director of Book Publications: Dr. Roy Y. Chan, Lee University, US
Director of Digital Production: Dr. Sahar Aghasafari, University of South Carolina, US
Director of Global Essay Project: Dr. Franca Nwankwo, Morgan State University, US
Director of Open Access: Dr. Sharif Uddin, Morgan State University, US
Managing Director: Dr. Chinwe Ihoma, Morgan State University, US
Associate Director: Dr. Patricia Timmons, Harvard University, US
Production Director: Rajendra Bista, STAR Scholars Network, US
Grants and Awards Director: Tina Pandey, STAR Scholars Network, US
Coordinator of Awards & Contracts: Dr. Fatima Babih, STAR Scholars Network, US

Subject: Education/Higher Education – United States

Library of Congress
US Programs, Law, and Literature Division
Cataloging in Publication Program
101 Independence Avenue, S.E.
Washington, DC 20540-4283

Printed in the United States of America
Typsett: GM Solutions
Cover Design: Christon Stewart

press.starscholars.org

About the Book

Current Perspectives on Intercultural and Global Competence

This book represents collective endeavors of experienced scholars, practitioners and students from around the world, to enhance and expand knowledge and understanding of the critical concept of intercultural and global competence emerging from insightful dialogues and work between members of the World Council on Intercultural and Global Competence, a global NGO.

Current Perspectives on Intercultural and Global Competence offers a compelling exploration of the evolving landscape of intercultural and global competence through a variety of lenses. This insightful book delves into the complexities of navigating the practical implications of getting along together across difference and similarity. With collective contributions from scholars and practitioners worldwide, this book presents a diverse array of perspectives from different disciplines, contexts, languages, and cultures. Through rich discussion and insights, contributors to this book invite readers to engage in delving further into the complexities of the crucial understanding needed to thrive in today's interconnected and yet often polarized world.

Editors

Dr. Darla K. Deardorff is Founding President of the World Council on Intercultural and Global Competence. She is also the UNESCO Chair on Intercultural Competence at Stellenbosch University (South Africa) as well as appointed faculty at other universities in Japan, China, the US and Canada. She has worked in the international education field for thirty years and is the author/editor of 14 books and over 60 other publications including the seminal work on intercultural competence, Sage Handbook of Intercultural Competence as well as the open access UNESCO Manual on Developing Intercultural Competence: Story Circles. Regularly invited to speak around the world, she is working on the intersections of intercultural competence with peacebuilding, gender equality and climate action.

Mizuho Tatebayashi, a Japanese scholar-practitioner, who is enthusiastic about intercultural communication and international education. Her roots lie in Japan, yet she had the privilege to explore outside the country during her undergraduate years, where she discovered the transformative power of cross-cultural experiences. As a doctoral student in North Carolina State University's Educational Psychology program, her focus centers on the development of intercultural competence and fostering enriching learning environments. She currently serves as an Executive Fellow at the World Council on Intercultural and Global Competence.

New Titles

*Bridging Cultures, Empowering Futures: Global Citizenship and International Education*Rethinking Hybrid and Remote Work in Higher Education*
Online Teaching and Learning in Asian Higher Education
Transforming Lives at the Institutional Level: Equity Promotion Initiatives Across the World
Making Learning Happen: Five Shifts Toward Student-Focused Education
Curriculum Theory and Pedagogy for Student Mobility: Research and Practice in International Higher Education
International Graduate and Doctoral Student Experience: Navigating Relationships, Resources, and Resilience
International Student Identities and Mental Well-Being
Faculty Engagement and Internationalization at Home in Iceland
Institutional Commitment to Global Engagement
Shaping a Humane World Through Global Higher Education: Pre-Challenges and Post-Opportunities During a Pandemic
Home and Abroad: International Student Experiences and Graduate Employability
Global Higher Education During COVID-19: Policy, Society, and Technology

https://press.starscholars.org/

This publication was made possible through the
generous support of
the Humane Letters Grant.

Contents

Foreword

As an international educator following the scholarship of Darla K. Deardorff, it is both a privilege and a profound responsibility to introduce "Current Perspectives on Intercultural and Global Competence," masterfully compiled by Darla K. Deardorff and Mizuho Tatebayashi. This seminal collection arrives at a pivotal moment in our history, echoing the visionary insights of Yuval Noah Harari in "Homo Deus," where he envisages humanity's future as self-made gods of planet Earth.

Harari challenges us to consider what destinies we shall set for ourselves and which quests we will undertake as we possess the capabilities to rein in famine, plague, and war. It is in this context that "Current Perspectives on Intercultural and Global Competence" becomes not just timely but urgent. It provides the 'secret sauce'—the crucial skills and understandings needed to manage and utilize our godlike powers responsibly. As we harness these abilities, intercultural competence ensures that our global interactions are marked by empathy and understanding rather than conflict and alienation.

Martin Luther King Jr.'s profound declaration that "We must learn to live together as brothers or perish together as fools," resonates deeply with the mission of this book. The work by Deardorff and Tatebayashi is a toolkit for navigating a future where global cooperation and cultural empathy are not optional but essential for survival and prosperity. This book empowers us to forge connections that transcend cultural and geographical boundaries, encouraging a collective approach to solving our interconnected world's multifaceted challenges.

The contributors to this volume bring diverse and powerful insights from their extensive research and practice worldwide. From exploring intercultural competence at the intersection of diverse cultural knowledge to developing skills that advance global goals, each chapter contributes to a holistic understanding of our potential as a global community.

Furthermore, this book's accessibility as an open-access publication underscores our commitment to inclusivity and the widespread dissemination of knowledge. It invites readers from all walks of life to engage with these ideas, participate in this crucial dialogue, and apply these lessons in varied contexts.

In embracing the perspectives and tools presented in this book, we step closer to realizing Harari's vision of *Homo Deus,* where our future as custodians of this planet hinges on our ability not only to coexist but to thrive together in understanding and respect. "Current Perspectives on Intercultural and Global Competence" is an indispensable guide for all who are committed to this journey towards a more equitable, peaceful, and sustainable world.

I am excited about this book's transformative potential and recommend it wholeheartedly to educators, policymakers, students, and anyone interested in the profound work of building a better future for humanity. This is our call to action: to learn, reflect, and embrace the intercultural competences necessary for us to truly prosper as the stewards of our world.

Uttam Gaulee, Ph.D.
Professor of Higher Education, Morgan State University
President, STAR Scholars Network

Acknowledgements

This book is the result of much hard work and collaboration among working group members in the World Council on Intercultural and Global Competence. Collaborating across languages, cultures, and yes, time zones, is "the norm" for working group members. This resulting text is strong evidence that intercultural and global competence - among working groups, teams and individuals - can indeed lead to greater insights and learnings. Deep appreciation is expressed to all those who contributed to making this volume possible.

We are indebted to the Humane Letters Grant Committee and external reviewers for their critical support, without which this project would not have reached completion.

We also recognize the following individuals for their roles in bringing this book to publication: Director of Book Publications: Dr. Roy Y. Chan, Lee University; Director of Communications: Dr. Bo Zhang, University of Hartford; Director of Digital Production: Dr. Sahar Aghasafari, University of South Carolina; Managing Director: Chinwe Ihoma, Morgan State University; Associate Director: Patricia Timmons, Harvard University; Production Director and Reference Checker: Rajendra Bista, STAR Scholars Network; and Grants and Awards Director: Tina Pandey, STAR Scholars Network, US and Dr. Fatima Babih, Coordinator of Awards & Contracts, STAR Scholars Network, US.

Introduction

The Context

"We must learn to live together as brothers or perish together as fools." These are the words of Martin Luther King Jr which are more prescient now than ever. With planetary devastation and human destruction wrought through wars, intercultural and global competence is urgently needed to bridge divides and facilitate humans working together to address global challenges that confront all of us as humans. While academics have debated and discussed concepts of intercultural and global competence (with the myriad related terminology) for over 70 years, much of that discussion has occurred predominantly in the Global North, given existing systems of power and even oppression, excluding many voices and perspectives. Given that the one key component necessary in this construct is that of seeing from others' perspectives (Deardorff, 2020), it behooves practitioners and scholars alike to continue to seek out varied perspectives. And regardless, in the end, it is about how humans can connect and understand each other better. Indeed, some may say that it goes beyond connection and understanding, to even loving our neighbor, locally and globally - to what Martin Luther King Jr saw as living together in Beloved Community with each other. This text, collectively written by both practitioners and scholars from around the world, is the result of coming together in community to further explore perspectives, recognizing that there are many perspectives and truths that exist.

The collective contributors of this volume are all members of the World Council on Intercultural and Global Competence, a global nonprofit non-governmental organization comprised of dedicated researchers, scholars, practitioners, students, and policymakers from all around the globe. The purpose of the World Council is to bring all of these constituencies together across languages, cultures, disciplines and sectors to learn from and with each other in advancing the praxis of intercultural and global competence around the world, in order to build a better world together. The World Council accomplishes these connections primarily through working groups on various topics related to intercultural and global competence. Membership in the World Council is intentionally kept free and accessible to all and at the publishing of this book, World Council has over 4000 in its membership from all over the world with less than half being in North America. Members interact and connect with each other through World Council's Workplace, where there are 20+ working groups in which anyone can engage and contribute. (To join the World Council, simply go to www.iccglobal.org and complete the brief online form to be sent an invite link to World Council's Workplace.)

This book is an ideal illustration of how these connections made through the World Council working groups can come to fruition for the betterment of us all. Each of the chapters represent the collaboration of those within working groups, learning from and with each other from many places around the world through various disciplines and languages. These chapters demonstrate results of intercultural collaboration of practitioners, students, and researchers. The purpose of this book is to share these collaborative learnings with a broader audience interested in these key topics so as to further discussions in these areas and beyond. This landmark publication of the World Council is intentionally published as open access so that all may be part of these continued discussions.

Book Overview

This comprehensive book is structured into three sections with a total eight chapters that provide deep insights into various aspects of intercultural competence development and practice, followed by three appendices which offer practical examples and explorations in specific contexts. The first section, Regional Perspectives on Intercultural and Global Competence, provides detailed explorations of intercultural competence development in multiple global regions, offering insights into the unique challenges, opportunities, and assessment methodologies. The three chapters in this section—"Intercultural Competence at the Intersection of Euro American and Islamic ways of knowing: Algeria a Case Study," "Exploring Intercultural Competence and Interculturality in Latin America's Higher Education: Four Case Studies," and "The Practice of Assessing Intercultural Competence – A Preliminary Global Study"— collectively lay the foundation for a deeper understanding of how diverse regions approach and cultivate intercultural competence. They provide a holistic view that informs the broader discourse on effective strategies and practices for navigating cultural diversity.

The Emerging Perspectives section, comprising "Underrepresented Voices in Intercultural Competence Scholarship: Exploratory Analysis of an Annotated Bibliography" and "Transcultural Education - A Framework for Supporting Students to Develop Commonalities in Cultural Complexity," critically examines both intercultural competence research and educational practices. The former chapter assesses the landscape of underrepresented voices in intercultural research, offering an annotated bibliography with 126 entries and recommendations for amplifying these voices. Meanwhile, the latter introduces a transformative approach aligned with UNESCO's 2021 proposal, providing educators with a framework for designing transcultural learning in higher education.

The third section, Practice Perspectives, delves into various applications of intercultural competence, offering practical insights and tips for educators and trainers in the field. "Virtual Exchanges: Experiences with 'Invisible Assumptions'" offers key recommendations for equitable North-South partnerships in Virtual Exchange/COIL, emphasizing underrepresented voices from the South. "Developing Intercultural Skills to Advance the United Nations' Sustainable Development Goals (UN's SDGs)" demonstrates the intentional inclusion of intercultural skills education through global case studies, illustrating their crucial role in addressing challenges outlined by the United Nations' Sustainable Development Goals. Meanwhile, "Challenges educators face facilitating intercultural competence in healthcare." delves into the significance of intercultural competence in healthcare, addressing challenges and introducing the profile of an intercultural nurse educator.

The three appendices of the book serve as practical examples or explorations of intercultural and global competence development in specific contexts. Appendix 1 thoroughly illustrates two Circle methodologies, the Global Intercultural Circle (GIC), and UNESCO Story Circles, which is featured in the World Council. The GIC is a community group addressing the challenge of engaging effectively with culturally different individuals. GIC employs diverse practices, from group gatherings to storytelling and culinary arts, aiming to enhance intercultural understanding and navigate conflicts constructively. UNESCO Story Circles is a structured yet adaptable methodology that has been successfully piloted by UNESCO in a variety of settings and contexts around the world and is used for the purpose of developing and practicing key intercultural competencies. Appendix 2 reports on a study in Brazilian higher education, investigating how internationalization impacts students' intercultural competence. Using a Mixed Methods Explanatory Sequential Study, the research provides the first local definitions of intercultural competence and interculturality, collectively constructed from participant feedback. Appendix 3 explores Japan's integration of intercultural competence with global human resources for economic objectives. It traces how the role of intercultural competence evolved alongside Japan's international relations, emphasizing higher education's role and addressing challenges to the development of intercultural competence in the Japanese context.

Through this rich exploration of perspectives on intercultural and global competence, the reader can grasp the immense complexities and challenges inherent in human connection and interaction. Given the current state of societies around the world, there is much work yet to do. The perspectives offered in this volume are one step toward building a better world together.

STARSCHOLARS
NETWORK

STAR
GLOBAL
Conference
KATHMANDU, NEPAL
VIRTUAL
DEC 8-11, 2024
IN-PERSON
DEC 12-14, 2024

Hosted by
KATHMANDU UNIVERSITY

Intercultural Competence at the Intersection of Euro American and Islamic Ways of Knowing

Algeria a Case Study

Yovana S. Veerasamy, PhD
Stony Brook University, United States of America

Lamia Nemouchi, PhD
De Montfort University, United Kingdom

Hadjer Hammadi, M.A.
University of Limerick, Ireland

ABSTRACT

Including intercultural competence (ICC) in curriculum is a meaningful step towards bridging differences and enhancing understanding across cultures. In this study we explore: Which ICC models are used within higher educational institutions in the Middle East and North Africa (MENA) region? Although culturally, ethnically and religiously heterogeneous, the region is predominantly Islamic. Using qualitative research methods we collected and analyzed documents on dominant ICC models used in the region and gave special attention to the use of ICC in foreign language training in Algeria. Western models of ICC dominate scholarship in the region, yet Islam, has its own teachings on what western cultures term ICC. Based on our findings, we advocate adopting fused models of ICC. Fusing western ICC models with Islamic ICC principles offers a decolonial approach to include perspectives marginalized by western epistemology to reflect cognitive and epistemic justice.

Keywords: Algeria, cognitive justice, intercultural competence, Islam, MENA region

INTRODUCTION

The Middle East and North Africa (MENA) region is a geographical location which encompasses Middle East and North African countries (OECD, 2022). The region is also known as the Arab world or the Middle East, namely the transcontinental area between Southwest Asia and North Africa (World Atlas, 2022). The geographic span of MENA includes 19 individual nation states: Algeria, Bahrain, Egypt, Iran, Iraq, Israel, Jordan, Kuwait, Lebanon, Libya, Morocco, Oman, Palestine, Qatar, Saudi Arabia, Syria, Tunisia, United Arab Emirates, and Yemen (World Atlas, 2022). Also, definitions of MENA countries vary, as such, the geographical region has been extended to include Muslim nations such as Afghanistan and Pakistan and even Cyprus (World Atlas, 2022). On the whole, the MENA region represents 6% of the world's population where the dominant language spoken is Arabic and at least 94% of inhabitants are Muslims (Pew Center 2015). Israel stands as an exception to this generality where Hebrew is the dominant language and Judaism the dominant religion. Other religions from the region include various Christian denominations (Roman Catholic, Coptic, Maronite, Orthodox, Protestant), Druze, Samaritans, Mandaeans, Yezidis, Zoroastrians (Rogan, 2009; Weitz, 2015). Waves of migrant workers in the 21st century have added Hinduism and Buddhism to the religious composition of the region (Pew Center, 2015).

Existing nation states within the MENA region were largely carved by former western colonial nation states. During the 19th and 20th century, dominant western European powers such as Britain, France and Italy sliced up former Islamic Ottoman Empire territories to create individual nation states based on European notions of statehood (Rogan, 2009). In the process, Europeans regrouped diverse ethnic groups for example Arab, Turk, Azerbaijanis, Persian, Kurd, Armenian, Berber, Copt, Nawar, Zazas and more with different religious beliefs and wider historical heritages under individual MENA nation states; also leaving their own individual cultural imprints upon this mixture of new nations (Rogan 2009; Weitz, 2015). By nature therefore most MENA countries are culturally diverse, and exist in a cross-cultural reality.

Although a controversial construct, in western scholarship, intercultural communication competence has been deemed to assist with navigating cross-cultural realities. Deardorff (2006) asserts that many terms are used to mean cross-cultural competence. The scholar uses the term intercultural competence (ICC) which she defines as "the ability to communicate effectively and appropriately in intercultural situations based on one's intercultural knowledge, skills, and attitudes" (Deardorff, 2004, p. 194). Deardorff (2006) further asserts that ICC, is a competence that can be learned and developed over time and which helps with understanding one's own culture. In this study, we use the term intercultural competence (ICC) to denote intercultural communication competence and cross-cultural competence. When looking at the MENA region, Raddawi (2015) recognizes the importance of ICC in the modern world, be it in the context of globalization or as a result of geopolitical scuffles or terrorist activities. Speaking of the Arab peoples, the scholar calls for better understanding of and between this diverse group of peoples, namely the largest ethnic group within the MENA region.

Finally, lingering effects of colonialism still persist in the region, and in Algeria, the largest and one of the most populous MENA nations, the effects of colonialism are particularly evident in the education system regardless of its historical penchant for Islam (Nemouchi, 2022; Calafell, 2020; Rogan 2009). Against such a complex backdrop, Zaharna (2009) has called for adopting innovative approaches to the study of ICC in the region. In this vein, to understand the ICC space in the region, it is imperative to identify ICC models utilized to foster intercultural interactions within and with the region. Also, identifying the source of ICC principles which are embedded within educational offerings in the region is pertinent. Adopting a novel approach to the study of intercultural competence, we explore: Which ICC models are used within higher educational institutions in the MENA region? Do they emanate from the west, from Islam, or from both? If from both, how does this unfold on the ground? Drawing on excluded cultural dynamics which remain on the periphery of western centric academia, this study shares data to broaden ICC literature.

LITERATURE REVIEW

According to Sastry and Ramasubramanian (2020), intercultural communication is dominated by Euro American perceptions. And Guilherme (2019) positions the absence of non-western ways of knowing and doing in the context of global cognitive and epistemic justice. For R'boul (2022) "non-western ways of knowing are not visible in the foundational scholarship of [intercultural]communication research" (p.76). Within the context of western cognitive universality, Arasaratnam (as cited in Alexander et al., 2014) notes that few privileged non-westerners are ever heard. Driven by the reality that excluding the ways of knowing of non-westerners is anathema to an academic discipline which seeks to include perspectives from world cultures to promote respect and understanding, there is a call to encourage non-western, non-white/ euro-centric or decolonial approaches to the study of ICC to include previously excluded perspectives (Dutta, 2020).

In the context of globalization, Raddawi (2015) states that ICC is a vital competence in the modern world. Admitting that as an academic discipline ICC emerged in the US in the 1960s, proliferated in Europe in the 1990s, Raddawi states that ICC is scarcely offered in MENA countries especially from the perspective of the region. Placing the MENA region in the socio-economic locality of the "Global South" (RGS, n.d.), it becomes vital to de-Westernize knowledge production in the region and develop frameworks to reflect its local cultural context (Alahmed, 2020). During this process, scholars who advocate for decolonial or postcolonial approaches warn against using binary approaches. They recommend embracing plurality to reflect diversity, while keeping in mind the distinct make-up and colonial histories of the region (Shome, 2019).

The cultural context of MENA countries is diverse and the region is heavily influenced by Islam due to Saudi Arabia being the birthplace of Islam. Nemouchi (2022), points out that Islam, has its own teachings on ICC. Islamic principles of ICC, emanate from the Quran to include concepts of anti- discrimination, equality and human dignity (Loi d'Orientation sur L'Education Nationale, 2008, p.11). Yet some scholars in the region warn against including ICC in educational offerings in fear of imposing "cultural violence" (our own translation from Arabic) through "acculturation" (our own translation from Arabic) while propagating ideas from the "Global North", especially under the guise of globalization (Bouali, 2008, p. 243-244). To include discourse on ICC from non-western and non-Euro perspectives, this study looks at intercultural competence models and principles utilized in curricula in the MENA region; discusses Islamic principles of ICC and analyzes ICC models utilized in Algerian public education offerings to offer practical context.

RESEARCH METHOD

We used combined qualitative research designs to collect and analyze data. First, we searched for publicly available documents (Merriam, 1998; Krippendorff,

2013); this allowed us to identify dominant ICC models and principles utilized in MENA countries in general. The selected documents for this study included three doctoral dissertations, 27 scholarly articles and chapters on ICC and education policy documents. Second, we analyzed ICC models used in the context of English language instruction in public higher education institutions in Algeria. We selected Algeria to explore dominant ICC models further because it is the largest and most populous country in the MENA region, and it is an Islamic state. According to Yin (2003), a single case study can be used to explore a phenomenon - here ICC models used in English language instruction. English instruction provided the context for analysis, as ICC models have long been associated with foreign/second language instruction (Borguetti, 2017). We coded the data, sorted and arranged the codes under themes to report our findings (Creswell, 2013). Under the final theme *ICC used in English Instruction* we report on Algeria specifically and in detail. Recurring discussions and rearranging of our data allowed us to cross-verify our analysis allowing for triangulation and validation.

Participants

Document analysis covered 13 MENA countries: Algeria, Egypt, Iraq, Israel, Jordan, Lebanon, Oman, Palestine, Saudi Arabia, Tunisia, Qatar, United Arab Emirates, Yemen. We looked at Algeria as a single case study.

RESULTS

We report our findings on the MENA region under three themes and share in depth analysis on Algeria.

ICC in HEIs in the MENA region

According to Alkharusi (2018), ICC is not commonly offered in academia in the MENA region and if it is offered, higher education institutions (HEIs) rely on western models of ICC. In his research on intercultural communication, a discipline that has traditionally been used to teach ICC in the region, the scholar notes that in recent years Middle Eastern universities have started offering ICC courses but has been largely limited to a few institutions such as:

> Cairo University [in Egypt], the Arab American University of Jenin in Palestine, the American University of Sharjah, the American University in Dubai, Zayed University in United Arab Emirates, King Saud University in Saudi Arabia, Qatar University,

Lebanese University, American University of Beirut (AUB), and
Sana'a University (Yemen) (Alkharusi,2018, p.2)

Yet, the scholar points out that HEIs in the MENA region " teach world
culture, culture from a critical perspective, human interaction and behavior,
communications, and international relations" (Alkharusi, 2018, p.3). These have
typically been "offered by Cairo University, Ahram Canadian University in
Egypt, Sana'a University in Yemen, Middle East University Jordan, Al-Iraqiyah
University, Zayed University, and Bayan College in Oman" (Alkharusi,
2018,p.3). However, since 2014, the Arab American University of Jenin in
Palestine has been offering a master's degree in literature and intercultural
communication(Alkharusi, 2018).

Models of ICC used in the MENA region

Analysis of ICC in the region relies on western models, regardless of the scholar's
ethnic background. For example, when looking at HEIs in Saudi Arabia, Karolak
and Guta (2015) state that the MENA nation prefers to adopt American
models of HEIs and relies on non-Saudi faculty members for instruction. When
exploring how female students interact with professors at one such university,
to assess the cultural influences on cross-cultural communication between Saudi
students and foreign professors from the students' point of view, the scholars used
Hofstede's (2001) five-dimensional model. In 2015, Harkness looked at sectarian
conflict between Kurdish and Iraqi students in Iraq and his definitions and
explanations of culture, ethnicity and identity were rooted in western scholarship,
namely in the work of Rodriguez et al. (2010). Analyzing how time is treated
during meetings as part of organizational structure in UAE, Kemp (2015), relied
on Hall's (1981) theory of time stating that monochronicity is associated with
Western culture, and polychronicity with Arab culture.

On a quest to understand how internationalization shapes cosmopolitan
citizenship, Yemini (2014) looked at internationalization as a tool to provide
youth with "cosmopolitan capital" at Palestinian-Arab high schools that serve
minorities in the Israeli education system. In her study, the scholar relied
on western scholarship to analyze the internationalization process. Using
Knight's (2004) model she concluded that internationalization as a process,
which helps develop cosmopolitan students, is viewed differently within the
Palestinian-Arab schools understudy; reflecting the complex and divided nature
of the country. Similarly, drawing on western concepts, Miettinen et al. (2018)
used a comparative lens to look at ICC within music teacher programs at Israeli

and Finnish HEIs. Relying on western scholarship from MacPherson(2010) and Deardorff (2006), the scholars stated in part that their study showed "how the execution of teachers' intercultural competences and skills might be hampered if the students are reluctant to engage in learning that goes beyond their cultural or religious beliefs" (Miettinen et al. 2018, p.83). This remains an ethical question that teachers need to consider carefully in order to avoid imposing values on their learners that contradict their cultural values, especially considering the power dimension that exists between teachers and students during the teaching/learning process. For some participants in the study, this was "their first opportunity to discuss diversity and interculturality in music teacher education with their colleagues" (p.83). As such, participants called for continued discussions to further address intercultural issues in music teacher education.

ICC used in English Instruction

Analysis of English language instruction in the region reveals that scholarship relies on western models to discuss ICC in programs. For example, in 2012, Salem undertook a doctoral study based on action research to look at English language instruction in Lebanon. Salem addresses action research, and the starting point of her work is western centric. The predominant ICC models relied upon by Salem were Byram's (1997) and Holliday et al.'s (2004) model. Daraiseh (2018) evaluated intercultural competence among undergraduate students enrolled in English language at Yarmouk University in Jordan; the scholar relied heavily on western definitions of culture and ICC to showcase that the cultural context of language matters noting that educators remove what they perceive as culturally inappropriate from English text books:

> The textbooks are designed by the faculty members (Jordanians) of the Language Center of Yarmouk University, who are significantly attempting to delete all cultural aspects which do not fit with Jordanian culture. It is assumed that these inputs may affect the students' English language as an output (Daraiseh,2018, p.504).

Analyzing textbooks and curricula, Hermessi (2017) investigated the cultural dimension of English education in Tunisia including how ICC is taught. His analysis relied on western scholarship, namely: Joiner (1974); Sheldon (1988); the "National Standards in Foreign Language Education Project" (1996) and Moran (2001). Concluding on his investigation of the place of culture in English education, Hermessi stated that: "Tunisian language policy-makers, do not have any ideologically-motivated or religiously-driven a priori objections to the consideration of culture in English education" (2017, p.217). And, the author states that there is no clear theoretical or pedagogical frame of reference for teaching culture in Tunisian schools.

In her doctoral study on English language instruction and ICC in Algeria, Nemouchi (2022) uses Byram's (1997/2021) model as a starting point for her analysis. Over the years, scholars have pointed to tensions with using western based models of ICC in Algeria and in response, Nemouchi looked at *Ijtihad*, an Islamic concept of ICC. Taking a critical stance, she acknowledges the different and complex perceptions of ICC in the context of Algeria (encouraging vs. resisting ICC) as they exist throughout the Arabophone, Francophone and Anglophone Algerian literature and concludes that there is space for ICC in English language instruction when the teaching objectives include knowledge, skills and attitudes with a specific focus on 'criticality' in order to avoid the imposition of 'Western' values on non-western cultures. In other words, if, for example, learners who identify as Arab-Muslim are equipped with criticality (which is highly valued in Islam as 'Ijtihad of thought') they can evaluate their own knowledge, attitudes and values and those they are exposed to through teaching ICC to avoid any imposition of values and to have the ethical dimension of ICC at the center. It is likely that the conceptualization of 'criticality' requires careful attention and a contextualized definition, this however, is a task beyond the scope of this chapter.

Algeria a case study

Algeria is located in North Africa and represents one of three countries of the Maghreb region; Morocco and Tunisia make up the other two countries (definitions of the Maghreb also include Libya, Western Sahara and Mauritania; World Atlas, 2022). Algeria has a unique nature.   Historically it has been an Islamic leaning nation with strong nationalist tendencies (Rogan, 2009). Ninety-four percent of its 42 million inhabitants live in the Northern less arid part of the country. The modern territory of Algeria has been subject to invasions by the Arabs, the Ottomans, the Romans and the French (Rogan, 2009). Arabs make up 75% of the modern Algerian nations while native Berbers or Kabyle peoples account for 25% of the population (Ruedy, 2005). Languages spoken in Algeria include Algerian Arabic known as 'Derija'; Amazigh or Tamazight, Shawi, Tergui, Mozabite namely Berber languages and French. In the 21st century, English has become a fashionable language to be learned, largely due to the presence of multinationals in the Algerian energy sector (Nemouchi, 2022).

Curricula in Algeria is at a unique juncture in the MENA region. In 1962, the Algerian government engaged in the Arabisation of instruction and adopted Modern Standard Arabic (language of the Holy Quran). More so, in National Education policy, the government has maintained that Algeria is an Islamic nation which respects islamic principles. Algeria is guided by Islamic principles such as 'tolerance and *ijtihad'* (Loi d'Orientation sur L'Education Nationale, 2008, p. 11, our own emphasis) which are similar to western ICC principles.

Ijtihad, is an Islamic concept that Nemouchi and Byram (forthcoming) discuss as a potential ICC element which draws from Islamic teachings. Its conceptualization highlights:

'the value of observation (التأمل, alta'amul), doubting and questioning legal principles (الظن, al-dhanu) and a strong sense of reasoning (العقلنة, al-aqlana), as opposed to mere imitation'. It draws on religious principles and scientific evidence emphasizing the importance of taking action on social issues' (Nemouchi & Byram,forthcoming).

Ijtihad of thought as a potential ICC element overlaps in meaning with critical cultural awareness (Nemouchi & Byram, forthcoming). More so, the national laws in question state that Algerian national identity has been shaped by Islam (Nemouchi, 2022).

Language instruction within HEIs is shaped by the national government, and English language instruction follows national curriculum content, although in some instances HEIs, compared to elementary and secondary school education, have more freedom in setting their own content (Nemouchi, 2022). At the Master's level, in the curriculum offered to English Language Teachers, students are expected to develop ICC while learning English as a foreign language (Nemouchi, 2022). Yet Asselah-Rahal and Blanchet (2007) state that in Algeria, students are taught foreign languages mechanically and are not expected to develop an appreciation for the cultural context of the language.

In fact, Risager (2006) posits that language and culture are separate, and different Englishes exist. Analyzing ICC and culture in English language instruction Nemouchi (2022) relied on several western scholars including Byram's (1997/2021) definition of ICC and further states that: "Kramsch (2013) argues that language gives meaning to cultural products and practices" (p.41).

Also, of relevance for western foreign languages, is the status of the French language in Algeria. French has foreign language status in Algerian policy, yet as a result of colonization, the French language is prominent in the education system and remains the language of instruction for some subjects in HEIs. In sum, although Algerian national education laws refer to Islamic principles of ICC, in practice western Anglo Saxon models of ICC dominate Algerian curriculum when teaching English as a foreign language and some subjects are taught in French.

DISCUSSION AND CONCLUSION

Analysis of ICC in the MENA region, shows that in most countries western models have been used to analyze the ICC space. As such, Islamic epistemologies remain on the periphery of ICC in the MENA region. To include voices and ways of knowing from different cultures and religions, diverse voices which reflect local cultural make up, belief systems and ways of knowing need to be included in ICC discourse. In the long term, this inclusion will help equalize relations between peoples and broaden the scope of the ICC field. Also, it helps legitimize knowledge from other forms of knowing and recognizes that intercultural is also political and colonial (R'boul, 2022). Existentially, Islamic ontologies of ICC have been marginalized as a result of power dynamics and colonial history. This situation has given rise to the elevation of frameworks from 'Western' nations and culture. As such, adopting a postcolonial approach to the study of ICC will help create a mindset which values local belief systems. This process however requires un-learning 'western' ways of doing (Roy & Shaw, 2012). Also using frameworks which are inclusive of local culture help promote cognitive equality (De Sousa Santos 2014; 2018). Transnational interdisciplinarity approaches to scholarship especially when including Islamic principles of ICC helps add context to ways of learning and understanding. In this context, adopting a "Global South" perspective, De Sousa Santos (2014), calls for 'intercultural translations' and raises questions about power relations and the agency of translators for an inclusive acknowledgement of different epistemologies.

In her study of the phenomenon of ICC models used in English language instructions, Nemouchi (2022) discusses Islamic principles of ICC and analyzes ICC models utilized in Algerian public HEI offerings. Although Algerian laws refer to Islamic principles, in practice western models of analysis and implementation of ICC dominate the field of ICC when teaching English as a foreign language in Algerian HEIs. What is surprising here is the fact that Algeria has long been a nation which prides itself on its Islamic heritage, yet Islamic ICC principles remain elusive in practice in English instruction at the tertiary level.

In Algeria, students are exposed to Islamic values during secondary education and are exposed to western models of ICC when enrolled in English instruction in HEIs.Nemouchi (2022), points out that Byram's ICC model does not aim to teach values which may contradict Islamic values, instead, she posits that, implementing Byram's model in English teaching practices, promotes the notion that the 'intercultural speaker' can be a middle ground that does not require the 'acculturation' that Bouali (2008) warns against.

IMPLICATIONS

Based on our findings we advocate adopting fused models of intercultural competence, namely we call for fusing western ICC models with Islamic ICC principles to offer a culturally inclusive model of intercultural competence in the MENA region. This fusion will draw on other ways of knowing, but since western models dominate the region, adopting fused models can be a practical way of including previously excluded ways of knowing. This direct call for including religious epistemologies in ICC models acknowledges that ICC models can follow a bottom up approach to reflect cultural inclusivity, but above all it calls for the inclusion of intercultural ways of knowing prevalent in the MENA region to promote cognitive justice. For example relying on the fundamental tenets of Bryam's ICC Model and Islamic Ijtihad results in a fused model which calls for: changes in attitude, nurturing critical awareness and critical cultural awareness and reasoning and adapting.

Figure 1: Fused Western and Ijtihad ICC Model

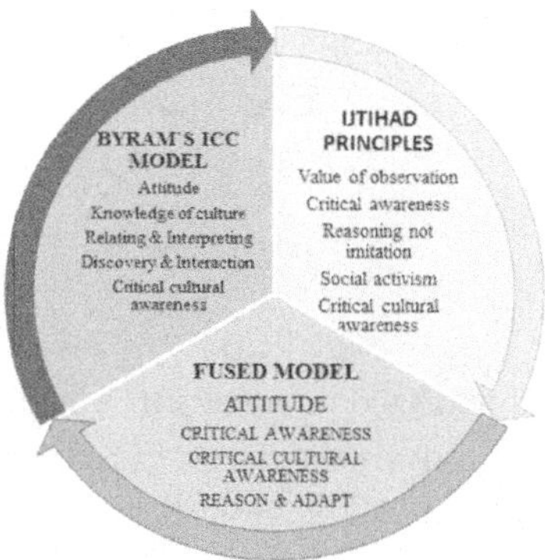

The use of frameworks which exist outside of whiteness or western models of knowing and doing and which draw from the Quran and Islamic teachings can help advance the implementation, analysis and assessment of ICC from an alternative perspective. Yet, based on the diversity of the region we should remain mindful of linguistic barriers when accessing knowledge from an Islamic perspective. In sum, the power dimensions of gatekeepers such as translators, editors, publishers, and more require critical analysis as we rely on 'intercultural translations' to access knowledge otherwise we risk perpetuating inequities. Such an approach acknowledges the complex cultural nature of the region while raising a flag on the dominance of knowledge by certain players, and epistemologies of ICC education. Our findings also reveal the need for a dialogic space between teacher and teacher-trainees (or students) to explore the complexity and sensitivity of intercultural issues to allow all parties to reflect on and question their own intercultural competence to better address ethical dimensions and power dynamics in classrooms.

In a post western colonial era, aspects of western discourse continue to dominate education systems and in most MENA nations, western models of ICC dominate scholarships, a conclusion also reached in existing research by R'boul (2022). This study examined documents covering 13 out of 19 MENA countries and utilized one country for in depth analysis; as such it is limited in scope and is not generalizable. Future research may consider extending our frame of analysis to cover MENA and Islamic nations worldwide. Investigating how a fused model of ICC can promote peace and understanding within the region and beyond is also in order. Lastly, approaches to including and measuring ICC in educational offerings can help advance its inclusion in curricula, as such we should ask:

1. How can we effectively design curricula to integrate nuanced and fused models of ICC in curricula ?

2. What are the potential benefits of doing so and how can challenges be addressed?

REFERENCES

Alahmed, M. A. (2020). Internalized orientalism: Toward a postcolonial media theory and de-Westernizing communication research from the global south. *Communication Theory, 30*(4), 407–428. doi:10.1093/ct/qtz037

Alexander, B. K., Arasaratnam, A. L., Avant-Mier, R., Durham, A., Flores, L., Leeds-Hurwitz, W.,Mendoza, L. S., Oetzel, J., Osland, J., Tsuda, Y., Yin, J., & Halualani, R. (2014). Defining and communicating what "intercultural" and "intercultural communication" means to us. *Journal of International and Intercultural Communication, 7*(1), 14–37. https://doi.org/10.1080/17513057.2014.869524

Alkharusi, M.J. (2018). Intercultural communication study in the Middle East. *The international encyclopedia of intercultural communication.* John Wiley & Sons, Inc.

Asselah-Rahal, S. and Blanchet, P. (2007). *Plurilinguisme et enseignement des langues en Algérie, Roles du Français en context didactique.* E.M.E. & InterCommunications.

Borguetti, C. (2017). Is there really a need for assessing intercultural competence?: Some ethical issues. *Journal of Intercultural Communication, 17*(2), 1–15. https://doi.org/10.36923/jicc.v17i2.736

Bouali, N. (2008). Acculturation in between the crisis of internationalization of values and the danger of integration. *Almawaqif Journal for Social and Historical Studies. N*(3), 243 - 250.

Byram, M. & Fleming, M. (eds) (1998). *Language learning in intercultural perspective – approaches through drama and ethnography.* Cambridge University Press.

Byram, M. (1997). *Teaching and assessing intercultural communicative competence.* Multilingual Matters.

Byram, M. (2021). *Teaching and assessing intercultural communicative competence: Revisited.* (2nd ed.) Multilingual Matters. https://doi.org/10.21832/9781800410251

Calafell, M. B. (2020). The critical performative turn in intercultural communication. *Journal of Intercultural Communication Research.* https://doi.org/10.1080/17475759.2020.1740292

Creswell, J. W. (2013). *Qualitative enquiry and research design: Choosing among five approaches* (3rd ed.). Sage.

Daraiseh, S. (2018). Intercultural competence among English learners at Yarmouk University Jordan. *US-China Foreign Language, 16*(10), 503-514.

De Sousa Santos, B. (2014) *Epistemologies of the South: Justice against epistemicide.* Routledge.

De Sousa Santos, B. (2018) *The End of the cognitive empire: The coming of age of epistemologies of the South*. Duke University Press.

Deardorff, D. K. (2004). *The identification and assessment of intercultural competence as a student outcome of international education at institutions of higher education in the United States*. Unpublished dissertation, North Carolina State University.

Deardorff, D. K. (2006). Identification and assessment of intercultural competence as a student outcome of internationalization. *Journal of Studies in International Education, 10*(3), 241-266.

Dutta, L. M. (2020). Whiteness, internationalization, and erasure: Decolonizing futures from the Global South. *Communication and Critical/Cultural Studies, 17*(2), 228–235. https://doi.org/10.1080/14791420.2020.1770825

Guilherme, M. (2019). The critical and decolonial quest for intercultural epistemologies and dis-courses. *Journal of Multicultural Discourses, 14*(1), 1–13. https://doi.org/10.1080/17447143.2019.1617294

Hall, S. (1981). Cultural studies: Two paradigms. In T. Bennett, G. Martin, C. Mercer, & J. Woollacott (Eds.), *Culture, ideology and social processes* (pp. 19–38). Batsford (in association with the Open University Press, London, 1981)

Harkness, G. (2015). In the zone: Female athletes and intercultural contact in Iraq. In R. Raddawi (Ed.), *Intercultural communication with Arabs* (pp. 295-306). Springer. https://doi.org/10.1007/978-981-287-254-8_4

Hermessi, T. (2017). An evaluation of the place of culture in English education in Tunisia. In S. Hidri & C. Coombe (Eds.), *Evaluation in foreign language education in the Middle East and North Africa* (pp. 203-220). Springer. http://www.springer.com/series/10129

Hofstede, G. (2001). *Culture's consequences: Comparing values, behaviors, institutions, and organizations across nations* (2nd ed.). Sage Publications.

Holliday, A., Hyde, M., & Kullman, J. (2004). *Intercultural communication: An advanced resource book*. Routledge.

Joiner, E. G. (1974). Evaluating the cultural content of foreign-language texts. *The Modern Language Journal, 58*, 242–244. doi:10.1111/j.1540-4781.1974.tb05106.x

Karolak, M., & Guta, H. A. (2015). Intercultural communication in the context of Saudi Arab tertiary education. In R. Raddawi (Ed.), *Intercultural communication with Arabs* (pp. 41-54). Springer. https://doi.org/10.1007/978-981-287-254-8_4

Kemp, L. J. (2015). Culturally different perspectives of time: Effect on communication in meetings. In R. Raddawi (Ed.), *Intercultural communication with Arabs* (pp. 163-178). Springer. https://doi.org/10.1007/978-981-287-254-8_4

Knight, J. (2004). Internationalization remodeled: Definition, approaches, and rationales. *Journal of Studies in International Education, 8*, 5-31

Kramsch, C. (2013) Culture in the foreign language teaching. *Iranian Journal of Language Teaching Research, 1*(1) 57-78

Krippendorff, K. H. (2013). *Content analysis: An introduction to its methodology.* Sage.

Loi d'Orientation sur l'Education Nationale, n°08-04 du 23 janvier 2008 (p. 36-38). *Bulletin Officiel de l'Education Nationale.* http://www.education.gov.dz/wp-content/uploads/2015/02/loi0804Fr.pdf

MacPherson, S. (2010). Teachers' collaborative conversations about culture: Negotiating decision making in intercultural teaching. *Journal of Teacher Education, 61*(3), 271–286.

Merriam, S. (1998). *Qualitative research and case study applications in education: Revised and expanded from "Case study research in education."* ERIC

Miettinen, L., Gluschankof, C., Karlsen, S., & Westerlund, H. (2018). Initiating mobilizing networks: Mapping intercultural competences in two music teacher programmes in Israel and Finland. *Research Studies in Music Education, 40*(1), 67–88. https://doi.org/10.1177/1321103X18757713

Moran, P. R. (2001). *Teaching culture: Perspectives in practice.* Heinle and Heinle publications.

Nemouchi, L. (2022). *Investigating the use of literary texts in a pedagogy to teach intercultural communicative competence in an EFL Master's course in Algeria.* [Unpublished doctoral dissertation]. Durham University, England.

Nemouchi, L. and Byram, M. (forthcoming). Challenges of Teaching Intercultural Competence and National Values: a case-study in Algeria. *Cambridge Journal of Education.*

OECD (2022). *The OECD and MENA.* https://www.oecd.org/mena/

Pew Center (2015). *Middle East-North Africa.* https://www.pewresearch.org/religion/2015/04/02/middle-east-north-africa/

R'boul, H. (2022). Postcolonial interventions in intercultural communication knowledge: Meta-intercultural ontologies, decolonial knowledges and epistemological polylogue. *Journal of International and Intercultural Communication, 15*(1), 75-93.

Raddawi, R. (Ed.). (2015). *Intercultural communication with Arabs: Studies in educational, professional and societal contexts.* Springer.

Royal Geographical Society (n.d.). A 60 second guide to the Global North/South d i v i d e . https://www.rgs.org/CMSPages/GetFile.aspx?nodeguid=9c1ce781-9117-4741-af0a-a6a8b75f32b4&lang=en-GB

Risager, K. (2006) *Language and Culture Global Flows and Local Complexity.* Multilingual Matters.

Rodriguez, L., Schwartz, S. J., & Whitbourne, S. K. (2010). American identity revisited: The relation between national, ethnic, and personal identity in a multiethnic sample of emerging adults. *Journal of Adolescent Research, 25*(2), 324–349.

Rogan E. L. (2009). *The Arabs : A history* (1st ed.). Allen Lane.

Roy, S., & Shaw, I. S. (2012). Intercultural communication in a conflict-torn world: Critical ques-tions/connections/implications. *International Communication Gazette, 74*(6), 507–508. https://doi.org/10.1177/1748048512454815

Ruedy, J. (2005) *Modern Algeria: The Origins and Development of a Nation.*(2nd Ed) Indiana University Press.

Salem, L., R. (2012). *Incorporating intercultural competence in English language teaching in a Lebanese university intensive English program context: An action research project.* [Unpublished doctoral dissertation]. University of Leicester, England.

Sastry, S., & Ramasubramanian, S. (2020). The subcontinent speaks: Intercultural communication perspectives from/on South Asia. *Journal of International and Intercultural Communication, 13*(2), 93–97. https://doi.org/10.1080/17513057.2020.1745440

Sheldon, L. E. (1988). Evaluating ELT textbooks and materials. *ELT Journal, 42*(4), 237–247. https://doi.org/10.1093/elt/42.4.237

Shome, R. (2019). Thinking culture and cultural studies—from/of the Global South. *Communication and Critical/Cultural Studies, 16*(3), 196–218. https://doi.org/10.1080/14791420.2019.1648841

The National Standards in Foreign Language Education Project. (1996). *The national standards for foreign language learning: Preparing for the 21st century.* The National Standards in Foreign Language Education Project

Weitz (2015). *Religious minorities in the Middle East.* https://www.fpri.org/article/2015/11/religious-minorities-in-the-modern-middle-ea

World Atlas (2022). *What are the MENA countries?* https://www.worldatlas.com/articles/what-are-the-mena-countries.html

Yemini, M. (2014). Internationalization of secondary education—lessons from Israeli Palestinian-Arab schools in Tel Aviv-Jaffa. *Urban Education, 49*(5) 471–498. https:// doi.org/ 10.1177/0042085913478622

Yin, R. K. (2003). Designing case studies. *Qualitative research methods, 5*(14), 359-386.

Zaharna, R. S. (2009). An associative approach to intercultural communication competence in the Arab world. In D. K. Deardorff (Ed.), *The SAGE Handbook of Intercultural Competence* (pp. 179-195). Sage.

Bios

Yovana S.Veerasamy, PhD, is a Consultant and Researcher in International Education. The focus of her research is internationalization policy, comparative internationalization policy, international student services especially in the virtual context, intercultural competence and VE/COIL. She is the founding coordinator of the MENA & IGC Working Group at the World Council on IGC. Email: parmeswaree.soobrayenveerasamy@utoledo.edu

Lamia Nemouchi, PhD, is a Lecturer in Education at De Montfort University, Leicester, UK. Her PhD at Durham University, Uk, focused on teaching ICC through literature in EFL classrooms in Algerian universities. Her research interests include: intercultural education, researching multilingually, social justice in education, and international and comparative education. Email:lamia.nemouchi@gmail.com

Hadjer Hammadi, MA, is a PhD candidate at the School of Modern Languages and Applied Linguistics at the University of Limerick in Ireland. Her research focuses on investigating intercultural competence and global competence of engineers in Algeria. Her research interests include: global competence, intercultural competence, intercultural education and training in workplace communication. She is the Coordinator of the MENA & IGC WG at the WC on IGC. Email: hadjer.hammadi@outlook.com

Appendix 1

"Les caractéristiques de la nation algérienne ont été ainsi façonnées par l'Islam qui a conféré au peuple algérien la dimension fondamentale de son identité "(Loi d'Orientation 2008, p. 10)

These guidelines, refer to implementing Islamic teachings that are explained briefly as :

[...] contribuer à promouvoir des comportements permettant : l'intégra tion sociale, l'amélioration des relations sociales et le renforcement de la cohésion sociale, et de l'environnement, le renforcement de la famille, du respect dû aux parents et des valeurs humanistes prônées par l'Islam : tolérance, générosité, sens moral, travail, ijtihad dans la pensée. (Loi d'Orientation 2008, p. 11)

(Nemouchi, 2022, p.33).

Chapter 2

Exploring Intercultural Competence and Interculturality in Latin America's Higher Education

Four Case Studies

Elizabeth Margarita Hernández López
University of Guadalajara, Mexico

Veronica Denmon
Argentina

María Elena Guerrero de Stöhr
University of Applied Sciences, Germany

Erika Shishido Lohmann
Distance Learning University of Applied Sciences, Germany

Natalía Hernández León
Colombia

ABSTRACT

Latin America is often perceived from the outside as a uniform and undifferentiated entity. However, the convergence in the use of the same language and the fact that some elements of a common past coincide do not in themselves ensure that there is homogeneity of conceptions or worldviews. In the specific field of intercultural education, it is assumed that the different Spanish-speaking countries reflect this diversity in the processes of Higher Education (HE).

Accordingly, this paper aims to explore some of the similarities and differences in the approach to intercultural competence and interculturality in some HE institutions, from Argentina, Colombia, Mexico and Peru. Data were collected through semi-structured interviews with program coordinators and findings indicate there is indeed diversity on how these concepts are approached bearing in mind the programs' own objectives and contextual characteristics. Despite this diversity, there is partial consensus when seeking for a harmonious interaction with the other.

Keywords: Argentina, Colombia, Higher Education, Intercultural Competence, Interculturality, Latin America, Mexico, Peru.

INTRODUCTION

In the field of international and intercultural education there are several concepts whose definitions, scope and perspectives possibly overlap and are used indistinctly and indiscriminately. In the case of this article, in Latin America, some of these concepts have arrived, to be translated into Spanish, from academic referents in other parts of the world while only a few others have originated locally. In our opinion, there is a lack of information in Spanish and from Latin America on the conceptualization of Intercultural Competence and Interculturality. In this sense and with the aim to open new perspectives that may contribute to a better understanding of the ways in which the notion of these terms is being developed in Higher Education Institutions in this region, this study explores how some Social Sciences and Humanities programs in Argentina, Colombia, Mexico and Peru embrace these concepts while exploring what differences and similarities exist.

LITERATURE REVIEW

This literature review stems from the idea of exploring the concepts of intercultural competence and interculturality applied in the specific field of intercultural/international education in Latin America. According to Medina-López-Portillo and Sinnigen (2009) the term of preference in the region is "interculturality" due to its historical status and descriptive character. In this sense, interculturality definitions appear to be based on the acknowledgement of elements from one's own culture and the adoption of new elements that are integrated when interacting with other groups (Capella, 1993). Interculturality is also perceived as the sharing of differences (Guerrero Arias, 2007, as cited in Medina-López-Portillo & Sinnigen, 2009) and ways to promote the relationship and active coexistence among different cultural groups (De La Torre 2006, as cited in Medina-López-Portillo & Sinnigen, 2009).

The problem with this concept is the plurality of meanings and its concrete use in politics and education (Corbetta, 2021). Regarding its contemporary use and meaning, Walsh (2009) argues that interculturality is conceived in three ways: relational, functional, and critical. The first view of interculturality as a relational one, refers to the contact and exchange among cultures. Functional interculturality is focused on recognizing cultural differences and diversity with the aim of including different groups through tolerance and dialogue. And the focus of critical interculturality is not only on difference and diversity as such, but by recognizing how that difference has been constructed within a colonial framework (Granados-Beltrán, 2016).

Within the field of intercultural education, approaches of a dominant narrative centered on Eurocentric knowledge are found in the production, organization and distribution of knowledge (Achinte, 2012), therefore Boaventura de Souza, (2018) emphasizes the need to give credibility to other epistemologies, and to other knowledge. When referring to ethno-education, mostly aimed at ethnic groups, Pérez (2005), however, stresses on the opening and reorientation of this approach to all socio-cultural groups in order to promote multiple knowledge and reciprocal relationships. Castro Suárez (2009) also suggests the need for interdisciplinary team building at educational institutions in order to work with and from many different ideological tendencies and perspectives.

Intercultural competency refers to the individual skills, knowledge, attributes, behavior, and attitudes needed to interact successfully with people from different cultures (Deardorff, 2006). Referring to the approaches presented above and analyzing them together with Deardorff's (2006) definition, we consider that the concept of intercultural competence is implicitly present here, even though the term interculturality is mentioned throughout.

As it is observed there does not seem to be clarity on how the concept of intercultural competence is defined, integrated or differentiated from the concept of interculturality. As a result, and bearing into account the researchers' context, the question that drove this study is: How is intercultural competence approached in some Social Sciences and Humanities programs in Argentina, Colombia, Mexico and Peru?

RESEARCH METHOD

This is an empirical study and as such, data presented here derive from four interviews conducted with Higher Education program coordinators in Argentina, Colombia, Mexico and Peru. We used convenience   sampling (Bryman,2016). Accordingly, the university's coordinators interviewed were those who replied to our invitation to partake in this research. Coincidentally, they were all females with different seniority in the post. Taking into account homogeneous sampling (Creswell, 2014), the criteria as to what universities select was based on being a pre graduate program, in the Social and Human Sciences, belonging to a public university, and explicitly containing the word: "intercultural" in its name. Nevertheless, maximal variation sampling (Creswell, 2014) was also allowed by taking into account either distance or face-to-face programs located in any of the country's regions. Given the flexibility that virtual interviews grant (Lobe et al., 2020), individual interviews using either Meet or Zoom, depending on the interviewee's preference, were arranged during the Fall 2022.

Ethical considerations included giving an informed consent, and promising confidentiality to the participants and the university in question (Van de Hoonaard, 2002). Bearing into account the potential that using the participants' native language in qualitative interviewing has (Welch & Piekkari, 2006), interviews were conducted in Spanish as a methodological consideration. Concerning the researchers, they shared the participants' native language and culture; nevertheless, being aware of the risk of developing myopia (Mercer, 2007), they were all unacquainted about the program in question. Thus, approaching potential candidates was reliant on a thorough internet search based on the criteria previously described.

Data was analyzed thematically. After iteratively reviewing data, researchers, individually, came up with a first categorization of codes (Saldaña, 2020). Then, they discussed the codes that inductively had emerged (Thomas, 2006), looked for similarities and came up with a second category of codes. The result was a set of four themes: Context, Curriculum design, Policy for interculturality and Understanding of concepts. Findings are presented following those themes.

FINDINGS

Argentina

Context:

The Bachelor's Degree in Intercultural Education is a two and a half year long virtual program (5 semesters), focused on training staff of the Argentinian educational system at all levels and modalities in the intercultural perspective. The program belongs to the Department of Social Sciences and Education of a national public university created in 2016. The program in itself was designed in 2020 and its implementation began in 2021, for which it does not yet have its first cohort of graduates. Its particularity lies in the fact that it is the first undergraduate degree in public education at the national level that addresses the intercultural dimension. As such, it outlines a general proposal, which is transversal to the system and not focused on any subject, language, or region in particular.

Curriculum Design:

The central objective of the program is to train professionals in the education system in the intercultural perspective as a cross-cutting paradigm, based on the idea that people live in heterogeneous environments and that they are simultaneously immersed in institutions and in diverse socio-community networks where they are confronted with different cultural uses and resources. The training seeks to promote awareness, considering the variety of realities of the learners in relation to their living conditions, the promotion of reflection, the review of strategies to address the different linguistic and cultural repertoires and the revaluation of knowledge produced in community spaces.

According to participant 1, the curriculum focuses on the realities of the local Argentinian context, drawing on the experiences of countries in the region with greater development and experience in intercultural education such as Mexico and Colombia. Some of its basic bibliographical references are, at a regional level, the texts of Elsie Rockwell and at national level, those of Gabriela Novaro, Ana Padawer, Ana Carolina Hecht and Silvina Hirsch.

As the focus of the Bachelors' Degree is on the national level and on the general intercultural problems faced by all teachers in the country, it does not offer students the opportunity to learn other languages (neither foreign nor local). The lack of teaching of other local mother tongues has to do with the prioritization of an inclusive and comprehensive approach. In Argentina, more than twenty different languages are spoken in addition to Spanish and none of them is hegemonic, so opting for one or more would end up excluding others. Instead, the program focuses strongly on the issues of multilingualism, the complexity of languages in contact and language policies.

Policy for interculturality:

Based on the interview, the degree is not linked to an explicit institutional policy of interculturality, but responds to a concern of the university to generate and develop a space in this field, based on the contributions of Anthropology. In addition, the institution promotes research projects in the area and works in coordination with the Teacher Training Institutes.

Participant 1 emphasizes that the degree has a national orientation. Compared to other existing training in the intercultural dimension offered in provincial areas and oriented to specific populations and/or languages, she stresses that what is interesting and innovative about this proposal lies in its outreach to all workers in the education system, and not only to those who work in intercultural schools.

Interculturality is addressed from a rights-based approach and is considered a fundamental human and educational right. Diverse linguistic and cultural repertoires coexist in the classroom. Each subject is crossed by multiple variables that interact in social relations, often reflecting inequality situations. The recognition of one's own diversity is a right that contributes to improving quality of life.

Understanding of concepts:

Interviewee 1 establishes a clear difference between the concepts of Interculturality and Intercultural Competence. Emphasizing that the structuring axis of the program is the intercultural perspective from a rights-based approach. Interculturality is considered as a fundamental human right and as a structural phenomenon, which must be approached structurally. Each person's life is a network of heterogeneous elements that is linked to other equally heterogeneous lives, immersed at the same time in institutions and communities. The intercultural perspective seeks to highlight these processes and relationships. From this point of view, it constitutes a concept that is cross sectional in society and the education system. According to the interviewee, the notion of competence implies the acquisition by a person of certain abilities to perform in a field. The concept of intercultural competence would respond to a more instrumental, functional, and individual-oriented vision. She clarifies that she is not against the competency-based approach, but she believes that a more structural approach to interculturality is needed.

Colombia

Context:

As a pioneer in its area, the program chosen for this analysis is the Bachelor's Degree in Ethnoeducation and Interculturality, from the Faculty of Education, at a public university in Colombia. After several denominations in the past (e. g. Ethnoeducation and Social Sciences), the current one, with an explicit focus on Interculturality, began four years ago, and its first alumni are expected to graduate in the first semester of 2024.

The territory where this University is located borders Venezuela and the Caribbean Sea. It is also the native territory of five indigenous peoples (Kogui, Arhuaco, Wiwa, Kankuamos, and Wayuu). The diversity of its population is also reflected in the student body as it is composed of people from almost all of these ethnic groups. Additionally, it is the eighth department in Colombia with the largest Afro-descendant population. This region has received migrants from the Middle East, Venezuela, and victims of forced displacement and FARC EP guerrilla ex-combatants who live today, after the Peace Agreement of 2016, in the Territorial Space for Training and Reincorporation of Pondores.

Curriculum Design:

This 8-semester program was designed through work groups with representatives of the Great Wayuu Nation, of the Afro-descendant people, with former guerrilla combatants, and, in addition, with graduates of the same degree who saw the need to make explicit the emphasis on Interculturality in the program.

The program bases are found, according to the interviewee, in "other-epistemes" and in consonance with its objectives: graduating alumni who are aware of and value ancestral knowledge and customs, share their education with the communities and "dynamize their life projects". Thus, the student body lives a process of self-recognition, learning the principles of otherness to relate to others from respect and differential approaches.

Observing the experience made by alumni under former denominations of the program, it is expected that the first graduates of the degree under the Interculturality approach will be mainly involved in projects related to the border, migration, the environment, social responsibility, higher education, research, ethno-educational centers and ethno-development plans, among others.

Regarding languages, it was mentioned that the program offers four levels, reading courses, conversational club and workshops in the Wayuunaiki language. Mastery of Wayuunaiki is valid to meet the requirement of a second language (along with Spanish), and the possibility of studying a third (English) is also offered.

Policy of Interculturality:

This program stems from the assumption of Colombia as a multi-ethnic and multicultural country and from the need to guarantee the survival of its ethnic people. It is based on the University's active participation and social responsibility to the progress and well-being of its communities in the "matrix of territory, body, and memory".

According to participant 2, its intercultural policy is intrinsic to the being and doing of the program. The collective aim is to preserve the knowledge, the "other-epistemes", the territorial and contextual view that communities possess: through its dialogues ("word circles") with, for example, indigenous and Afro-Colombian groups with whom these concepts are articulated in their day-to-day work and life.

During the interview, emphasis was repeatedly placed on the relevance of "interculturality in action" and on how crucial it is for them to "go to the territory" and bring it into the classroom. These inclusive practices are described as social, community, and ancestral. Interculturality lives "within the university" in the diversity of the people it is composed of and with whom its own education and narratives are built.

Understanding of concepts:

Within the program, they are still discussing the possible differences between the concepts of intercultural competence and Interculturality. Interculturality is the "rewriting process" that starts from self-recognition and otherness and occurs in practice in "encounters and disagreements" within the system. Similarly, intercultural competence refers to "being relevant to the territory" and the ability to share with others, starting from one's knowledge, without losing oneself. The competence manifests itself in everyday life by recognizing oneself and others and finding similarities and differences.

The concept of (de)colonization is also mentioned, firstly, in relation to the "badly told" story we have received and to those "own-knowledges" that were tried to be erased. Secondly, with respect to the human body itself and to the communities' "other-aesthetics". In this regard, being able to show unashamedly their nose, their hair, for example; is also perceived as an intercultural competence. This process, which has required effort, is developed with practice, in the relationship with others.

We find here the program's intention to question these facts, enabling the "own narratives" to "weave history" from the people and taking care of languages as an ancestral treasure.

Mexico

Context:

The B.A. program is named: Development and Intercultural Management and it was created in 2011. After a feasibility and contextual analysis, Central Mexico resulted as an eligible location for the establishment of this program given its very strong multicultural context as it is a city, where migrants and laborers transit regularly due to its location and-or the heavy presence of multinational companies.

This constant migratory flow is reflected on the diversity of the students' enrolled in this program. Thus, the student body belongs to Northern and Southern regions in Mexico, as well as to the country's capital city. However, this diversity, acknowledged as a distinctive characteristic of the program, does not entail students from ethnic communities. They are welcome to enroll and the interviewee had remembrance of a student from an ethnic community previously enrolled, notwithstanding, their presence in the program is not evident.

Curriculum design:

The B.A.'s length is 6 semesters and it aims to train professionals to respond to specific problems of Mexican society. Through the interdisciplinary formation of the curriculum with subjects such as anthropology, education, sociology and even psychology, it intends for students to grasp knowledge that can be translated into proposals and programs of intercultural development deriving from three areas of expertise: intercultural social mediation, management of cultural heritage, and science, technology and culture.

As part of the curriculum, it is mandatory to take a language throughout the career. During freshman level students opt for a foreign language; be it English or French. While during their second and third year, they can decide on a foreign and-or a native language such as Otomi or Nahuatl. The graduate profile is diverse and it entails incorporation to public as well as private sectors. As such, graduates have joined civil organizations, governmental offices in areas related to gender equality and LGBTQ+ communities, teaching positions while some others have pursued postgraduate studies.

Policy for interculturality:

Participant 3 acknowledges an institutional document containing the educational model which guides the curriculum's intercultural positioning. Such document indicates an approach to interculturality that goes beyond the relationship between cultures and delves further into a more critical, more transformative view of the social domain. In alignment with this, it is stated that the educational model has as core values: openness to diversity, flexibility and inclusion.

Associated with constructivist views, it is recognized that the collaborative construction of learning that takes place in the classroom is more powerful. Although the program's focus is not openly stated as a decolonizing one, as part of the curriculum, authors referred to were: Catherine Walsh, Boaventura de Sousa and Gunther Dietz; researchers known for their empowering and emancipatory studies in the field. Notwithstanding, this program is differentiated from those offered at Intercultural Universities in Mexico targeted to educate and prepare indigenous students to return to their communities and work towards a social transformation of their territorial space.

Concerning the stance taken towards intercultural competence, the need to explicitly approach it from a global perspective is asserted. In this sense, participant 3 claimed this global vision is not new and it is implicitly present in the program when topics such as discrimination and racism, for example, are covered. Nevertheless, it should be made an explicit objective of the program. Supporting this, there are local or regional matters that are tackled within the program, but similarly students should be aware of a global perspective. Reinforcing this attempt to integrate this international component and as part of the comprehensive evaluation the B.A. is undergoing, it is the initiative to establish links with international universities to internationalize the program.

Understanding of concepts:

When asked about the concepts of interculturality and intercultural competence a difference was acknowledged. Intrinsically related, interculturality is understood as a focus whilst intercultural competence is the means to achieve it. Key skills to achieve the latter concept are: the possibility of dialogue and conflict resolution. Allowing a dialogical construction and managing conflict are central to the social exchange with others. In this sense, dialogue, openness, learning and transformation are what, according to the interviewee, define intercultural competence.

Nevertheless, an important argument regarding the use of the word "intercultural" was made. It was claimed its meaning was undervalued and attached like a last name to every program that existed without deepening into its meaning more profoundly. This calls for reflection towards the use or abuse of the word intercultural from a discourse stance.

Peru

Context:

The undergraduate Intercultural Ecotourism program belongs to a Peruvian intercultural national university located in the Andean and Amazonian region of Peru. It was created 30 years ago as a professional school attached to a traditional national university. Its political purposes of regionalization were considered, along with two other professional schools, as justification and foundation for the creation of the new National Intercultural University in 2010. In 2019 it offered its first admission exam. This program is currently under the process of curricular restructuring by an organizing commission of the Ministry of Education. As part of this, its name is being reconsidered for one that does not include the word "intercultural".

Curriculum Design:

Taking advantage of the geographical location and biodiversity of the area through the implementation of health and professional education services, among others; this program's objectives and purposes address regionalization and decentralization policies for the Andean-Amazonian communities. As a result, this promotes economic dynamics, such as tourism.

The program offers different admission modalities. The extraordinary modality aimed at students from native origin, offers each year 40 vacancies. 10 of these places are reserved and subsidized for students from Andean-Amazonian communities with the purpose of encouraging their participation. The admission exam differs from the ordinary one in that it is partly conducted in the applicant's native language and questions are adapted to their own context. The native language is restricted to the admission exam, as the courses are given in Spanish during the B.A. According to the interviewee, it is not possible to offer native language courses or bilingual courses, because the Ministry of Education has established that the teacher must have an academic degree. However, two native language courses have been implemented since this semester: Andean and Amazonian, but from a historical perspective.

Policy for interculturality

Participant 4 expressed they had "an intercultural program" in its name and content, but not in its regulations and actions, as the courses could not be offered bilingually, neither could they hire teachers from indigenous communities, nor offer classes in indigenous languages, in addition to the fact that the teaching staff had not received any intercultural training which was very limiting for them. The profile of a graduate student of a traditional program university and that of an intercultural university is different because students at intercultural universities are not only provided with professional qualifications, but are also promoted through education, cultural identity and interculturality. In this regard, the traditional graduate student could result in being an ecologist, ecotourism project consultant, manager. This is a different profile to that of a student from the Andean-Amazonian communities, who after completion is expected to return to their communities and work there.

The university's perspective regarding its intercultural policies for the coming years is to elaborate a proposal adjusted to the curriculum's reality and the students' profiles. For this reason, a year ago they started meeting with other national intercultural universities to promote exchange programs and lobby a joint request to the Ministry of Education for a new regulation, which would also include bilingual classes, the teaching of Andean and Amazonian languages and the qualification of teachers in subjects such as methodology and intercultural awareness. They also wish to promote exchanges with traditional and intercultural universities at national and international level.

Understanding of Concepts:

The term intercultural competence is described by participant 4 as the action of "setting something above something or someone else" in order to achieve a goal. This concept, according to the interviewee, is part of globalization and is a term that does not have much meaning for them. Interculturality, however, is understood as respect for the individual's way of life and the practice of their roles in a globalized world. It is also understood as the promotion of one's own cultural identity and its interaction with others, fostering social inclusion and respect for the other.

It was also mentioned that in some cases the term interculturality is abused in the university context among the students from the cities and have the possibility to finance themselves their studies, so they demand free education, computer's donation, subsidy of the university cafeteria and free accommodation, just because they are studying in an intercultural university. There have been cases where the university has refused to give these facilities and services to students not belonging to an indigenous community and as a result, they have bad mouthed about the institution claiming they have been discriminated against.

DISCUSSION AND CONCLUSIONS

Returning to the research question that frames the present study, we observe in the four programs a trait of similarity: the consideration of intercultural competence as a set of skills to be developed, as a means to an end. Depending on the program and university, these skills are focused more on the individual or on the interactional level. For instance, the Colombian case emphasizes the ability of sharing with others without losing oneself while the Mexican program stresses collaborative construction of learning. Although not rejecting the idea of competence, the Argentinian program does not consider it aligned with the interculturality rights-based approach to which they adhere to. Peru's program, the only one of the four taught in an intercultural university, considers intercultural competence as part of globalization and the asymmetry of relations that it creates, and as such this concept does not fit for the purposes of this program.

The decolonial perspective of interculturality is clearly perceived, firstly in the case of Colombia and, to a much lesser extent, in the case of Peru. Alongside the critical vision, there is a transformative vision, without necessarily representing a contradiction, latent throughout the programs. They do not adopt a position of rejection, but seek to achieve a common goal: to educate citizens with a vision for living in a globalized world, contributing to the construction of a more democratic and equitable society.

Another interesting finding was the claim made by the Mexican interviewee about the abuse of the word "intercultural", which resonated with the example provided by the Peruvian coordinator about non-ethnic students demanding concessions just by belonging to an "intercultural" university. This raises awareness for the building of a much more critical understanding of the term. One that transcends a superficial conception of it as a merely rhetorical or politically correct formulation for one that is transformative and goes beyond the limits of recognition and inclusion.

With the exception of the Argentinian program, it is observed an intention of integrating a global perspective in the students' formation process. There is willingness to internationalize the programs and to extend the scope of their relationships through collaboration, engagement and exchange initiatives with other Higher Education institutions. There is also recognition about the need to prepare students to interact and evolve in a larger world, beyond their own community or region, seeking mutual enrichment.

Based on our research, we realized that we have a diverse panorama in which different local contexts contribute to the whole region's diversity. Accordingly, we acknowledge Latin America is not a homogeneous block, but a compound mosaic, built with many pieces combined to achieve a purpose. Considering the perspective of Medina-López-Portillo and Sinnigen (2009), where it explains that in the United States there is a consensus on the usage of the term Intercultural Competence whilst in Latin America, contrastingly, there is a preference for the use of the concept interculturality. From the development of this study, we can conclude that on the one hand, it was difficult finding literature specifically addressing intercultural competence in Latin America. On the other, among the interviews' data collected, interculturality was the concept most frequently employed. The participants refrained from explicitly using the term competence and preferred referring to skills and abilities. On that basis, we question whether it is relevant to separate the concepts: interculturality and intercultural competence within the Latin American region or whether it may be worth exploring a more nuanced approach; one which contemplates global perspectives while being more representative, unique, and applicable to the diverse range of local contexts found in the region. Despite the appreciation of a diverse mosaic, a block representation would be necessary to be taken more into account in the international arena, where Latin America could have a stronger presence. This entails greater organization and cooperation between communities and HE institutions inside and outside the region with the final purpose of achieving solid recognition.

LIMITATIONS

We acknowledge that this was a small-scale study, which did not aim to generalize its findings. Nevertheless, we recognize that collecting data on a larger scale would be of benefit to better understand how the concepts of: intercultural competence and interculturality, are used in several programs and countries. Bearing in mind the differences that exist between public and private universities, a further study could seek to gather data from private universities; a section that we had not explored and that could contribute to a more rounded understanding of these terms within the Latin American context. Another area that warrants further investigation is collecting data from students as insiders of programs with an intercultural focus as to explore their perspectives on the impact of these programs in their life.

REFERENCES

Achinte, A. (2012). Epistemes "Otras": ¿Epistemes disruptivas?. *Kula. Antropólogos del Atlántico de Sur. 6,* 22-34. https://www.revistakula.com.ar/wp-content/uploads/2014/02/KULA6_2_A LBAN_ACHINTE.pdf

Boaventura de Sousa, S. (2018). Epistemología del Sur: un pensamiento alternativo de alternativas políticas. Geograficando. *En Memoria Académica. 14*(1), e032. https://memoria.fahce.unlp.edu.ar/art_revistas/pr.8844/pr.8844.pdf

Bryman, A. (2016). *Social research methods.* Oxford University Press.

Capella Riera, J. (1993). Interculturalidad e interdisciplinariedad: Un planteamiento epistemológico desde la educación. *Allpanchis, 25*(42), 11–39. https://doi.org/10.36901/allpanchis.v25i42.768

Castro Suárez, C., (2009). Estudios sobre educación intercultural en Colombia: tendencias y perspectivas. *Memorias. Revista Digital de Historia y Arqueología desde el Caribe, 10,* 358-375. https://www.redalyc.org/articulo.oa?id=85511597013

Corbetta, S. (2021). *Políticas educativas e interculturalidad en América Latina Estado del Arte. (2015-2020). Oficina para América Latina del Instituto Internacional de Planeamiento de la Educación de la Organización de las Naciones Unidas para la Educación, la Ciencia y la Cultura.*

Creswell, J. W. (2014). *Research design* (4th ed.). Sage.

Deardorff, D. K. (2006). Identification and assessment of intercultural competence as a student outcome of internationalization. *Journal of Studies in International Education, 10,* 241-266.

Granados-Beltrán, C. (2016). Critical Interculturality. A path for pre-service ELT teachers. *Ikala, Revista De Lenguaje Y Cultura, 21*(2). https://doi.org/10.17533/udea.ikala.v21n02a04

Lobe, B., Morgan, David L. y Hoffman, K. A. (2020). Qualitative data collection in an era of social distancing. International. *Journal of Qualitative Methods, 19.* https://doi.org/10.1177/1609406920937875

Medina-López-Portillo, A., & Sinnigen, J. H. (2009). Interculturality versus intercultural competencies in Latin America. In D. K. Deardorff (Ed.), *The SAGE handbook of intercultural competence* (pp. 249–263). Sage. https://doi.org/10.4135/9781071872987.N13

Mercer, J. (2007). The challenges of insider research in educational institutions: Wielding a double-edged sword and resolving delicate dilemmas. *Oxford Review of Education, 33*(1), 1-17.

Perez, J. C. R. (2005). Inclusión social, interculturalidad y educación. *Universidad   Pedagógica   Nacional.* https://www.academia.edu/62039191/Inclusi%C3%B3n_Social_Interculturali dad_y_Educaci%C3%B3n?email_work_card=title

Saldaña, J. (2021). The coding manual for qualitative researchers. *The coding manual for qualitative researchers,* 1-440.

Thomas, D. R. (2006). A general inductive approach for analyzing qualitative evaluation data. *American Journal of Evaluation, 27*(2), 237-246.

Van den Hoonaard, W. C. (Ed.). (2002). *Walking the tightrope: Ethical issues for qualitative researchers.* University of Toronto Press.

Walsh, C. (2009). Interculturalidad crítica y educación intercultural. *Este artículo es una ampliación de la ponencia presentada en el Seminario "Interculturalidad y Educación Intercultural", organizado por el Instituto Internacional de Integración del Convenio Andrés Bello, La Paz, 9-11 de marzo de 2009.*

Welch, C., & Piekkari, R. (2006). Crossing language boundaries: Qualitative interviewing in international business. *MIR: Management International Review, 46*(4), 417–437. http://www.jstor.org/stable/40836096

Bios

ELIZABETH M. HERNANDEZ LOPEZ, PhD, is a Research Lecturer in the Modern Languages Department, University of Guadalajara, Mexico. Her major research interests lie in the area of Intercultural Communication, Internationalization of Higher Education and Teacher Training and Development. Email: elizabeth.hlopez@academicos.udg.mx

VERONICA DENMON, is a B.A in Literature, specializing in Argentine and Latin American authors. Her major research interests lie in Intercultural Communication and Intercultural Education. Email: veronicadenmon@gmail.com

MARIA ELENA GUERRERO DE STÖHR, M.A. in Intercultural Education, Migration and Multilingualism, is a postgraduate in Translation, Applied Language and Cultural Studies, and lecturer of IC Management Ibero-America. Her research interests lie in Women Migration, Labour Migration, Integration and Inclusion.Email: guerrero@hs-worms.de

ERIKA SHISHIDO LOHMANN, MSc, is a certified trainer & coach and consultant for intercultural and digital competence, Lecturer in Intercultural Psychology at a distance learning university of applied sciences in Germany. Her areas of interest are Distance Leadership, Change Management, People & Culture. Email: erika.shishido@interkulturelles-coaching-hamburg.de

NATALIA HERNÁNDEZ LEÓN is currently studying her masters degree in Inclusive and Intercultural Education. She has been working for 10 years on Colombian Higher Education Institutions' internationalization strategies and on intercultural competence courses design. Email: nataliahernandezleon@gmail.com

Chapter 3

The Practice of Assessing Intercultural Competence

A Preliminary Global Study

Curtis Chu
Setsunan University, Japan

Callie K. DeBellis
Meredith College, United States of America

Chris T. Cartwright
Portland State University, United States of America

Freeda B. Khan
University of Toronto, Canada

Chang Pu
Berry College, United States of America

Wenjun Tang
Civil Aviation Flight University of China, China

With contributions by *Bettina Hansel, Constatina Rokos, Emily Pelka, Esra Sari, Francisco José de Alencar Costa, Leysiane Pazini, María Cruz Cuevas Álvarez, Mariko Takahashi, Peyman Sabel,* and *Yusuke Torii*

ABSTRACT

While there are numerous methods for assessing intercultural competencies, it is important to know why and how practitioners of global learning are conducting the assessments. The goals of this preliminary global study are to explore the trends and practices of intercultural competence assessment in all regions of the world and establish a foundation for conducting this global mapping again in the future. A total of 227 responses were gathered using a survey offered in nine languages with 19 questions, and both qualitative and quantitative analyses were conducted. Most of the respondents were in higher education, and 57% of respondents assess intercultural competence. Over 80% use mixed methods to assess and we compiled their quantitative tools and qualitative methods. Respondents shared how intercultural competence is defined; the purposes and reasons for assessing; and the barriers to conducting assessments. Individuals seeking resources for assessments could refer to the common assessment methods from respondents; stakeholders could refer to barriers mentioned by respondents to make improvements; and scholars could refer to our suggestions on how to improve this study in the future.

Keywords: Assessment Methods, Assessment Tools, Educational Outcomes, Global Learning, Intercultural Competence Assessment, Global Learning

INTRODUCTION

The assessment of Intercultural Competencies (ICC) is essential for practitioners of global learning as it sheds light on the skills, knowledge, and attitudes that individuals need to develop to be engaged global citizens. Our study aimed to highlight these practices around the world, exploring the culturally nuanced and complex nature of our shared assessment work and the panorama of possibilities when engaging in the practice of assessing intercultural competence development. Furthermore, as we set out on this task we believed that the role of developing ICC is best supported by a well-grounded yet flexible assessment practice. Our goal is now to highlight assessment trends we discovered around the world and guide readers to think deeply and with greater acuity about how to adapt their practice to best support the competency development of intercultural professionals globally.

There is no one way to do assessment as it is a process specific to the institution and organization and the course or program being measured. However, learning from others about the intricacies of assessment practices is a valuable and useful exercise. Much of the assessment conducted around the globe focuses on methods developed in Western cultures; in order to diversify that prevailing perspective we chose to engage colleagues from outside of North America and Europe to highlight voices from those outside of the West and learn from their expertise. In order to reach this goal, we circulated our survey globally through a variety of networks and in nine different languages: English, French, German, Japanese, Mandarin, Persian, Portuguese, Spanish, and Turkish. As stated in the title of this chapter, this is a preliminary study of these practices and we feel we have uncovered some clear patterns that can guide readers toward initiating or even refining their current practice.

LITERATURE REVIEW

Intercultural Competence Assessments

Assessment is an integral part of the educational process in higher education and one that is, at times, fraught with uncertainty, anxiety, and a fair amount of trepidation. This is understandable since there are over 140 assessment tools and counting (Deardorff, 2020), all with varying goals and objectives and purporting to measure intercultural competence and all its facets. Many definitions of intercultural competence exist but for the purpose of this study, it is defined as the "the ability to communicate effectively and appropriately in intercultural situations based on one's intercultural knowledge, skills and attitudes" (Deardorff, 2006). Hence, dimensions of ICC assessed usually include intercultural knowledge, skills (e.g., communication), and attitudes (e.g., intercultural attitudes) (Deardorff, 2004).

Intercultural Competence is a complex construct, and the assessment of intercultural competence is an even more daunting task complicated by the myriad of assessment tools currently available. However, many benefits of assessing intercultural competence have been recorded in empirical studies. It can help recruit or select job candidates if they possess the desired traits (e.g., negotiation) related to ICC that employers value (e.g., Stevens et al., 2014), track students' or trainees' progress regarding acquiring or improving their ICC-related knowledge and skills (e.g., Allen, 2022), and evaluate and develop ICC training programs (e.g., Ang et al., 2007).

The process of assessment is an important undertaking to the individual, the program, and the organization in order to achieve the best results and to help learners develop their intercultural competence (Deardorff, 2009, 2020). Prior to embarking on the assessment selection process, practitioners should ideally review several considerations such as the purpose of the assessment, the target audience, what outcomes are being assessed, and which assessment tool or method is best and why (Fantini, 2009). Once these questions are answered, learning objectives can be developed using frameworks such as Deardorff's process model of intercultural competence (Deardorff 2015, 2020) or the AAC&U VALUE rubrics (Rhodes, 2010). ICC assessment methods have evolved as ICC research expands.

While many quantitative assessment tools exist, an important function and consideration is the definition of the construct and its theoretical meaning it proposes to measure (Richter et al, 2023). In the study by Richter et al (2023), the authors conducted a systematic review of 68 assessment instruments supplemented with a survey of experts to evaluate assessment tools and key aspects of the construct itself. Their findings indicate a lack of theoretical grounding in the assessment itself or it proposes a narrow view of the construct and its subdomains. Practitioners are also recommended to select instruments that are valid, reliable and appropriate for the purpose it aims to measure, such as the Behavioural Assessment Scale for Intercultural Communication, the Cross-Cultural Adaptability Inventory, the Cultural Intelligence Scale, and the Intercultural Development Inventory to name a few (Schnabel et al, 2015).

Qualitative methods can provide more elaborated responses and highlight the developmental processes which help assess and understand the complex nature of ICC learning outcomes. In Luo and Chan's (2022) systematic review of 34 qualitative studies on ICC assessment from 2007 to 2021, written reflection is the most commonly adopted method, and ICC was mostly assessed by the written mode (e.g., written reflections, essays, written responses to question prompts, reports) and verbal mode (e.g., interviews, discussions), followed by the performative mode (e.g., lived experiences, student actions in natural interactions).

While scholars disagree on any one type of tool to use, they do agree on the need to use a multimethod, multi-perspective mix of formative and summative assessments with intentional objectives and a longitudinal approach that encompasses the learners' development over time (Fantini, 2009; Deardorff, 2009, 2015, 2020; Blair, 2017). In future iterations of this research, we encourage scholars to look at how well works cited in these literature reviews are applied globally because they may have been biased to the US or Western Europe.

RESEARCH METHOD

In this collaborative work, World Council on Intercultural and Global Competence (WCIGC) – Intercultural Competence Assessment Working Group members volunteered to contribute in ways such as research design, translation, distribution of survey, and data analysis. Figure 1 below shows the process of how this research was conducted.

Figure 1. Flow Chart of Research Process

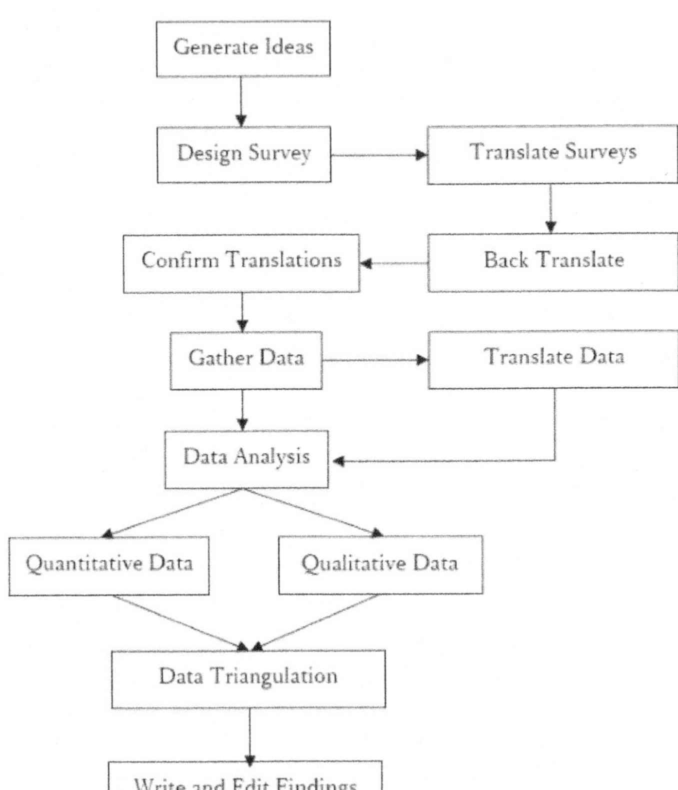

We began generating ideas at a monthly working group meeting in September of 2022, where members of the working group discussed ideas and volunteered to contribute to different stages of this research. Then, two members (Sari and Sabet) created a draft survey for data collection, and it was shared with all working group members to view and discuss before finalizing the survey. After feedback on the draft was gathered, the editors of this chapter (Chu, DeBellis, and Cartwright) established a final version in English, which consists of 19 questions (see Appendix 1). As this is a preliminary study, we purposely devised items that could easily be quantified or coded. Our goal was to set a precedent that could be built upon by future researchers .

In an attempt to conduct a global mapping of ICC assessment practices which is inclusive of different regions, the survey was translated into nine languages by the following contributors of this research: French (Tang), German (Rokos), Japanese (Tang), Mandarin (Chu), Persian (Sabet), Portuguese (Pazini), Spanish

(DeBellis), and Turkish (Esra). Then, the surveys were back-translated into English by different contributors (Chu, Cruz, Hansel, José, Pelka, Tang, and Takahashi). The editors of this chapter confirmed the back-translations matched the contents of the finalized version, and then the surveys were created in Google Forms and Microsoft Forms. They were distributed widely for six weeks through global networks that included, but were not limited to, members of the WCIGC, NAFSA (the North American International Education Association), SIETAR (the Society for Intercultural Education, training, & research), The Forum for Study Abroad, WISE (Workshop on Intercultural Skills Enhancement), etc.

A group of volunteers translated the responses into English and compiled them into a Google spreadsheet. It was shared with different scholars around the world for analysis; a person for quantitative analysis (Khan) running descriptive statistics in Excel; a person for qualitative analysis (Pu) coding open-ended responses with Nvivo; a person for triangulation (Tang); and a person for graphic representation (Cruz). The primary editors of this chapter then reviewed all data and analysis for the final presentation. This research began from drafting survey questions in September, 2022, and the first draft was completed in January, 2023.

RESULTS

A total of 227 responses were gathered in six weeks. It is interesting to note that 129 participants from the survey or 57% do assess intercultural competence as part of their work while 98 participants or 43% do not.

The majority of respondents who completed the survey were from (in order of frequency) the United States of America (35%), China (11%), Mexico (8%), Japan (5%), Germany (5%), Canada (4%), and Australia (3%). While 50 countries were represented and all continents were covered, which is a good representation of the world geographically, it is important to note that the majority of respondents were from the US, as shown in Figure 2.

Figure 2. Representation map of respondents

When asked what type of institution they worked in most respondents stated they were from 1) undergraduate education institutions, 2) graduate education 3) community/technical/vocational colleges and 4) primary/secondary schools. Details can be found in Figure 3 below.

Figure 3. Institution or field of respondents

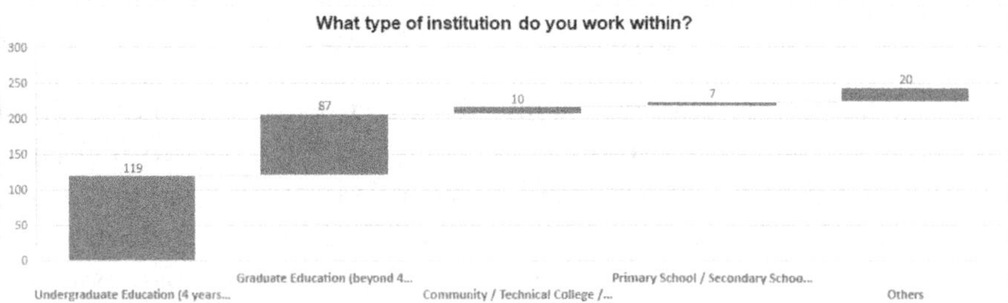

It was no surprise that the majority of the respondents in the survey worked in academic settings: either in 1) an academic unit or 2) in student services. Others mentioned working in areas such as research, teaching, central services and very few worked in the private sector or as volunteers. Assessment of intercultural competence is predominant in higher education as the researchers and members of the WCIGC are fellow educators.

Respondents worked in every discipline, but the top four were university settings, arts and science, business, and languages. Many academic disciplines were listed from engineering, education, computer science, gender studies, history, and nursing, to name a few, to more general services applicable to all students such as international programs, study abroad, student development and even continuing studies, as shown in Figure 4. The variety of academic units listed signifies the extent to which intercultural competence has proliferated through many parts of educational institutions and is not limited to traditional areas such as study abroad.

Figure 4. Academic unit in which the respondents are working

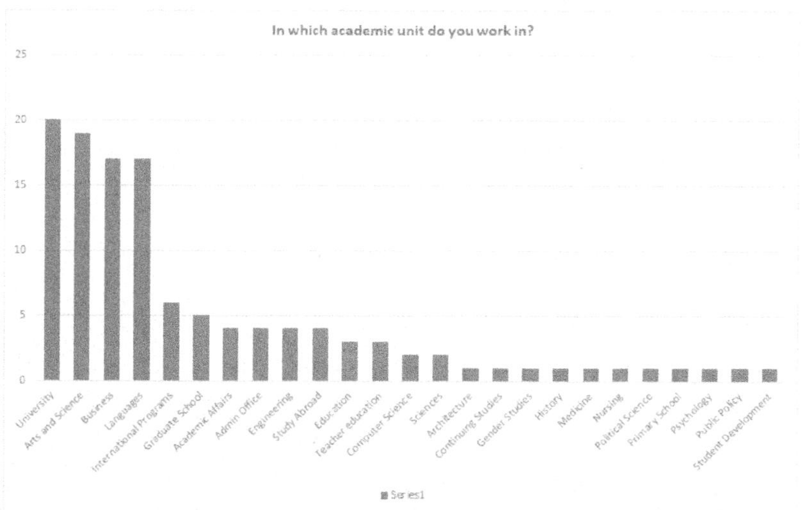

When asked about their role, the top four responses were 1) Instructor/Trainer 2) Administrative/Manager 3) Instructor/Trainer/Administrator/Manager, and 4) Instructor/Professor/Trainer. There was significant overlap of roles with many listing multiple titles encompassing the complex nature of intercultural competence and ultimately which department and/or position bears the responsibility for assessment. It is evident that most respondents identify as educators/ instructors/trainers and less so as project leaders or managers.

Learners served by the respondents of this survey ranged from local (in-country) students to a mix of international, study abroad, and local students, as shown in Figure 5. Given that many educational institutions have a diverse student body it makes sense to have students that are local and international, both who want to stay local and study abroad.

Figure 5. Learners served by the respondents

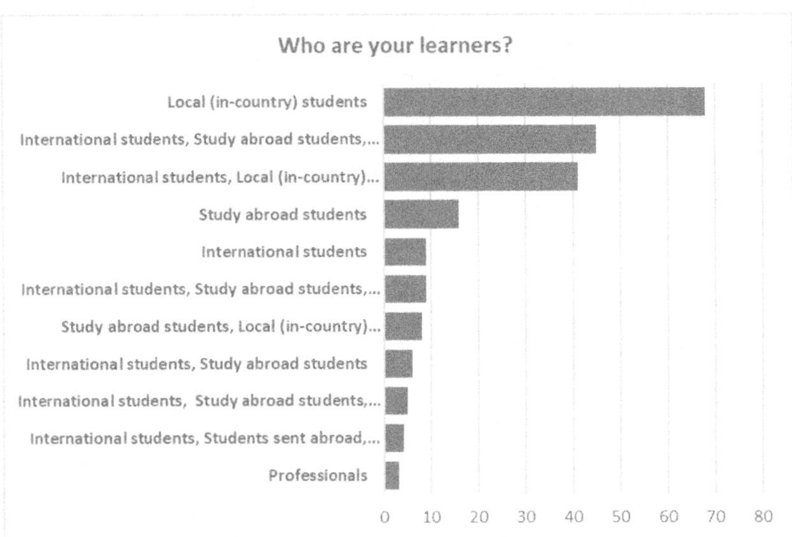

Respondents defined intercultural competence as a set of skills, dispositions/attitudes, awareness, and knowledge. Among skills, communication is the most prominent skill mentioned in the responses followed by listening, critical thinking, interacting with people from varied cultures, bridging cultural differences, adapting to new environments, and language. In regards to disposition/attitudes, some keywords are mentioned, such as openness, empathy, respect, and tolerance. When it comes to awareness and knowledge, these include awareness of one's own culture as well as knowledge of another culture.

The most addressed aspects of intercultural competence in the assessments are skills, particularly communication skills. Other skills mentioned by the respondents are recognizing, analyzing, assessing cultural elements and differences, effectively interacting/working with people from varied cultures, adapting to multicultural environments, critical thinking, problem-solving/conflict resolution, and recognizing biases/stereotypes. The second focus of their assessments is to see if the students have developed or demonstrated an awareness/self-awareness regarding culture, identity, behaviors, and beliefs. Attitudes mark the third place in the assessments, including openness, acceptance, resilience, empathy, respect, curiosity, and tolerance.

From the respondents who confirmed they do assessments, they acknowledged the use of mixed methods, using both quantitative and qualitative methods as the most frequently cited. Participants who stated they only conducted qualitative methods using case studies, observations, practicums, etc. were second and quantitative assessments utilizing surveys and psychometric tools came in last. This finding is in line with the scholarly research that emphasizes the use of mixed methods and a combination of qualitative and quantitative data is best utilized for assessment purposes (Fantini, 2009; Deardorff, 2009; Blair, 2017). Figure 6 below shows the distribution of these assessment practices.

Figure 6. Which approach is being used to assess ICC

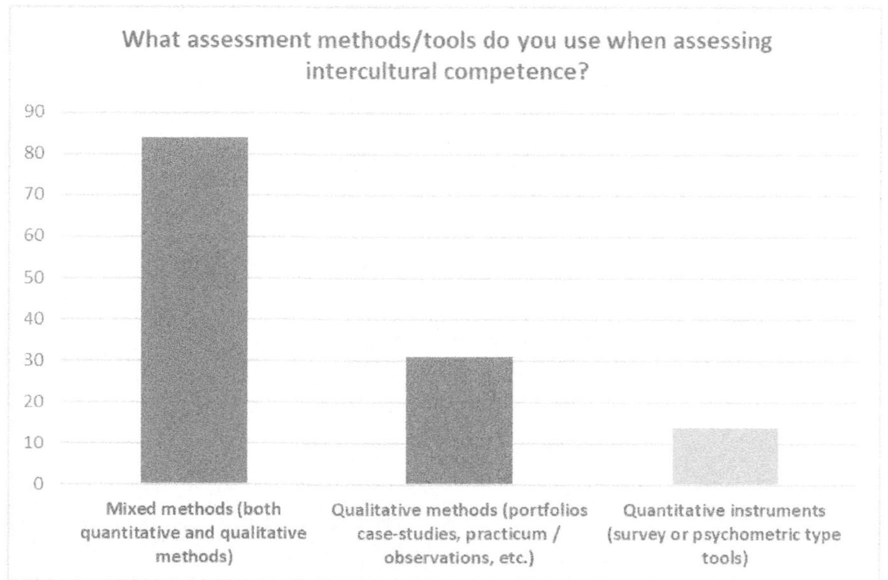

The survey respondents listed several quantitative tools employed in their assessment work (a full list can be found in Appendix 2). Respondents also listed out qualitative assessment tools, including coursework, e-portfolio, case/simulation studies, reflective journals, open-ended questionnaires, observations, discussions, role plays, etc. Additionally, self-designed surveys and tests were used as well. However, it is interesting to note that among those who use either qualitative or quantitative ways of assessing, more respondents employ qualitative measures than quantitative ones. We may assume that there's a tendency in higher education to collect direct evidence through qualitative measures while assessing intercultural competence instead of only using surveys or inventories from the learner perspective (Deardorff, 2011). It is still interesting to note that assessments are being conducted in either a qualitative or quantitative fashion rather than combining the two to obtain optimal results and learning.

When asked how they use the ICC assessment, the majority of respondents stated it was to assess the learning, meaning the data is shared with learners for instructional purposes, or for administrative staff. The assessment of learning where the data is shared with instructors/trainers and staff only for the purpose of program or course improvement or accreditation was secondary, as shown in Figure 7. This data clearly indicates the majority of participants use assessment for the learners to help them improve and develop their intercultural competence and not for the improvement of academic programs of study. Where possible, data should be shared among students and the organization as it would benefit both and would undoubtedly enhance the student's learning and assist the organization to improve their own assessment practices.

Figure 7. How are ICC assessment data being used

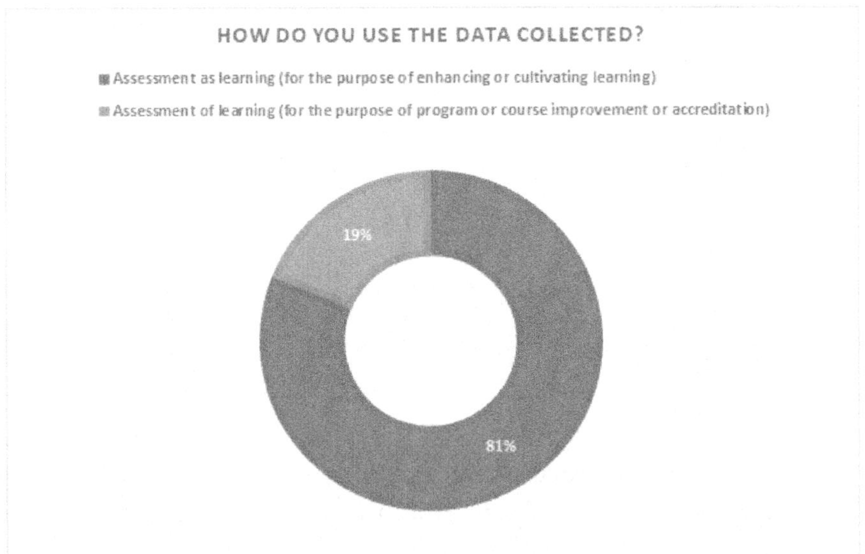

Respondents use both formative and summative assessments as the format of their ICC assessment practice, however, the most frequent use is for 1) formative assessment and 2) summative assessment as secondary. Others also use the assessments for diagnostic purposes to help determine levels of intercultural competence for the program or course of study, as shown in Figure 8.

Figure 8. Formative or summative ICC assessment practices

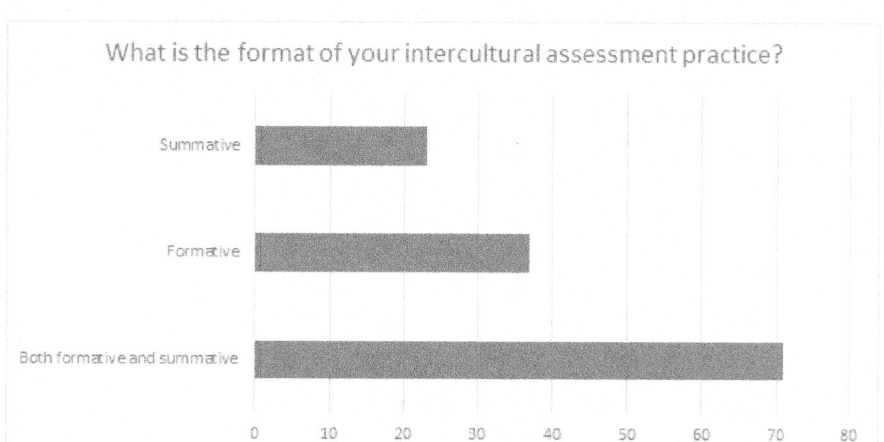

When asked about the level or scale of ICC assessment most indicated it was at the course/cohort level, then at the departmental/program-wide level, and then a combination of departmental, organizational and campus-wide levels, as shown in Figure 9 below.

Figure 9. The scale of ICC assessments

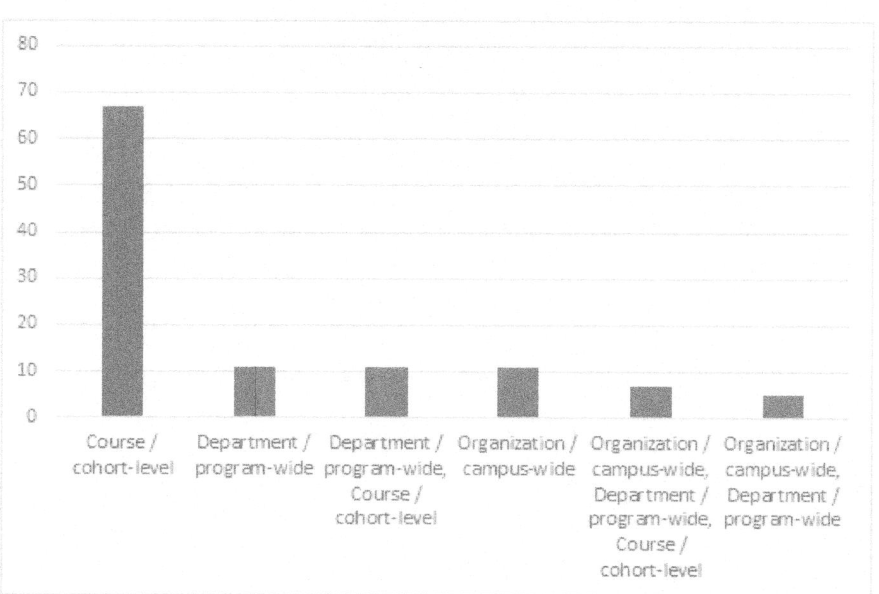

When asked if the respondents assess ICC for internationalization initiatives, accreditation, and research for publication, many chose internationalization. Some also had a combination of the three reasons indicating an overlap of uses and multiple rationales for example equity, diversity, and inclusion, career development, developing strategic frameworks, and optimizing advising tools, as shown in Figure 10. Given the multitude of reasons participants provided, assessment is being used to address multiple rationales. If the assessment is to be done well, more thoughtful consideration of the goals is necessary at the outset to prioritize the outcomes.

Figure 10. Purposes for assessing ICC

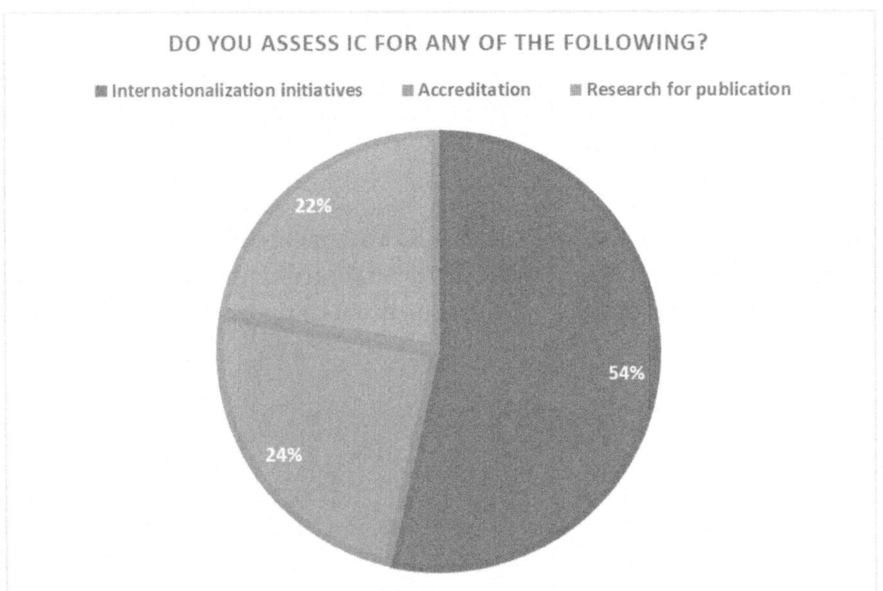

When using an assessment method, participants were asked what they used it for and the top four reasons were (in order of frequency) 1) needs assessment and analysis for individual development, 2) pre and post-measurement of the program's impact, 3) individual development and/or team development and 4) career/academic advising, as shown in Figure 11. Whatever the reason, the assessment that is aligned with the objectives and goals of the program or course is paramount.

Figure 11. Reasons for assessing IC

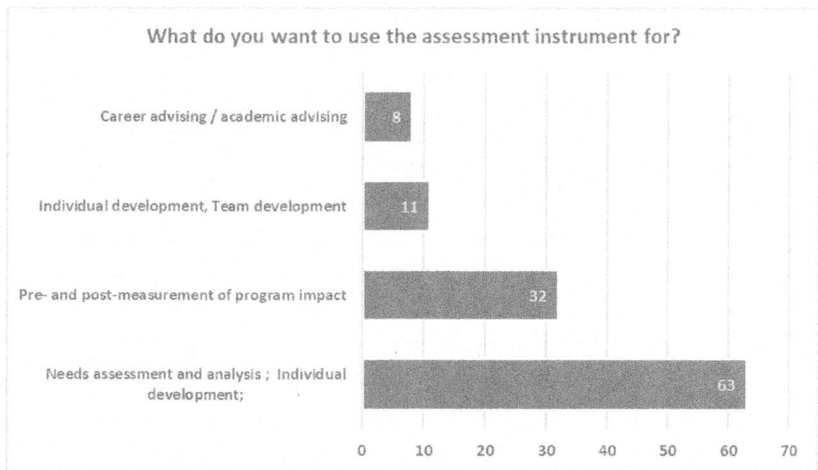

The respondents also indicated that if provided with unlimited support, they would reinforce the assessment of intercultural competence by implementing both qualitative and quantitative measures, integrating IC assessments into the curriculum, creating new ICC activities/programs/experiences, as well as providing training to faculty/staff, and conducting ICC assessment research. These statements reflect some of the previously mentioned constraints which limit the practice of ICC assessment in some institutions. We can sense a willingness for engagement and participation from the respondents in terms of developing the ICC training and assessment in their institutions. It can also be explained by the fact that they volunteered to participate in our survey.

For those who did not conduct assessments, many of the reasons cited were budgetary constraints, lack of time, staffing, other resources, or lack of support and leadership from the organization which made it difficult to move forward. Having key stakeholders as part of the assessment process is a vital part of assessment and without senior leadership support, it becomes siloed and cumbersome, limiting additional input and resources to fully optimize the endeavor.

It is worth noting that the top three reasons that prevented respondents from assessing ICC include 1) not being integrated into the curriculum, 2) limited knowledge of ICC assessment or not knowing about the available ICC assessment tools, and 3) not being perceived as an institutional priority.

DISCUSSION, CONCLUSIONS, AND IMPLICATIONS

This survey provides a preliminary glimpse of the assessment of intercultural competence that is being conducted worldwide and some of the opportunities and challenges associated with them. The fact that only 57% of the participants report that they assess ICC in their work is troubling. Clearly, we have not impressed upon the leadership of this field, especially in higher education, that the improvement in learning outcomes for individual learners as well as programs is worth the investment to support a practice of ICC assessment. As intercultural competence evolves in higher education and other sectors, more emphasis on assessments is needed to provide learners with accurate and comprehensive evidence of their intercultural competence development. In the same vein, programs, courses, and academic units would also benefit from a clear roadmap of assessment practices in order to provide much-needed data to create the framework for further development to achieve their ICC goals. While this research was illuminating and helped recognize and grasp assessments in a more conscientious manner, more research is required to further develop the mapping of ICC with regular surveys.

The results of this research are not surprising to those rare few who are engaged in identifying and developing intercultural competence in their work, especially those in educational settings where this research pool is situated. However, at each cut of the data, there are facets revealed that can be worthy of examination for deeper insights. We'll start our discussion with overall participation and global reach, and then drill down from there.

The overall participation rate ('N') of 227 is both pleasing and insignificant. It is pleasing that in an initial study from a newish organization (WCIGC) with only 3000 members and a mighty, but small, working group of approximately 240 members, we did not expect more than 30-50 respondents total. Conversely, given that we focused our research on people in educational settings who are engaged in intercultural development, we had hoped and worked to secure many, many more respondents. Try to imagine all of the schools and colleges in the world that are working toward growing global understanding or citizenship, and only 227 could respond? We posted our survey to association discussion boards, Facebook, and LinkedIn Groups, as well as to the World Council for Intercultural and Global Competencies listserv. Our online metrics informed us that we'd made it available to over 200,000 people. But how many of us are invited almost weekly to take just 10 minutes of our precious time to answer a few questions and click through without giving the request another thought? Is the participation rate low because potential participants are overwhelmed with requests, have no time, were not asked in a way that they felt was appropriate for their attention, or are the educators doing intercultural development work truly not engaged in assessment work? We believe the answer is a 'both and'; (a) we could have approached potential participants in more effective ways and (b) the practice of assessing for intercultural competencies is not (yet) foundational to many who do this work.

The analysis above tracks easily to the global distribution of respondents to our survey. Getting responses for 50 different countries from around the world is satisfying when one is attempting to find global perspectives. Conversely, the fact that the majority of the 50 countries are represented by a singular respondent is troubling. Interculturalists have long known that a single individual of a cultural group can never be considered representative of anything other than that individual's singular perspective and experience. The fact that the 3 largest groupings of respondents and languages were from the United States of America (English), Mexico (Spanish), and China (Chinese) is intriguing in that we have insights from North America as well as East Asia. However, this may be more the result of the working networks and the languages used by of the research team assembled for this project and the membership of the World Council. Was our distribution network and choice of languages skewed, or is the practice of assessing ICC still too rarefied to gauge with any acuity? Again, we submit that both conclusions are possible.

Again, because the membership of the World Council works predominantly in educational settings, especially higher education, we expected and received the majority of responses from this sector. What is surprising was the number of responses from participants conducting ICC assessment work in graduate education settings (82 or 36%) and in fields other than language and liberal arts (business as an example). Given that ICC in higher education was dominated by undergraduate international education where for both incoming international students and outgoing study abroad students engaged in language and broadly defined 'cultural' learning, these result mirror shifts toward inclusion of ICC in more disciplines that can be found in studies such as the Institutes of International Education's (IIE) annual Open Doors report (IIE, 2022).

We find the plethora of roles that respondents offered to be emblematic of the multitasking type of duties in which people who do this work must engage. They may be primarily paid either as an instructor or an administrator, but must straddle multiple responsibilities as they attend to such divergent roles and constituencies in order to carry out this work.

The definitions of intercultural competence and the learning objectives employed to reach intercultural competences are intriguing. Previous scholars (Bennett 2008; Byrum 1997; Deardorff 2006, 2009, 2015, & 2020; Fantini 2009; Savicki 2020, Vande Berg, Paige & Lou 2012) have all laid out definitions of ICC that are either more succinct or comprehensive than those offered by our participants. However, the respondents' definitions are more colloquial and therefore more applied than those offered by our respected scholars and therefore worth consideration. We know of no study that compiled learning objectives tied to ICC, so our initial findings here are insightful for those either initiating ICC development work, or seeking to polish or refine an already launched initiative.

The highest percentage finding in this whole study was the preference for mixed-method assessment practices. Over 80% of respondents report adopting this practice and this can be considered a win for the field. Research has shown that the assessment of intercultural competency is complex and requires multiple methods and time-sequenced assessments in order to find evidence of ICC either initially, or as a result of a treatment (course, experience, training, etc.) Many are using only qualitative or quantitative assessment methods, which may be as much of an issue of access and infrastructure to support mixed method work as it is to mindset, preference, or comfort level with either format. In general, our respondents who engage in assessment are on the right path for moving this work forward for their learners and for their institutions.

The fact that the majority are practicing assessment of intercultural competence doing both formative and summative assessments and are sharing the data with their learners demonstrates that they are supporting learners in seeing how they can grow in terms of ICC. The majority are also leveraging their assessment of ICC to support individual development for their learners for a variety of reasons, but centering their work on course level and individual development is evident.

There is an intriguing anomaly in the data surrounding the purpose and level of assessment work being conducted. A slight majority of respondents (54%) report that they conduct assessment of intercultural competence for the purposes of supporting a campus internationalization initiative. A greater majority report that they conduct assessment of ICC at the course (67%) level. But only 22% report doing this work tied to accreditation and 5-11% report using assessment data beyond the course level (department-wide, campus-wide, etc.) This lack of tie to campus accreditation and much aggregation of data to enlighten the campus community of what is or could be developed in terms of intercultural competence is troubling. Is internationalization not tied to overall campus accreditation? Are departmental, unit/school level, or campus level learning objectives devoid of global/intercultural competencies? Are we truly training our learners to be full participants in our deeply diverse and interconnected world? These results are baffling and worth further consideration.

We'll end with where the results started, the fact that a very slight majority (57%) of our respondents practice assessment of intercultural competencies as foundational to their work, leaving 43% not doing so for a variety of valid reasons. Building on our discussion on the levels of assessment and its ties to the overall learning outcomes of a degree or plan of study, we see this slim adoption rate as evidence of a lack of leadership and buy-in from leadership in our field. The evidence of the positive impacts of intercultural competence is compelling and significant (Paige, Fry, Stallman, Josić, & Jon, 2009; Vande Berg, Paige, & Lou, 2012). The evidence of the positive impacts of a practice of assessment-supported intercultural development (Acheson, Jin, Stahl, & Yngve, 2021) is again compelling and significant; however, our work is not being valued enough to become a catalyst for change within our organizations in order to support the implementation of intercultural competence identification and development on the scale that it is needed.

Improvements for future mapping study:

No study can be completed without unearthing areas of deficit. Here are a few areas that we feel could be improved by scholars who take this work up after us. (The WCIGC has committed to replicating this study in future years to build upon these initial results.)

Overall and global response rate:

- Take more time to attract and empower an even wider and more globally diverse team to conduct this study to ensure the survey reaches more possible respondents, in languages that they can access, and in the necessary time frames in which they can respond.

Diversify the representation of team members by work sectors:

- Government, NGOs, corporate, and consultant/coaches all develop intercultural competence as a part of their work and many have an assessment practice associated with this work, but our study was aligned too closely to higher education to be of interest or value to those outside of higher education.

Survey instrument:

- Refining the survey instrument is required, as data from several items would have been more valuable if the respondents had been supplied with simplified options to choose from.

Extended studies:

- Ask for data, examples, and case studies of the impacts of assessing intercultural competence, may belong to a different study, but we feel that it is necessary to convince leadership to support our work more fully.

- Another possible study could be to investigate whether participants who are indeed conducting IC assessments are doing so in sufficient and effective ways.

Conclusion:

We set out to conduct an initial study of the practice of assessing intercultural competencies in higher education settings. We feel we have completed that task. Practitioners and future scholars can find both insights into what is being done in ICC assessment and how as well as the antecedents for future research. We thank the World Council for Intercultural and Global Competencies for this opportunity and the dedicated team that volunteered to join us in this work. We offer these results with both pride and humility of what we have accomplished in this short study and what is yet to be found. Thank you.

REFERENCES

Acheson, K., Jin, L., Stahl, A., & Yngve, K. (2021). Introduction: Special issue on assessment as pedagogy in education abroad. *Frontiers, 33*(1), 1–10. https://doi.org/10.36366/frontiers.v33i1.624

Allen, T. J. (2022). Assessing intercultural competence using situational judgement tests: Reports from an EMI course in Japan. *Open Journal of Social Sciences, 10*(13), 405–427. https://doi.org/10.4236/jss.2022.1013029

Ang, S., Dyne, L. V., Koh, C., Ng, K. Y., Templer, K. J.,Tay, C., Chandrasekar, N.A. (2007). Cultural intelligence: Its measurement and effects in cultural judgement and decision making, cultural adaptation and task performance, *Management and Organization Review, 3*(3), 335-371

Bennett, J. M. (2008). Transformative training: Designing programs for culture learning. In M. A. Moodian (Ed.), *Contemporary leadership and intercultural competence: Understanding and utilizing cultural diversity to build successful organizations* (pp. 95-110). Sage.

De Meyer, A. (2012). Reflections on the globalization of management education. *The Journal of Management Development, 31*(4), 336-345.

Deardorff, D. K. (2004). *The identification and assessment of intercultural competence as a student outcome of international education at institutions of higher education in the United States.* [Unpublished doctoral dissertation, North Carolina State University, Raleigh.] (Publication No. AAT 3128751)

Deardorff, D. K. (2004). In search of intercultural competence. *International Educator, 13*(2), 13–15.

Deardorff, D. K. (2006). Identification and assessment of intercultural competence as a student outcome of internationalization. *Journal of Studies in International Education, 10*(3), 241-266. https://doi.org/10.1177/1028315306287002

Deardorff, D. K. (2009). *The SAGE handbook of intercultural competence.* Sage. https://doi.org/10.4135/9781071872987

Deardorff, D. K. (2011). Assessing intercultural competence. *New Directions for Institutional Research, 2011*(149), 65.

Deardorff, D. K. (2015). *Demystifying outcomes assessment for international educators: A practical approach.* Stylus Publishing.

Deardorff, D. K. (2020). Defining, developing and assessing intercultural competence. In G. Rings & S. Rasinger (Eds.), *The Cambridge handbook of intercultural communication* (pp. 493-503). Cambridge University Press. https://doi.org/10.1017/9781108555067

Eisenberg, J., Lee, H., Brück, F., Brenner, B., Claes, M., Mironski, J., & Bell, R. (2013). Can business schools make students culturally competent? Effects of cross-cultural management courses on cultural intelligence. *Academy of Management Learning & Education, 12*(4), 603-621.

Fantini, A. (2009). Assessing intercultural competence: Issues and tools. In Deardorff, D. K. (Ed.), *The SAGE handbook of intercultural competence* (pp. 456–476). Sage Publications.

Graduate Management Admission Council. (2016). *Connecting with the core motivations of business school candidates: Global graduate management education segmentation study.*

Institute for International Education, (2022) Open Doors; Retrieved November 2022 from https://opendoorsdata.org/

Jalali, M. (2021). Developing and assessing intercultural competence through ethnographic interviews in the domestic context of teacher education in Iran, *Issues in Language Teaching, 10*(2), 119-144.

Kurpis, L. H., & Hunter, J. (2017). Developing students' cultural intelligence through an experiential learning activity: A cross-cultural consumer behaviour interview. *Journal of Marketing Education, 39*(1), 30-46.

Luo, J., & Chan, C. K. Y. (2022). Qualitative methods to assess intercultural competence in higher education research: A systematic review with practical implications. *Educational Research Review, 37*, 100476. https://doi.org/10.1016/j.edurev.2022.100476

McMillan, C., & Overall, J. (2016). Management relevance in a business school setting: A research note on an empirical investigation. *The International Journal of Management Education, 14*(2), 187-197.

Paige, R. M., Fry, G. W., Stallman, E. M., Josić, J., & Jon, J.-E. (2009). Study abroad for global engagement: the long-term impact of mobility experiences. *Intercultural Education, 20*(sup1), S29–S44. https://doi.org/10.1080/14675980903370847

Richter, N. F., Schlaegel, C., Taras, V., Alon, I., & Bird, A. (2023). Reviewing half a century of measuring cross-cultural competence: Aligning theoretical constructs and empirical measures. *International Business Review, 32*(4), 102-122.

Rhodes, T. L. (2010). *Assessing outcomes and improving achievement: Tips and tools for using rubrics.* Association of American Colleges and Universities.

Savicki, V. (Ed.). (2020). *Developing intercultural competence and transformation: Theory, research, and application in international education.* Stylus Publishing, LLC.

Stevens, M. J., Bird, A., Mendenhall, M., Oddou, G. (2014). Measuring global leader intercultural competency: Development and validation of the Global Competencies Inventory (GCI). In *Advances in global leadership* (pp. 115-154). Emerald Group Publishing Limited.

Vande Berg, M., Paige, R. M., & Lou, K. H. (2012). *Student learning abroad: What our students are learning, what they're not, and what we can do about it* (1st ed.). Stylus Publishing, LLC.

Appendix 1

IC Assessment Questionnaire V3

<u>Section I</u> *{Who is assessing? Who is being assessed?}*

1. Where in the world do you practice?

2. What type of Institution do you work within?

Primary School/Secondary School *(K-12)*

Community/Technical College/Vocational *(2 years of less)*

Undergraduate Education *(4 year or more)*

Graduate Education *(beyond 4 years)*

Other: *(Please list)* ____________________

3.   Which field in higher education do you work in?

Academic Unit: ____________

Student Service Unit: __________

Other: ____________________

4.   Role; What is your role in your Institution? *(check all that apply)*

Learner

Instructors/Trainers

Administrators/Managers

Assessment Personnel

Other: *(please specify)* ____________________

5. Learners; Are your learners *(check all that apply)*

International Students?

Study Abroad students?

Local *(in-country)* Students

Other: ____________________

6.Do you assess intercultural competence as a part of your work?

Yes __ *(Please skip question 7 & continue with questions in and beyond Section I)*

No __ (Please answer question 7 and submit. Thank you.)

7.Why Not? ______________________________

<u>Section II *{What is your Practice of Assessing IC?}*</u>

8.How do you define IC? ______________________

9.What components of IC are most valued in your context? ____________

10. What is the learning objective(s)/goals that you are assessing when you assess IC? ______________________

11. What assessment methods/tools to you use when assessing IC? *(check all that apply)*

· Quantitative instruments *(survey or psychometric type tools)*?

· Qualitative methods *(portfolios, case-studies, practicum/observations, etc.)*?

· Mixed Methods *(both Quantitative & Qualitative methods)*?

· Please briefly list tools or practices: ______________________

12. How do you use the IC assessment data collected? *(check all that apply)*

· Assessment *as* learning *(data shared with learners as well as instructional & administrative staff for the purpose of enhancing or cultivating learning)*?

· Assessment *of* Learning *(data shared with instructors/trainers and staff only for the purpose of program or course improvement or accreditation)*?

· Other, please explain: ______________________

13. What is the format of your IC assessment practice? *(check all that apply)*

·   Formative; (*singular assessment at either the start or end of the course/training/program of study*)?

·   Summative; (*pre-post format assessment – so at least twice at the start & end of the course/training/program of study*)

·   Both?

14. Level or Scale of IC Assessment *(Check all that apply)*

·   Organization/Campus-Wide

·   Department/Program-Wide

·   Course/Cohort-Level

·   Other __________

<u>Section III *{Why Assess IC?}*:</u>

15. What do you want to use the assessment instrument for? *(Chose all that apply)*

·   Needs assessment and analysis

·   Pre- and post-measurement of program impact

·   Individual development

·   Team development

·   Re-entry (Post Study Abroad Debriefing)

·   Career advising/academic advising

·   Other (explain) ________________

16. Is your assessment of IC to be used for any of the following? *(Check all that apply)*

·   Accreditation

·   Internationalization initiatives

·   Research for publication

·   Other, please explain. _________________________

Section IV *{What if? What barriers?}*

17. What if there were no limitations to assessing IC in your context *{full budget, no time limits, willing/collaborative stakeholders, etc.)* What would you do to assess IC? _________________________________

18. What barriers do you face today that keep you from assessing IC? _________________

Optional Follow up:

If you would like a copy of the IC Assessment Planning Form as our 'Thank you for completing the survey; please leave your name & email below. Also, if you would like to follow-up with us about this survey, please leave your name & email below.

1.Name: _________________________

2.Email Address: _______________________

Appendix 2

Quantitative Assessment Tools Reported by Survey Respondents
(listed in alphabetical order)

Aptitude, Knowledge, and Skills Scales (A.S.K.S.2)	Intercultural Conflict Style Inventory (ICSI)	Global Competencies Inventory (GCI)
Beliefs, Events, and Values Inventory (BEVI)	Intercultural Communication Competence Scale	Global DISC
Cross-Cultural Adaptability Inventory (CCAI)	Intercultural Competence Test	Global Equity Standard (GES)
Cross-Cultural Perspectives Scale	Intercultural Development Inventory (IDI)	Global Engagement Measurement Scale (GEMS)
Cultural Agility	Intercultural Effectiveness Scale (IES)	Global Learning Rubric
Culture Calculator	Intercultural Knowledge and Competency Rubric	Globe Smart Inventory (GSI)
Culture Connector	Intercultural Leadership Matrix (self-designed tool)	Multicultural Awareness Knowledge and Skills Survey (MAKSS)
Cultural Intelligence Scale (CQS)	Intercultural Readiness Check (IRC)	My Cultural Awareness Profile (MyCAP)
Cultural Mapping Inventory (CMI)	Intercultural Sensitivity Scale (ISS)	Scale of Intercultural Empathy
Inclusive Behaviors Inventory (IBI)	Interpretative Co-Actional Perspective (ICAP)	National Survey of Student Engagement (NSSE)
Inclusion Competence Inventory (ICI)	Intercultural Hermeneutics (IH)	Offender Assessment Index (OAI)
Intercultural Awareness Scale (IAS)	Global Aptitude Test	3 Colors of Worldview

Bios

CURTIS CHU, PhD, is an assistant professor in the Global Education Center at Setsunan University, Japan. He is interested in internalization in education, intercultural competence, virtual exchange, global citizenship, and translanguaging. Email: curtis2020@gmail.com

CALLIE K. DEBELLIS, M.A, is an Assistant Professor of Spanish in the Department of World Languages and Cultures and Director of Meredith in Italy in the Office of International Programs, Meredith College. Her research interests lie in the areas of intercultural competence assessment, international education, and community-based learning. Email: debellis@meredith.edu

CHRIS T. CARTWRIGHT, MPA, Ed.D, is a consultant and adjunct instructor in International and Global Studies, Portland State University. His primary interest lies in the assessment and development of intercultural, inclusion, and global competencies. Email: cartwrightc57@gmail.com

FREEDA BUKHARI KHAN is a Ph.D. student at the University of Toronto. She is a qualified administrator for the Cultural Intelligence (CQ) Assessment and the Intercultural Development Inventory (IDI) to measure intercultural competence. Her research interests are in the internationalization of higher education, intercultural competence, cultural intelligence, and global citizenship. Email: freeda.khan@Rotman.Utoronto.Ca

CHANG PU, PhD, is an associate professor of teacher education at Berry College, USA. Her current research interests include Teaching English for Speakers of Other Languages, Intercultural Competence, Virtual Exchange/COIL, and Teacher Education. Email: cpu@berry.edu

WENJUN TANG, PhD, is an Assistant Professor at the Department of Foreign Languages, Civil Aviation Flight University of China. Her major research interests lie in the area of Computer-assisted language learning and Global Competence Education. Email: wenjun_0308@qq.com

Chapter 4

Underrepresented Voices in Intercultural Competence Scholarship Exploratory

Analysis of an Annotated Bibliography

Grace Lee-Amuzie
The Penn State University, United States of America

Horane A. Diatta-Holgate
University of Notre Dame, United States of America

Kris Acheson
Purdue University, United States of America

Kyra Garson
Thompson Rivers University, Canada

ABSTRACT

In this chapter, our working group reports on . the "state of the field" amplifying underrepresented voices in intercultural research—that is, what have these voices already contributed, in which disciplines do those voices seem most welcome, and what are the apparent gaps in representation. Our first step was to construct an annotated bibliography that gathered and cataloged some of these contributions. Contributions to the annotated bibliography were made by eight regular working group members coming from several global regions (see acknowledgements); the analysis was conducted by a core group of four members (the authors listed above). The bibliography now includes 126 entries. This chapter offers an analysis of the themes and gaps of the collected literature and makes recommendations for further amplifying underrepresented voices in this area of scholarship.

Keywords: access, global literature review, minoritized scholars, representation, state of the field critique, thematic analysis

INTRODUCTION

The global experience of the COVID-19 pandemic coupled with the reckoning of racial injustice and increasing recognition of social inequality have forced many disciplines to more explicitly grapple with questions about equity, marginalization and access (Cooper & Nagel, 2022; Evered et al., 2023; Laurencin & McClinton, 2022). While the definitions, conceptualizations, and models applied in intercultural communication and competence scholarship and practice have varied across time and context (Spitzberg & Changnon, 2009).), given these recent events, there is reason to pause and reflect on the extent to which the scholarship of our discipline reflects the experiences of members across various marginalized groups. Through this project, we wanted to explore how or whether intercultural research has taken the time to include and understand the perspectives of those outside dominant discourses. In this chapter we attempt to highlight some of the people, perspectives, regions and disciplines in intercultural scholarship and practice which have not always been presented as salient.

When our working group convened, we articulated the goal of opening spaces for and amplifying underrepresented voices in intercultural research. We decided rather than doing a traditional review of literature we wanted to construct an annotated bibliography (Purdue O.W.L., 2022) that gathered and cataloged some of these contributions. Most existing annotated bibliographies were discipline specific, for example limited to Business, and the most recent interdisciplinary example we found (Casmir, 1987) did not intentionally seek underrepresented voices so the majority of entries are from the North / West. Therefore, we decided that we needed to review the current "state of the field" with a focus on underrepresented scholarship. We wanted to explore what these voices have already contributed (whether we've been listening or not), in which disciplines those voices seem most welcome, and what the apparent gaps in representation are.

Before we discuss our findings, we will describe our own journey as intercultural scholars, reflecting on what brought us to this project. In the early stages of the project after deciding that we would undertake the seemingly impossible task of developing this annotated bibliography, we took some time during one of our meetings to reflect on why we joined a working group focused on underrepresented voices. The reflections that follow are from the authors of this chapter as well as members of our initial working group.

For us as lifelong learners there are things that we're just not aware of…there's a real need and a responsibility for us as a community to make space for other voices and we have not always in our place of privilege made the effort to do that. (Kris)

…Looking at Deardorff's Sage Handbook (2009) , I remember thinking there's got to be other perspectives about this framing it [intercultural development] from different cultural and linguistic backgrounds (Kyra)

My interest was piqued largely because of the gaps that I was observing at the time, some of which I didn't even realize because I was sort of in my own little world working. (Horane)

As an Asian and multilingual scholar with marginalized identities, I also recognize that there are other voices that are even further marginalized. (Grace)

For each of us, curiosity was a driving force, a desire to know and seek out what else was out there. What were other ways of thinking about the concepts and frameworks we were using and thinking about in our research and practice? We also realized there was a need, and gaps not only in our knowledge and understanding, but in the field, regarding diverse voices and perspectives. Grace and Kyra's reflections highlighted the role of *identity* in intercultural scholarship. Whose voices are heard or amplified, in what contexts or venues? As we developed the bibliography *identity* became an important theme as we experienced challenges with navigating various sources and recognizing our own limitations. We discuss this later in the chapter.

By the end of this chapter, our hope is that readers will become even more curious, and inspired to continue the conversation within intercultural scholarship and practice across disciplines. We hope readers will become more intentional about including, listening and amplifying a greater diversity of voices and perspectives to enrich our understanding of ourselves and one another. We wanted to explore the following questions:

1. What are the themes in the included scholarship?

2. What gaps emerged, and what are some reasons for those gaps? (Who we are? What do we have access to? Whose voices do we make room for or give credibility to?)

3. What are the implications of these findings? Where do we go from here?

In the subsequent sections we describe the methods and scope of the bibliography, the criteria for inclusion and exclusion of sources. Then we discuss the process of analysis and some salient themes and gaps we identified. We conclude with implications of this work and recommendations for future directions to continue this work. We want to acknowledge that this bibliography does not represent an exhaustive list of all the perspectives from various marginalized peoples.

METHODS AND SCOPE

Our approach to address the aforementioned questions was organic and process-oriented. Unlike a traditional literature review, which discusses various select publications in relation to each other in narrative form, an annotated bibliography collects in list form and offers commentary on a set of literature, usually guided by inclusion and exclusion criteria, in order to facilitate access to the sources for readers and to support analysis of the relationship between included parts and the whole (Purdue O.W.L., 2022; University of North Texas, 2023). Scholars in various fields have used an annotated bibliography to present an overview of the published literature and to show the direction being taken in research on their topics of interests, (e.g., Macinco & Sarfield, 2002), to provide more attention to certain areas and to identify suggestions for action (e.g., Wright & Tsao, 1983), or to provide researchers and practitioners with access to important contributions in the field (e.g., Kendall et al., 2010).

Contributions to our annotated bibliography were made by eight regular working group members coming from several global regions (see acknowledgements); the analysis presented was conducted by a core group of four members (the authors listed above). The bibliography now includes 126 entries. The working group met monthly and sometimes biweekly in synchronous online working sessions. In these sessions, each team member made individual contributions to a table in a shared Google spreadsheet based on publications they had found, listing each citation (e.g., author, title, year, link) along with certain inferred details such as topic, discipline, description, and region. Strategies we used to find sources to include varied. Some of us used keyword searches by topic and region in scholarly indexes or library sites. Others perused our physical bookshelves and digital drives for relevant literature, searched through issues of specific journals that publish in this area, and mined anthologies, handbooks, and citation lists to discover relevant works to include or authors and topics to search further. We also intentionally sought out work from particular regions or cultural groups that seemed to be missing.

As we worked to construct the bibliography, questions arose about what exactly we were looking for. We needed to come to a shared understanding of how we should decide whether to list a publication. Thus, part of our process was to articulate detailed inclusion and exclusion criteria. As the project developed, we sought feedback on our criteria and processes from the larger World Council community via two platforms -- a blog (Authors., 2021a), and a live webinar presented in cooperation with the Intercultural Resources Working Group (Authors., 2021b). The finalized criteria for the project are listed below.

Inclusion Criteria (all must be met to be included):

- Brings underrepresented voices (defined as from underrepresented regions of the world, minoritized populations, non-dominant perspectives and ideologies, etc.) into the scholarly literature;

- Explicitly related topically to intercultural competence and cognate fields (IC relations, IC communication, IC education and training, IC assessment, conflict resolution, peace studies, global management, multicultural studies, language and culture learning, international education);

- Work from a critical perspective, regardless of the identity of authors, that ethically amplifies non-dominant epistemologies and ontologies and local knowledge;

- Articles that critique—specifically with regard to intercultural interactions—the histories, systems, theoretical frameworks, or practices that colonize or suppress underrepresented voices;

- Publications in any language may be included (titles at least must be translated into English in the annotated bibliography; note whenever a source is available in multiple languages).

Exclusion Criteria (if any are true they are excluded):

- Scholarship in these fields that represents "dominant" ideologies, discourses, cultural perspectives, theoretical frameworks, social identities, and regions of the world;

- Texts and media not in scholarly venues (e.g., popular music, blogs);

- Work that represents underrepresented perspectives from an outsider's perspective (e.g., anthropological study of an Indigenous population by a White scholar; "Nothing about us without us"); and

• Cultural, anthropological, or sociological studies of a single culture without emphasis on the intercultural.

Categories for Analysis

We began by searching for publications from different regions, populating a spreadsheet with entries that included the bibliographic source, and hyperlink when available, the topic / discipline with a short description, and the region/nation of the author. Each of us initialed the entries we made so that we could provide additional details as we moved forward. As we talked through the sources we were compiling, it became clear that we needed additional categories and a refining of our initial categories. Our broad categorization of topic/discipline became topic, discipline of scholar, discipline of publication, thematic category, and key ideas. We also realized that we needed to include the paradigm of the work and the methodological approach.

The topic and thematic categories evolved organically as we began to see patterns. For example, several entries were clearly dealing with aspects of identity, whereas others were focused on communication. Thematic categories emerged as we identified patterns in the key ideas which allowed us to differentiate between sources that were centered on specific topics such as global citizenship education, Indigenous knowledges, geopolitics, linguistics, or intercultural development. Refining and adding categories ultimately allowed us a richer analysis across the categories, as we were able to discover the prominent paradigms by region, year of publication, or discipline of the scholar. We were also able to identify thematic categories that were more prominent in specific regions or disciplinary publications. Table 1 provides a summary of the final categories.

Table 1: Categories for Analysis

Category	Sub-Categories
Publication date	Sorted by decade 1950s to present
Region of publication - 8 United Nations regions (UN, 2019)	Sub-Saharan Africa Northern Africa and Western Asia/MENA Central and Southern Asia Eastern and South-Eastern Asia Latin America and the Caribbean Australia and New Zealand Oceania Europe, Northern America/Global North Global, Multiple categories
Country/nation of author	By country or multiple countries
Paradigm	Critical, interpretivist, social scientific
Methodological Approach	Qualitative (e.g., case study, ethnography, discourse analysis) Quantitative (e.g., psychometric assessment, questionnaire) Theoretical (e.g., critique, commentary)
Thematic Category	Adaptation/acculturation/assimilation Critical global citizenship Critiques of dominant voices/alternate paradigms (e.g., subversion of Eurocentrism, postcolonialism) Cross-cultural interactions Identity (e.g., linguistic, racial, ethnic, gender, intersectionality, marginalization/exclusion) Indigenous knowledge Intercultural competence development Migration/refugee experiences Other
Discipline of Scholar and Discipline of Publication	For example, African studies, anthropology, applied linguistics, Black studies, business, communication, cultural studies, education, political science, psychology, sociology

Each entry also included topics drawn from the language used in the texts and a description which provided us with detailed information. These topics and descriptions later helped inform our analysis as the bibliography grew and we refined the thematic categories for analysis.

Analysis Processes

Our approach was to base inductive thematic analysis (Alhojailan, 2012) on the categories included in our annotated bibliography. To address the above questions, our team sorted the bibliography by different categories (region, discipline of scholar, discipline of publication ,themes, and year of publication). Descriptive statistics were computed through excel, based on the different sorting category. The implications of the findings were discussed in several team meetings. The next section will present the findings of our analysis and discuss their implications for the "state of the field", as well as propose concrete actions we all can take to address gaps the analysis identified.

RESULTS AND DISCUSSION

Themes

Our first task in the thematic analysis was to identify which themes were present and which were most prominent. Two themes had the most entries; together these two themes account for roughly half of the annotated bibliography. These two most popular themes were Identity (n=30) and Critiques of Dominant Voices (n=28). Identity was a complex theme that included several subcategories, such as Racial/Ethnic Identity (n=19), Linguistic Identity (n=5), and Intersectionality (n=6). Critiques of Dominant Voices also included several subthemes, for example expositions of Eurocentric assumptions that Western scholarship could be universally applied and criticism of colonial legacies. A middle tier of four themes which each held a significant number of texts included Critical Global Citizenship (n=17), Cross-Cultural Interactions (n=14), including 5 on Bias/Discrimination), Intercultural Competence Development (n=12), and Indigenous Knowledge (n=10). Two smaller themes were also present: Migration (n=6) and Cultural Phenomena such as Adaptation, Acculturation, Assimilation (n=5).

Interestingly, patterns appeared in the themes when we sorted the bibliography by methodological approach. The texts that featured theoretical development overwhelmingly represented the themes of Identity, Critiques of Dominant Voices, and Critical Global Citizenship. These three themes were also dominant in qualitative research, but qualitative studies also featured a number of texts on Indigenous Knowledge and Cultural Phenomena. Finally, quantitative research tended to document Cross-Cultural Interactions and Intercultural Competence Development. These patterns are not necessarily surprising, since some themes may naturally lend themselves to particular ways of knowing -- that is, scholars critiquing eurocentric theories will likely engage in theoretical development and those trying to establish when and why learners develop intercultural competence (or don't) may be prone to leverage the predictive power of empirical quantitative methods.

Many themes seem to be tied to the positionality of the authors themselves. Said another way, who scholars are seems connected to the topics of the scholarship they are producing and the questions they ask. It makes sense, given their positionality as historically minoritized voices in the research community, that the bibliography would be rife with critiques of dominant voices, a focus on bias/discrimination in cross-cultural interactions, and centering of Indigenous knowledge. Among the works in these themes, a couple of the earlier contributions seem to have been particularly influential for future research, based on the high number of citations that those works have garnered over the years as well as the streams of related research that they helped inspire. In this bibliography, an example of those paradigm-shifting early pieces is Molefi Asante's (1983) work on Afrocentrism. In addition to the influence of identity in theme generation, it is also worth noting that many themes also seem to stem from the tenets and values of the critical research paradigm, which encourages attention to power and subjectivity and promotes agency towards social change. Example themes that emerge naturally from critical scholarship are explorations of socially constructed identity, particularly intersectional conceptualizations of identity, critiques of dominant voices, and critical global citizenship. Readers interested in discovering more about these themes are encouraged to explore the annotated bibliography on their own.

Representation and Gaps

To see regional representations in our bibliography, we conducted a content analysis of the publications and coded data using the UN's 7-region category (UN, 2019) to indicate what region the publications represent. In determining whose voice publications represent, we looked at both research context/site and researcher's origin (where it was stated in the text or easily discernible from public information). When context and researcher differed, we labeled based on context and made a note of researcher' origin. Table 2 presents the counts of the seven regions. The most dominant region was Eastern and Southeast Asia (N=35), followed by Europe and North America (N=33). The most underrepresented were Central and Southern Asia, the African Diaspora, Oceania and Australia/New Zealand.

Taking a closer look at each region, we also found that many regions were often dominated by a few countries. For example, the vast majority of Eastern and South-Eastern Asia were from China, South Korea, and Japan. South Asia is dominated by India, and Sub-Saharan Africa by South Africa. Latin America, Australia, and New Zealand mostly represented Indigenous perspectives. It is worth noting that there are underrepresented voices even among underrepresented regions. Table 2 summarizes the regional representation.

We also analyzed the content of the annotated bibliography according to the discipline of scholars, presented in Table 3. Scholars come from a range of disciplines, with the largest number of authors (N=33) either employed as faculty of communication in higher education institutions or self-identifying in their writing as communication scholars. We also see the social and behavioral sciences as dominant with very few contributions from the natural sciences and technology, or what is often known as STEM (Science, Technology, Engineering, Mathematics). To get a sense of the transdisciplinarity of these publications, we compared the discipline of each scholar to the discipline of the publication venue (that is, journal scope, professed book audience, publisher focus, etc.). Interestingly, scholars in some disciplines appear to be more transdisciplinary than others. For example, manuscripts in Sociology publications were often

Table 2: **Regional Representation**

Region	N
Sub-Saharan Africa (including African Diaspora)	19
Northern Africa and Western Asia / MENA	22 (9 Middle East; 13 Northern Africa)
Central and Southern Asia	5 (South Asia)
Eastern and South-Eastern Asia	35
Latin America and the Caribbean	14 (7 Latin America; 7 Caribbean)
Australia, New Zealand and	4
Europe and Northern America/ Global North	33 (10 Europe and 13 North America)
Oceania	2
Global/Multiple Regions	12

written by scholars who are not in the Sociology field themselves. On the contrary, Communication, Linguistics, Education, and Psychology showed the highest percentage of alignment between author discipline and publication discipline, suggesting more insular or siloed cultures within those fields, without as much cross-pollination from other areas of study.

Another category of our content analysis was the paradigm of research. For this category, based on either explicit claims of the authors about their work or clues such as the nature of the research questions, the methodological choices made, and the genre expectations fulfilled (macro-organization, for example), we coded bibliography entries as one of the following: social scientific/post-positivist, interpretive, or critical. The paradigm content analysis yielded a clear pattern of dominance by critical scholars, with 65% of entries, followed by interpretivists with 30%. Only 10% of publications stemmed from social scientific or post-positivist perspectives.

Table 3. Counts by the Field of Scholars

Field of Scholars	N
Communication	33
Intercultural Communication	10
Education	7
Sociology	8
Psychology	8
Political Science	6
Linguistics	7
Business	5
Literature	5
Public Health	3
African Studies	2

Moving past the initial audit, we looked at the relationships between various categories of content analysis. Several patterns emerged when we looked at the interaction between region and discipline of scholars. When analyzed based on the discipline of scholars, most regions were dominated by Communication and Intercultural Communication, representing at least 50% of publications. One of the least diverse regions in terms of discipline was the Caribbean, which featured Literature scholarship. Some of the most diverse regions were Africa and East/Southeast Asia. We also compared time of publication and discipline. When analyzed by decade, Communication was consistently dominant across the time periods of pre-2000, 2000-2010, and after 2010. The diversity of disciplines represented in the bibliography increased after 2000, however. When exploring the impact of time period on paradigm, critical scholars remained dominant throughout. This is particularly interesting because, at least in Communication Studies, which was the most prolific discipline, critical studies were minoritized in a strongly social scientific field before 2000 (Martin & Nakayama, 2013). On the other hand, the plethora of examples from a critical paradigm is not surprising in a collection of literature from underrepresented voices, since it encourages social critique and more intentionally makes space for nondominant perspectives (Miike, 2013). These findings align with what other scholars, for example Kotthoff and Spencer-Oatey (2009), have noted previously -- that the methods of inquiry naturally follow from the disciplines that dominate an interdisciplinary space, and that inclusion of more voices in those spaces benefits scholarship both in terms of ideation and diversity of ways of knowing.

CONCLUSIONS AND IMPLICATIONS

Throughout this project we had moments where our work prompted discussions that yielded what our team considers to be important lessons learned along the way. We highlight a few of those issues here before presenting a few conclusions of the bibliographic analysis. One recurring conversation involved critically reflecting on our own positionality and privilege based on our identities as intercultural scholars in the North American/Western context. This dialogue often included reflecting more generally on how scholar identities have not been thoroughly considered within the field, especially when it comes to how we go about researching and using research that involves people from underrepresented and marginalized backgrounds. This omission, beyond the issue of exclusion, can cause further trauma to people who have already historically experienced violence through genocide, colonization, forced migration, cultural erasure, and other forms of oppression. There were a few points of tension that ignited important conversations which perhaps have been raised by different scholars but have not been taught or communicated as widely as some of the models and frameworks developed in the Global North (particularly the US and Europe).

An example was how research conducted by scholars who do not identify with the population in which they are conducting their investigation was to be evaluated and reviewed. While on the one hand the scholar's work may bring attention to the issues facing the specific population, on the other hand there is sometimes no acknowledgement of the historical trauma these groups have experienced and the ills that continue as result of the residue from groups and systems that as scholars we come from and represent. Careers are built on these works; subsequent promotion and advancement benefit the authors but not the communities and peoples who they conduct research with. We initially wondered if we should look up the backgrounds of the different authors, or review their names to see if there is a connection between the scholar and the community or peoples they are writing about. While we tempered our initial thoughts on this issue, we do want to emphasize the problem of representation that is common in scholarly research (Alcoff, 1991). In the end we concluded that it would not be our place to try and link authors' identity with their work in the community where this was not explicitly stated in the publication. However, one practice we should develop in our discipline is to acknowledge privilege and power and make efforts to build authentic relationships when working within historically marginalized communities.

We acknowledge that the makeup of our research group was influential in this collection of sources and analysis. Where and how far and deep we could cast our search net were both enabled and limited by our linguistic capacities, background knowledge in various disciplines, and research interests. In our group, we had a few multilingual speakers who could access publications in other languages; however, we were obviously limited by our own knowledge of languages and by accessibility of texts in the places where we are used to finding research. For example, one of the reasons why South East Asia was overrepresented in our bibliography is because two of the researchers speak Korean and Japanese, respectively, and are familiar with those academic contexts. Had our group included speakers of other languages from other underrepresented regions, we might have been able to find more publications written in other local languages in those areas. Being aware of this significant limitation, throughout the duration of our project, we made efforts to recruit new members who represent underrepresented perspectives and languages, however, our efforts were also limited by the fact that most members of our group were based in privileged regions of North America. We were faced with the reality of just how limited knowledge we had about publication venues that did not use English as primary language of publication or knowledge about scholars doing intercultural work with groups that did not involve native English speakers. Therefore, the themes, patterns and gaps we have identified are far from being a complete, accurate picture.

The inaccessibility of non-English texts also reflects structural inequity that exists in our specific field and the broader academia (Anderson & Hellman, 2021; Sonn, 2019) the language used in global intercultural research is English. The current research and publication process that privilege English publications marginalize multilingual scholars from underrepresented regions and scholarly work published in languages other than English. Not surprisingly, the majority of the publications included in our bibliography are English publications. As a field, we should be more intentional about creating room for marginalized non-English or multilingual voices. Creating space for multilingual scholars and rewarding collaborative projects that represent marginalized voices and include multilingual scholars from marginalized communities can be helpful. Also, it is important to identify and include scholars from marginalized communities from the very beginning of a research project in order to form a diverse group and to develop a thoughtful collaboration plan that is inclusive of underrepresented voices and their perspectives. Our discussions often came back to the questions:

- What counts as scholarly research?

- How does our scholarly focus limit underrepresented voices who value other kinds of knowledge generation and/or knowledge sharing?

- How does the preference for peer-reviewed processes function as gate-keeping both in terms of capacity/willingness to engage in the process as an author and the socially constructed expectations of reviewers that must be met?

- How are systemic inequities perpetuated and reinforced in ways that limit access to research funding, publication venues, and institutional and professional profiles (Wellmon & Piper, 2017).

We also wondered what this work would look like if it were not limited to written texts. What would it look like to include music lyrics, spoken word poetry, documentaries and other films, oral histories, visual arts, and more?

Although the problem of underrepresentation remains a serious one, from the increasing number of texts from more recent decades in our annotated bibliography we can conclude that publishing venues and processes seem to be more accessible now than they were pre-2000 for minoritized scholars and/or communities. However, it could also be the case that a higher number of these scholars have been trained and are actively publishing (not necessarily that the environment is more welcoming), or underrepresented communities have more relationships with scholars who publish in traditional research venues. Regardless of the reason for the increase in contributions we found in later years, the fact remains that these voices are still dramatically underrepresented in scholarship as a whole. Even accounting for the natural effect of the limit to English language publications, the US and Europe saturate intercultural research publications. Other English-speaking nations are not as visible in the corpus of research as a whole. Even within these dominant regions of the world where there appears to be a saturation in IC research among dominant social groups, there are some underrepresented voices that also need to be amplified (e.g. Roma, Greek, stigmatized immigrant communities). Obviously more work remains to be done to enable a wider range of voices to be heard within our field.

In this project, we set out to document, as thoroughly as our time and combined expertise allowed, the many wonderful contributions of underrepresented voices to intercultural scholarship. During this process,we have celebrated both the ingenuity of these scholars and the difficult journeys they may have endured to gain visibility. But, we also uncovered quite a few ugly truths, such as some of the ways and reasons more voices have been excluded (including by our own team) and the many gaps that we were not able to fill with our annotated bibliography. In the end, we may have generated more questions than we began with. We have also, though, generated motivation, at least among our team, to accept more of the burden for seeking out knowledge not at our fingertips and to commit to continually driving our field towards greater inclusion. In the end, we are left with two suggested actions (neither original, as others have been advocating for these imperatives for years):

1. At an individual level, intentionally seek out scholarship from perspectives that differ from your own. Note that this action could require going beyond usual search habits that may not return results from underrepresented voices (Martínez-Bascuñán, 2014).

2. At institutional and disciplinary levels, critique and alter structural barriers to full participation in scholarship by the full range of potential contributors (Doubeni et al., 2022).

ACKNOWLEDGEMENTS

We four authors of this chapter would like to acknowledge the labor of early group members who have not been involved in this analysis and reporting stage of the annotated bibliography project. We were aware at the working group's conception that our team, ironically, was not very diverse, and made an effort to recruit additional members, many of whom contributed entries to the bibliography along the way. We are grateful for the time, efforts, and support of all the World Council members who have participated in our meetings, attended our webinar, read our blog, or otherwise provided support to our work.

REFERENCES

Alcoff, L. (1991). The problem of speaking for others. *Cultural Critique, 20,* 5-32.

Alhojailan, M. I. (2012). *Thematic analysis: a critical review* of its *process and evaluation.* In WEI international European academic conference proceedings, Zagreb, Croatia.

Andersen, D., & Hellman, M. (2021, May 21). Thinking in a foreign tongue: The problem of English language dominance in social research. *Nordic Studies on Alcohol and Drugs, 38*(3), 207–211. https://doi.org/10.1177/14550725211010682

Authors. (2021a, March 19). *Listening to underrepresented voices.* World Council on Intercultural and Global Competence. https://iccglobal.org/2021/03/15/listening-to-underrepresented-voices/

Authors. (2021b, March 22). Listening to underrepresented voices. In H. Ibrahim & I. Golubeva's *Decentering Intercultural Competence Research and Practice Webinar Series*. World Council on Intercultural and Global Competence.

Casmir, F. L. (1987). International, intercultural communication: An annotated bibliography. Special communication module. ERIC Clearinghouse on Reading and Communication Skills.

Cooper, D. H., & Nagel, J. (2022). Lessons from the pandemic: climate change and COVID-19. *International Journal of Sociology and Social Policy, 42*(3/4), 332-347.

Deardorff, D. K. (Ed.). (2009). *The SAGE handbook of intercultural competence.* Sage. https://doi.org/10.4135/9781071872987

Doubeni, C. A., Corley, D. A., & Peek, R. M. (2022). Advancing diversity, equity, and inclusion in scientific publishing. *Gastroenterology, 162*(1), 59-62.

Evered, J. A., Castellanos, M. E., Dowrick, A., Germani, A. C. C. G., Rai, T., de Souza, A. N., & Grob, R. (2023). Talking about inequities: A comparative analysis of COVID-19 narratives in the UK, US, and Brazil. *SSM-Qualitative Research in Health, 3*, 100277.

Kendall, G., Knust, S., Ribeiro, C. C., & Urrutia, S. (2010). Scheduling in sports: An annotated bibliography. *Computers & Operations Research, 37*(1), 1-19.

Laurencin, C. T., & McClinton, A. (2020). The COVID-19 pandemic: a call to action to identify and address racial and ethnic disparities. *Journal of Racial and Ethnic Health Disparities, 7*, 398-402.

Macinko, J. A., & Starfield, B. (2002). Annotated bibliography on equity in health, 1980-2001. *International Journal for Equity in Health, 1*(1), 1-20.

Martin, J. N., & Nakayama, T. K. (2013). *Intercultural communication in contexts* (Vol. 6). McGraw-Hill.

Martínez-Bascuñán, M. (2014). Why should we think of structural injustice when speaking about culture?. *Revisiting Iris Marion Young on normalisation, inclusion and democracy*, 17-32.

Miike, Y. (2013). The Asiacentric turn in Asian communication studies: Shifting paradigms and changing perspectives. In Asante, M. K., Miike, Y., & Yin, J. (Eds.), *The global intercultural communication reader* (pp. 125-147). Routledge.

Purdue OWL® - Purdue University. (2022). *Annotated bibliographies.* Annotated Bibliographies - Purdue OWL® - Purdue University. (n.d.). https://owl.purdue.edu/owl/general_writing/common_writing_assignments/annotated_bibliographies/index.html

Sonn, J. W. (2019). Dominance of English in social science: the case of economic geography. *International Journal of Urban Sciences, 23*(2), i–ii. https://doi.org/10.1080/12265934.2019.1611005

Spencer-Oatey, H., & Kotthoff, H. (2009). Introduction. In H. Kotthoff & H. Spencer-Oatey (Eds.), *Handbook of intercultural communication* (pp. 1-8). Mouton de Gruyter.

Spitzberg, B. H., & Changnon, G. (2009). Conceptualizing intercultural competence. In D. Deardorff (Ed.), *The SAGE handbook of intercultural competence* (pp. 2-52). Sage Publications, Inc.

United Nations (2019). *The Sustainable Development Goals Report 2019.* https://unstats.un.org/sdgs/report/2019/regional-groups/

University of North Texas at Dallas. (2023). *Annotated bibliography vs. literature review.* Retrieved July 6, 2023, from https://www.untdallas.edu/learning/writing/academic-writing/annotated-bibliography-vs-literature-review.php

Wellmon, C., & Piper, A. (2017). Publication, power, and patronage: On inequality and academic publishing. *Critical Inquiry.* https://criticalinquiry.uchicago.edu/publication_power_and_patronage_on_inequality_and_academic_publishing/

Wright, T., & Tsao, H. J. (1983). A frame on frames: an annotated bibliography. In Wright, T. (Ed.), *Statistical methods and the improvement of data quality* (pp. 25-72). Academic Press.

To access the Annotated Bibliography discussed in this chapter, be sure to view the Bibliography accessed through the following link: https://docs.google.com/spreadsheets/d/1-Beyhuy5G_TrEqENCWTXO3QN D_K6sA6B/edit#gid=755392493

Bios

Grace Lee-Amuzie is the Director of the Center for Intercultural Leadership and Communication and Assistant Professor of Language and Writing Studies at Penn State University (Abington). She provides leadership in developing initiatives and resources for equity pedagogy. Her research explores social justice issues in higher education. Email: exl457@psu.edu

Horane A. Diatta-Holgate is the Program Director for Inclusive Pedagogy in Kaneb Center for Teaching Excellence at the University of Notre Dame. Horane works with faculty and graduate students on applying inclusive teaching principles and practices in course design, developing their intercultural competence as well as embedding diversity, equity and inclusivity throughout their course and curriculum. Email: hholgate@nd.edu

Kris Acheson directs Purdue University's Center for Intercultural Learning, Mentorship, Assessment and Research (CILMAR). She is a thought leader in the development and assessment of intercultural competence and the creator of the open access resource site for intercultural, global learning, and DEIJ professionals, the Intercultural Learning Hub at www.hubicl.org. Email krisac@purdue.edu

Kyra Garson is the Intercultural Coordinator, Thompson Rivers University. Her research interests include critical pedagogies, multicultural group work and critical internationalization studies. Her work has been recognized by the Canadian Society for the Study of Higher Education, the Canadian Bureau for International Education, and the British Columbia Council for International Education. kgarson@tru.ca

Chapter 5

Transcultural Education

A Framework for Supporting Students to Develop Commonalities in Cultural Complexity

Tobias Grünfelder
Zeppelin University, Germany

Julika Baumann Montecinos
Hochschule Furtwangen University | HFU Business School, Germany

Heidi Smith
University of Edinburgh, Scotland

Jessica Geraldo Schwengber
Zeppelin University, Germany

Abstract

In 2021, the United Nations Educational, Scientific and Cultural Organization (UNESCO) proposed a new social contract for education and pedagogy to be organized around building the capacities of students to work together to transform the world. Against this background, this chapter introduces the concept of transcultural education as a promising relational approach to help students learn first-hand how to cooperate and develop commonalities in a world that is shaped by cultural complexity. Building on the authors' experience as educators and the results of an international and interdisciplinary Delphi study on transcultural competence, this chapter offers a framework on how to design and structure transcultural learning in higher education. In this practical resource for educators, the crucial role of content organization, shared experiences, debriefing, and cultivating communities of practice is emphasized in order for students to develop transcultural competences.

Keywords: *Transcultural education, higher education, transcultural competence, social learning, experiential learning, communities of practice*

A need for transcultural education

In 2021, the United Nations Educational, Scientific and Cultural Organization (UNESCO) published "a new social contract for education", claiming that "pedagogy should be organized around principles of cooperation and solidarity, building the capacities of students to work together to transform the world" (UNESCO, 2021, p. 60). This chapter aims to show how transcultural education contributes to such a new social contract and helps students to *learn through cooperating with others.* The focus is on the role of education and educators in supporting students to develop competences for successfully navigating a world that is shaped by cultural complexity with manifold resources and varied interests of nations, organizations, groups, and individuals.

The time in which this is written has shown that cultural aspects matter and cultural differences receive increasing attention, for example, geopolitical concerns and/or global challenges such as pandemics and ecological crises. At the same time, the need, willingness and ability to cooperate across cultures are gaining importance. Existing and future global challenges are not solvable with the mindsets, worldviews and tools of a single discipline or cultural perspective. The corresponding competences to deal with cultural complexity for mutual benefit such as intercultural competence (Deardorff, 2006), intercultural intelligence (Ang & Van Dyne, 2008) and transcultural competence (Baumann Montecinos & Grünfelder, 2022) thus become a major concern for universities that acknowledge this complexity and offer their students meaningful, experiential learning journeys. The task of transcultural educators is to,

> "be the producers of something new and not just maintaining the status quo as a product of our own culture. In the past, cultural education has focused more on how we are products of culture and not enough on how we are producers of culture. Transculturalists should take the lead in studying how we, as teachers and students, are the producers of culture" (Aldridge et al., 2014, p.116-117).

To address the potentials and challenges of transcultural learning as a life-long, multi-layered relational process lies at the core of the framework developed in this chapter. Therefore, we explicitly build on a relational understanding (Emirbayer, 1997; Donati, 2011; Gergen, 2009; Wieland, 2020) and its implications for concepts of competence (Spitzberg & Changnon, 2009). Against this backdrop, on the following pages, the transcultural approach is sketched out as a relational understanding of education and thereby offers an invitation to rethink the success factors of cooperation across cultures by focusing on developing new commonalities. Transcultural education is then presented in the form of a framework for how to design and structure transcultural learning. We build on our previous research (Baumann Montecinos et al., 2021; Smith, 2020), our teaching experiences with students, and the ongoing exchange with our working group "Transcultural Cooperation & Leadership" at the World Council on Intercultural and Global Competence. The resulting framework can be applied to teaching in informal contexts, schooling and higher education.

Transculturality and transcultural competence

Spitzberg and Changnon (2009) argue "competence is still largely viewed as an individual and trait concept and is almost always measured accordingly" (p.44). Mollenhauer (2023) agrees that often the term "intercultural competence suggests that such an interpersonal process is shifted to the individual" (p.132). However, to detach individuals from contexts and to suggest that individuals possess a fixed set of competences (e.g., a collection of values, attitudes, knowledge, understandings, skills and behaviors) is reducing the actual complexity of the corresponding learning processes. Considering the definition of intercultural competence as "the ability to communicate effectively and appropriately in intercultural situations based on one's intercultural knowledge, skills and attitudes" (Deardorff, 2006, p.247), the question can be raised if such an individual-focused concept might benefit from a relational complement in order to sufficiently capture the complexity and reciprocity of cooperation and learning.

Transculturality as a relational, commonality-focused concept is used in many different disciplines with manifold meanings and interpretations (Antor, 2020; Bolten, 2020; Glover & Friedman, 2015). In general, transculturality mostly emphasizes the existence of cultures in relational webs of interconnections and permeations, the ongoing processes of exchange, and the role of commonalities (Benessaieh, 2010; Welsch, 1999). In such an understanding, the prefix "trans" defies and neglects binaries, implies a movement and process not in-between, but across and beyond, and thus points towards the creation of new commonalities beyond existing cultures, thereby reconstructing the status quo.

Building on these conceptual foundations, a focus on a relational view and on developing commonalities in contexts of cultural complexity summarizes the results of an international and interdisciplinary Delphi study on transcultural competence (Baumann Montecinos & Grünfelder, 2022) and is central to the transcultural approach in this chapter[1]. By emphasizing the context-dependence and dynamics of cross-cultural interaction as constant processes of constructing shared meaning, practice and experience are considered to play a crucial role. In a nutshell, transcultural competence can be defined as

> "a general competence of individuals or organizations to intentionally develop new commonalities in contexts of cultural complexity. It refers to the ability and willingness to engage in context-specific processes of constructing new shared meaning and action beyond existing practices by shared experience and mutual learning [...]. The new commonalities are based on a sense of belonging to a heterogeneous community of experience rather than on overcoming one's own identity in a process of homogenization. New forms of cooperation and the expansion of existing cooperation corridors may be the goals and results of applying transcultural competence" (Grünfelder & Baumann Montecinos, 2023, p.25).

This approach is inspired by discussions on concepts such as mutual adaptation (Bennett, 2013, 2020) and third-culture building (Bhabha, 1994; Casmir, 1993, 1999), and connecting these concepts to a relational understanding. In doing so, the relational roots of intercultural communication should not be overlooked (Bennett, 2023). Similarly, adherence to specific terms (inter-, cross-, multi-, transcultural) should not hinder an examination of possible contributions of a relational view. Overall, it is not about which term is used but about the meaning and nuances attached to it.

Transcultural education for higher education

Transcultural education in higher education can be defined as a "pedagogy aiming to engage students from different cultures and disciplines with the purpose of guiding them through ideas and processes of working together in a way that respects differences, acknowledges common ground, and seeks to co-create new knowledge" (Ermine, 2007). The purpose hereby is to

> "provide spaces for relational learning opportunities for students to engage with people across multiple layers of cultures [...] in concrete, cooperative activities. By taking part in activities that require the identification and development of commonalities, the students experience learning from and with each other, and thus hone their ability to cooperate across cultures, which can in turn create new shared meanings and actions" (Baumann Montecinos et al., 2021, p.241).

The following aspects of such an understanding should be pointed out in particular: Firstly, such learning can be described as a lifelong and intentional developmental process (Deardorff, 2016; O'Dowd & Dooly, 2020) that requires self-reflection, cultural humility, and a commitment to continuous growth (Deardorff, 2016; Vande Berg et al., 2023). It involves being aware of one's own cultural biases, actively seeking cultural knowledge, and developing skills to mutually adapt and create a "third culture" (Bennett, 2013). Thereby, secondly, a fundamental role is ascribed to experience and particularly to shared experience. In line with Wulf (2010), "to experience other people and cultures is central to the development of children and adolescents. People can only understand themselves as reflected by and through the reactions of other human beings and cultures" (p.4). Accordingly, transcultural education aims to design experiential learning opportunities which help students "understand themselves" in cultural terms and thus create conditions for better futures based on empathy and cooperation. This also builds on the so-called contact hypothesis (Allport, 1954) that emphasizes that intergroup contact under appropriate conditions can effectively reduce intergroup prejudices. Thirdly, the key role of the facilitators in supporting learners' development is to be recognized (O'Dowd & Dooly, 2020; Helm, 2017; Deardorff, 2016). Educators need to address the issue of cultural diversity carefully. They are called upon to create transcultural learning spaces "in which students bring together different sets of knowledge from different knowledge traditions and start a conversation between them" (Zohar & Newhouse 2019, p.132). Educators provide students with opportunities for shared experiences, activities, and dialogues and make students aware of cultural differences without stereotyping or overemphasizing them. Fourthly, out of transcultural learning spaces, "different kinds of sayings, doings, and relatings" (Smith, 2022, p.55) can emerge which form a transcultural community of practice. Communities of practice may be a goal and outcome of transcultural education for some educators. Most importantly here, relational learning, understood as social and experiential processes, is at the center of these communities, where educators and students may "change together" (Cadman & Song, 2012, p.16). Hence, "[t]he practice of transcultural pedagogy aims to create a learning environment where all students want to be, have agency, and can connect the cognitive and the social" (Smith, 2020, p.52).

In view of these particular aspects of transcultural education, several goals of such learning formats can be identified, one main aim being to strengthen students' transcultural competence by enabling them to engage in processes of shared practice. Students learn by doing, through cooperation, which allows them to better understand themselves and others, developing new commonalities and a sense of belonging to a community. By experiencing and engaging with cultural differences, students develop an ethnorelative view that enables them to see the world through a lens that acknowledges how their cultural beliefs, values, and ways of living represent only one out of many possible and acceptable ways of living (Bennett 2013, 2017; Allport, 1954). Linking those expected learning outcomes to Kwame Anthony Appiah's work on cosmopolitanism (2006), being a member of the global community comes with responsibilities. Appiah emphasizes that every human being matters, that we have a shared obligation for one another, and that conversations are valuable in themselves. In this spirit, to value conversations and to keep communication going, to practise cooperation and to experience the co-creation of new meanings and actions across cultures are essential elements of transcultural learning.

How to design and structure transcultural learning in higher education

The conditions for transcultural learning in higher education can be created in many different formats. Importantly, transcultural learning is emergent and cannot be forced. The following framework (Figure 1) is derived from previous works (Baumann Montecinos et al., 2021; Roberts, 2003) and aims to serve as inspiration for designing and structuring relational learning for education groups with different cultural backgrounds.

The focus is on formats where students from different cultures and/or universities are brought together for cooperative tasks or challenges. Despite this scope, some of the insights may also be helpful in "standard" classroom settings with a culturally diverse group of students. In the following, selected elements of Figure 1 are explained in more detail and the boxes provide educators with questions to ponder.

Figure 1: Transcultural learning in higher education framework

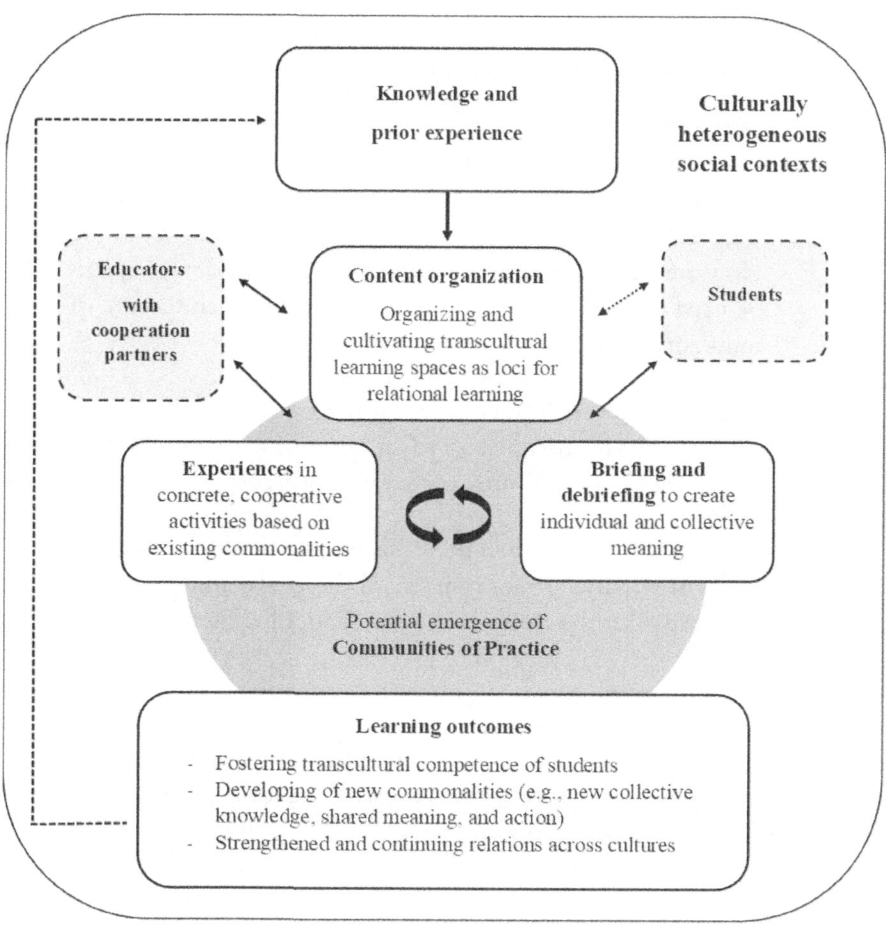

Culturally heterogeneous social contexts

The phrase "it takes a village to raise a child" originates from an African proverb and conveys the message that it takes many people ("the village") to provide a safe, healthy environment for children, where children are given the security they need to develop and flourish. This emphasises the importance of the social environment for learning as a relational process that is embedded in the respective context, and highlights that the responsibility of educating goes beyond the teacher and involves the entire social system. Accordingly, universities and educators can benefit from a diverse social environment and foster this by actively interacting with other universities, organizations and educators. The thematic design of courses and student projects may intentionally address and nurture such a beneficial social environment. With this ambition, a specific theme of a course (e.g., sustainability in the food industry) can focus on analyzing the given context and identify options to connect the theme with the course's specific context. In this manner, the social environment can be seen as an opportunity in which a learning journey for students can be designed.

Culturally heterogeneous social contexts

The following guiding questions may help address the social environment of the teaching format:

- How are learning spaces on campus designed and what spaces can be used in the surroundings (including the architecture of the university, parks and museums in reach)?

- Who are relevant stakeholders and what different cultures do we have within the university (e.g. professional cultures, regional cultures, national cultures, corporate cultures)?

- What specific topics does the social environment offer (focus areas of the university, current concerns of the local community, burning questions that the students bring in from their lifeworlds)?

To analyze the social environment and to keep the specific context continuously in mind requires educators to spot opportunities for unique and authentic learning experiences. Being aware of this social embedding as both a condition and an opportunity is an important step towards a transcultural approach to education.

The actors involved are categorized in the framework as students, educators and cooperation partners, but have in common that in an ideal relational teaching format, they engage in a joint process in which they continuously change and develop by learning from and with each other. The different roles, backgrounds and prior experiences that they bring shape the specific constellation of a learning format that is designed, prepared and moderated by the educators, but for whose success and ultimate learning outcome the students assume explicit co-responsibility.

Knowledge and prior experience

Taking a social constructivist perspective on knowledge, where knowledge is socially constructed and based on prior experience in social interactions, what is taken to be true and objective is the result of social processes that take place in historical and cultural contexts. Furthermore, a relational view on knowledge presupposes to view knowledge in constant flux (Clemens, 2021). In this view, socially created knowledge is not something that someone possesses, but which emerges as a result of a relation between the situation (context/environment) and the entities or subjects involved (educators/students) (Clemens, 2021). A relational view on knowledge would thereby reject an epistemology of possession (Cook & Brown, 1999; Burr, 2003), since knowledge "(...) is not something that a person has or doesn't have but is something that people do together" (Burr, 2003, p.9). In such a perspective on knowledge, the learning context within which knowledge is produced is of relevance - what some scholars in the social learning literature call situated learning. For example, Lave and Wenger (1991) proposed the concept of communities of practice (CoPs) as a corresponding locus of situated social learning which may be one of the learning outcomes of transcultural education.

Knowledge and prior experience

In terms of knowledge and prior experience, some helpful guiding questions to be considered are:

- What is considered as valuable knowledge in a specific discipline and what knowledge is overlooked?

- What prior experience is used to design and structure the course?

- Is knowledge from different cultures and perspectives included?

Content organization

A crucial part for every educator is the course structure and organization of content: the choice of topics and the sequencing of course content ideally utilizing a wide variety of learning experiences.

Regardless of the structure, integrating activities and switching up content delivery modes helps to maintain student interest, along with individualising learning (Wilson & Korn, 2007) and motivation through relevance of content to students (Bradbury, 2016). Furthermore, Dewey and Bentley (1949) argued that traditional education often does not allow learners to grasp the relationship between the content and real life situations.

When content and course organization occur only online or indoors removed from places and spaces beyond the classroom, learning becomes more abstract, less connected and less situated. An important part of transcultural learning is to focus on the ongoing interactions present between, students and students, students and educator(s), students and the content, and students and spaces and places. From our experience as educators, the first sessions of any course are crucial to set the stage and atmosphere of the whole course. It is important to invest time in the first session(s) increasing person to person, and person to place interactions with a focus on relationships. In order to facilitate content within transcultural learning spaces "intentional pedagogy", which supports "students in unpacking the what, how, and why of the learning presented" (Smith, 2020, p.46) is essential. When it comes to content organization, transcultural learning requires more structure and preparation to ensure multiple cultural perspectives are included which offer a wide variety of perspectives as well as learning experiences that support learners from diverse educational backgrounds. "What is required is an approach to such transcultural learning spaces that affords different kinds of sayings (ways of presenting content), doings (activities) and relatings (relationships between students, educators and places), until a transcultural community is developed" (Smith, 2020, p.55). Where activities or learning experiences are incorporated to intentionally disrupt traditional approaches to learning, educators need to be prepared to facilitate discussions and learning.

Content organization

Here are some helpful guiding questions to assist with content selection and organization:

- Why are we here and what is the core content?

- How can the content be related to real-life situations?

- How can the content be discovered by students in multiple ways?

- Have I scheduled enough time for debriefings and reflections?

Experiences

The first initial experience, not unlike the importance of a first meeting with someone new, the content organization and learning design of the first five minutes of the class are extremely important in the transcultural learning space. This initial experience can be as simple as welcoming each individual as they enter the learning space with their name. Another way is to go for a walk with students, stopping along the way as students share their personal stories a few at a time. In between, students have the opportunity to speak with each other, one on one. In such an activity, it is important to invite engagement, and accept some may choose not to share. As educators, this is an opportunity to share our stories as well and enables students to gain an insight into who we are, and why we are here.

This simple, but powerful beginning is one way in which to accelerate the development of a CoP. Commitment from all educators and students is required, however levels of commitment can vary. Such an activity as described here, is a perfect example of what Dewey and Bentley (1949) reminded us of, in that all genuine education comes about through experience but that does not mean that all experiences are genuinely or equally educative. Experiential learning, learning by doing with cooperation, widens the opportunities to offer and guide students through meaningful experiences which generate new knowledge. We argue, this is the aim of all transcultural educators.

According to Whitehead's (1929) philosophy of education, the attempt to educate a person by merely focusing on objective content—on inert ideas, scraps of information, bare knowledge—while disregarding the subjective form or emotional pattern of that person's experience can never be successful. "Education is the acquisition of the art of the utilisation of knowledge" (Whitehead, 1929, p.4). Education cannot be dissected from practice. Widening content selection, being creative in course design and being willing to take risks which include experiential learning opportunities in a range of places and spaces within and beyond the direct learning context, where students are encouraged to undertake their own self-directed learning beyond the classroom, is central to transcultural learning.

Experiences

Some helpful suggestions and questions to consider when developing learning experiences:

- How to encourage students to create their own meaningful experiences (e.g. take notes during the course by hand in a

> notebook, create opportunities for learning together beyond the classroom – reading groups, providing feedback on assessment to each other, testing out ideas explored in class in a wider context)?
>
> - Which activating experiences can be included (e.g. learning log or personal journal on thoughts, ideas, and learnings from classes and beyond)?
>
> - How can experience be created among interactions between students/educators/contents/places/spaces?

Widening content selection, being creative in course design and being willing to take risks which include experiential learning opportunities in a range of places and spaces within and beyond the direct learning context, where students are encouraged to undertake their own self-directed learning beyond the classroom, is central to transcultural learning.

Briefing and Debriefing

Previous research on transcultural competence has emphasized that the perception and evaluation of cultural diversity depend, among other things, on being able to reflect on one's experiences and ascribe meaning to them for oneself (Baumann Montecinos & Grünfelder, 2022, p.45). Accordingly, briefing and especially debriefing, enabling individual and collective meaning making, play a key role in the learning process along students' collective experiences. Reflection should be particularly highlighted as a building block here, especially for our context of transcultural education.

Briefing not only means giving information on the "what" and the "how" of an input or activity, but it emphasizes the "why", aiming to convey the relevance and motivate the students to engage and take ownership of their learning. Throughout and after the learning journey, debriefing then enables participants to connect their experiences to their prior knowledge and experience, as well as to more general questions and to the wider world. Debriefing questions are chosen intentionally, with sufficient attention to the emotional level, by the educator to moderate this process of reflection, which takes place individually and collectively at the same time.

Briefing and Debriefing

Examples of debriefing questions in transcultural education formats are:

- What happened? What did you experience? What did you learn? What was new to you?

- How did you feel about it?

- What did you observe within the group? How would you describe the behavior of yourself and the other participants?

- What was your role in the group process? How would you describe others roles in the group process? How would you describe your group communication?

- What did it mean to you to be part of this collective learning experience?

- In which ways did the diversity of the group shape the outcome?

- Did you develop new shared meaning and action within your group? How did you do that? What was helpful?

- Based on what you have learned today, what would you do differently if you were exposed to a similar activity again?

In a similar way, Schoel, Prouty & Radcliffe (1988) designed a three step model for debrief questions: What? So what? Now What?, and David Kolb, one of the forefathers of experiential education philosophy, believed that in order to truly learn from experience there must be time for reflection (1984). Not only is sufficient time needed for debriefing, but also timing. Participants should be given the opportunity to reflect on their own experiences before any instructor feedback or constructive criticism is offered. The purpose of the debriefing session is not to serve as a lecture, but rather as an open-ended forum. A skilled debriefer recognizes when certain issues or events are particularly impactful for learners and helps students to explore them thoroughly.

Communities of Practice (CoP)

CoPs are loci of situated social learning. Through transcultural learning CoPs can be cultivated by educators. A CoP is a group of people who share a common concern, a set of problems, or an interest in a topic and who come together to fulfil both individual and group goals (Wenger, 1999, Wenger et al., 2002, Wenger et al., 2015).

Communities of Practice (CoP)

To define a community as CoP, some elements have to be present (Wenger, 1999):

- **Domain:** Community members have a shared domain of interest, competence and commitment that distinguishes them from others. This shared domain creates common ground, inspires members to participate, guides their learning, and gives meaning to their actions.

- **Community:** Members pursue this interest through joint activities, discussions, problem-solving opportunities, information sharing and relationship building. The notion of a community creates the social fabric for enabling collective learning.

- **Practice:** Community members are actual practitioners in this domain of interest, and build a shared repertoire of resources and ideas that they take back to their practice. While the domain provides the general area of interest for the community, the practice is the specific focus around which the community develops, shares and maintains its core of collective knowledge.

The *domain* that connects participants in a learning community is what leads to the formation of the *community* itself. Wenger (1999) defines the learning process as a negotiated enterprise. Triggered by a common domain, through mutual engagement participants in the learning community develop a repertoire of negotiated practices. *Practices* are the traditional outcome of CoPs, as the term CoP itself suggests. The relation between practices and knowledge is a debated theme in the literature. Is also knowledge a possible outcome of CoPs? Do practices include knowledge? Traditionally, practices are conceived as the pragmatic part of knowledge. Practices relate to knowing, namely doing, acting, and knowledge to the intellect (Cook & Brown, 1999). In the CoP literature, knowing and knowledge are complementary which makes the dichotomy between knowledge and practices meaningless (Wenger et al., 2002; Weick & Roberts, 1993; Cook & Brown, 1999). Both are situated and continuously reconstructed in relational learning processes. In this view, knowledge embedded in practices is also part of learning outcomes of learning within CoPs.

Learning outcomes

Possible learning outcomes could be the fostering of students' transcultural competence, the cultivating and emergence of CoPs, the development of new commonalities and to strengthen the relations across different cultures. Here, CoPs are presented as a potential outcome of transcultural learning. This would be in line with the goal of transcultural education to create spaces (either physical or online) for relational learning and with UNESCO's call to design learning spaces in such a way that students come into contact with each other and thereby form a community.

The common domain that connects culturally heterogeneous students in an actual learning process may vary from situation to situation. Transculturally competent students would be able to form a community to pursue different common domains: solving an assignment together, writing a paper together, organizing an event, etc. Engagement in a common domain can occur both in and out of the classroom, depending on the domain and the specific situation. However, once the community is built, the role of the educator may change: from active designer of transcultural learning content to cultivator of the community. This view of transcultural learning as a process that leads to the creation of CoPs which then foster the development of new knowledge and practices has other implications for educators. In particular, it is important to recognize that new knowledge that may emerge is linked to prior knowledge and experiences. UNESCO (2021) highlights that critical examination of established, dominant knowledge is central to a pedagogy of solidarity and that not much attention has been paid to the silencing and exclusion of collective memories, aspirations, cultural traditions, and indigenous knowledge in education and knowledge communities.

At this point, the importance of assessment needs to be recognized. Different assessment approaches, methods, and tools can be used (Deardorff, 2011, p.74-76; Fantini, 2009; Paige, 2004; Byram, 1997) to measure the learning of students - which is beyond the scope of this chapter. Finally, the framework is in itself a learning cycle and builds on the experience of educators and students. Transcultural learning can be described with Figure 2, the three-step model (Baumann Montecinos, 2022; Wieland, 2019; Baumann Montecinos et al., 2019), which focuses on developing new commonalities and cultivating CoPs.

Figure 2: Transcultural Learning Model

3 Development of new commonalities
- Common perspectives
- Community of practice

2 Identification of existing commonalities
- Ability to cope with polycontextuality, polycontexturality and polylingualism
- Dialogue, interaction and common experiences

1 Recognition of cultural diversity
- Intercultural knowledge and skills
- Non-normative observation and analysis

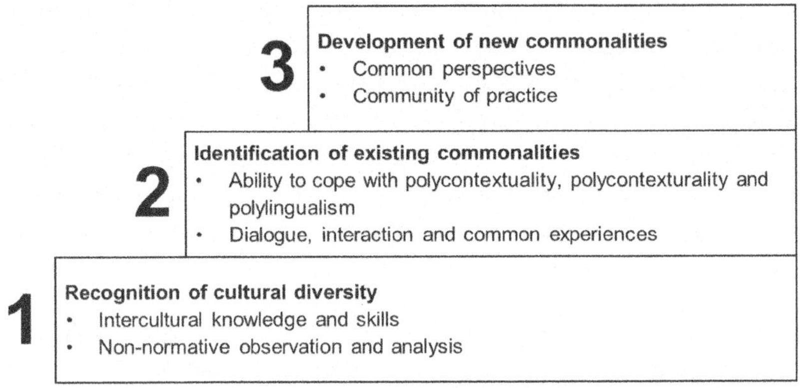

We offer the following table as a tool to evaluate your existing teaching with using the three-step model of transcultural learning.

Transcultural learning model for students and educators
Step 1: Recognition of cultural diversity
Students should be given opportunities to strengthen their own cultural self-awareness and self-reflective consciousness. The recognition of cultural diversity implies that students should be aware of cultural differences and should value, respect, tolerate, and sometimes even endure them. Based on this awareness, it is then a matter of adopting an attitude of non-normative observation and analysis, which involves recognizing one's own cultural shaping and the relevance of possible conscious and unconscious biases, as well the probability of not being oneself the (only) expert on a concrete situation.

Questions to ponder:
Do students have the opportunity to explore their own cultural background and that of their fellow students? Do they practice cultural self-awareness and assume agency?

- Do students get aware of their own cultural "glasses" (including unconscious biases)?

- Do students gain a deep understanding of culture and its impact?

- Do students learn to postpone their judgment?

- Do students demonstrate empathy and appreciation for other people and seek to understand how they feel and what informs their perspective?

- Do students value the interactions without making any judgments?

- Are students aware of and questioning their possible privilege and power, including asking themselves how they can use it to make a change that disrupts inequalities?

Step 2: Identification of existing commonalities

Students should be able to identify existing commonalities and differences in various contexts. Students train their ability to cope with polycontextuality (the diversity of different contexts, e.g. ...), polycontexturality (different decision logics, eg. ...) and polylingualism (different language games, e.g. ...) and to find commonalities. Commonalities can serve as a vehicle to start a mutual learning process and are the starting point and reference point for cooperation. Commonalities make it possible to enter into dialogue and interaction and thus have common experiences. In this spirit, students should be able to make meaningful experiences while cooperating (to have common experiences).

Questions to ponder:
- Did students have the opportunity for dialogue, interactions, and collaborative experiences?

- Do students train to listen actively, carefully, and with maximum receptivity?

- Are students able to think in overarching contexts, to see beneath the surface and to explore underlying intentions?

- Are students able to recognize differences and commonalities in culturally complex situations?

- What are shared challenges and problems that can be addressed and solved?

Step 3: Development of new commonalities:

Shared and common practices and experiences of the students may lead to the creation of new common perspectives and commonalities over time. New commonalities among the students can be anything, from newly gained knowledge to new ways of communicating with each other. New commonalities in terms of shared perspectives and a sense of belonging can lead to a productive community of practice.

Questions to ponder:

- Did new commonalities (shared understandings, meanings, and actions) emerge among the students?

- Did students discover that learning comes from listening and engaging in the dialogue process and that developing a complex understanding means the possibility of creative and innovative insights, thus, they learned how to cooperate in different cultural settings?

- Did the students experience a sense of belonging (to the course, group, etc.)?

- Are the opportunities for CoPs?

- Did students need to cooperate and work together that is allowing them to create shared meaning and actions?

- Did the students learn how to facilitate relational processes (e.g., to organize and structure group meetings)?

Transcultural education as a catalyst for change

Transcultural education shifts the role of an educator toward facilitating mutual learning experiences and cultivating learning communities. Designing and creating transcultural learning spaces in universities builds the capacities of students to work together and to transform the world. Transcultural competence, the ability and willingness to engage in context-specific processes of constructing new shared meaning and action beyond existing practices through shared experience(s) and mutual learning is a key competence in a world shaped by cultural complexity. This chapter is an invitation to think and act together in building the futures of transcultural education as a joint endeavour, a starting point, the beginning of a process of dialogue and co-construction. Transcultural education is an ongoing relational process that meets the UNESCO call for a new social call for education (2021), and begins now, through the ideas and efforts of educators around the world and those who work and learn alongside them.

References

Aldridge, J., Kilgo, J. L., & Christensen, L. M. (2014). Turning culture upside down: The role of transcultural education. *Social Studies Research & Practice, 9*(2), 107-119.

Allport, G. W. (1954). *The nature of prejudice.* Perseus Books.

Ang, S., & Van Dyne, L. (2008). Conceptualization of cultural intelligence: Definition, distinctiveness, and nomological network. In S. Ang, & L. Van Dyne (Eds.), *Handbook of cultural intelligence: Theory, measurement, and applications* (pp. 3-15). M. E. Sharpe.

Antor, H. (2020). Interculturality or transculturality? In G. Rings & S. Rasinger (Eds.), *The Cambridge handbook of intercultural communication* (pp. 68-82). Cambridge University Press. doi:10.1017/9781108555067.006.

Appiah, K. A. (2006). *Cosmopolitanism: Ethics in a world of strangers.* W.W. Norton & Co.

Bradbury, N. A. (2016). Attention span during lectures: 8 seconds, 10 minutes, or more? *Advances in Physiology Education, 40*(4), 509-513. doi:10.1152/advan.00109.2016.

Baumann Montecinos, J., Schwengber, J., & Grünfelder, G. (2021). Transcultural education: The transcultural caravan as a relational learning journey. In J. Baumann Montecinos, D. Fischer, & A. E. H. Heck (Eds.), *Kooperation, governance, wertschöpfung - Perspektiven auf eine relationale okonomie* (pp. 227-262). Metropolis.

Baumann Montecinos, J., & Grünfelder, T. (2022). What if we focus on developing commonalities? Results of an international and interdisciplinary Delphi study on transcultural competence. *International Journal of Intercultural Relations, 89,* 42-55. https://doi.org/10.1016/j.ijintrel.2022.05.001.

Baumann Montecinos, J. (2022). Transcultural cooperation in global networks: A contribution to the research program of Relational Economics. In L. Biggiero et al. (Eds.), *The relational view of economics* (pp. 193-212). Springer.

Baumann Montecinos, J., Grünfelder, T., & Wieland, J. (2023). *A relational view on cultural complexity: Implications for theory and practice.* Springer International. https://doi.org/10.1007/978-3-031-27454-1.

Bennett, M. (1993). Towards ethnorelativism: A developmental model of intercultural sensitivity. In M. Paige (Ed.), *Education for the intercultural experience*. Intercultural Press.

Bennett, M. (2013). *Basic concepts of intercultural communication: Paradigms, principles, & practices*. Intercultural Press.

Bennett, M. (2017). Developmental model of intercultural sensitivity. In Y. Kim (Ed.), *Encyclopedia of intercultural communication*. Wiley.

Bennet, M. (2023). The relational roots of intercultural communication. In J. Baumann Montecinos, T. Grünfelder, & J. Wieland (Eds.), *A relational view on cultural complexity: Implications for theory and practice*. Springer International. https://doi.org/10.1007/978-3-031-27454-1.

Benessaieh, A. (2010). Multiculturalism, interculturality, transculturality. *Transcultural America*, 11-38. https://doi.org/10.2307/j.ctt1ch78hd.4

Bolten, J. (2020). Rethinking intercultural competence. In G. Rings & S. Rasinger (Eds.), The Cambridge handbook of intercultural communication (pp. 56-67). Cambridge University Press. https://doi.org/10.1017/9781108555067.005

Burr, V. (2003): *Social constructionism*. Routledge.

Byram, M. (1997). *Teaching and assessing intercultural communicative competence*. Multilingual Matters.

Cadman, K., & Song, X. (2012). Embracing transcultural pedagogy: An epistemological perspective. In X. Song & K. Cadman (Eds.), *Bridging transcultural divides: Asian languages and culture in global higher education* (pp. 3–28). University of Adelaide Press.

Casmir, F. L. (1993). Third culture building: paradigm shift for international and intercultural communication. In S. A. Deetz (Ed.), *Communication Yearbook* (Vol. 16, 437-457). Sage.

Casmir, F. L. (1999). Foundations for the study of intercultural communication based on a third culture building model. *International Journal of Intercultural Relations, 23*(1), 91-116.

Clemens, I. (2021). Wissen und der homo connectus. Überlegungen zu einem grundbegriff der erziehungswissenschaft aus einer relationalen perspektive. In M.

E. von Eschenbach & O. Schäffter (Eds.), *Denken in wechselseitiger beziehung. Das spectaculum relationaler ansätze in der erziehungswissenschaft.* Velbrück Wissenschaft.

Cook, S. D., & Brown, J. S. (1999). Bridging epistemologies: The generative dance between organizational knowledge and organizational knowing. *Organizational Science, 10*(4), 381–400.

Deardorff, D. K (2006). Identification and assessment of intercultural competence as a student outcome of internationalization. *Journal of Studies in International Education, 10,* 241–66.

Deardorff, D. K. (2011). Assessing intercultural competence. *New Directions for Institutional Research, 2011*(149), 65–79. https://doi.org/10.1002/IR.381

Deardorff, D. K. (2016). Outcomes assessment in international education: Changing the paradigm. In R. Coelen, J. Beelen, & H. De Wit (Eds.), *Global and local internationalization* (pp. 81–89). Brill.

Dewey, J., & Bentley, A. F. (1949). Knowing and the known. Beacon Press. *The ANNALS of the American Academy of Political and Social Science, 268*(1), 224–224. https://doi.org/10.1177/000271625026800166

Ermine, W. (2007). The ethical space of engagement. *Indigenous Law Journal at the University of Toronto Faculty of Law, 6*(1), 193–203.

Fantini, A. (2009). Assessing intercultural competence: Issues and tools. In D. K. Deardorff (Ed.), *The SAGE handbook of intercultural competence.* Sage.

Glover, J., & Friedman, H. (2015). *Transcultural competence: Navigating cultural differences in the global community.* American Psychological Association. https://doi.org/10.1037/14596-000

Grünfelder, T., & Baumann Montecinos, J. (2023). Delphi study on transcultural competence: Summary and reflections on a call for a relational approach. In J. Baumann Montecinos, T. Grünfelder, & J. Wieland (Eds.), *A relational view on cultural complexity - Implications for theory and practice.* Springer International. https://doi.org/10.1007/978-3-031-27454-1

Helm, F. (2017). Critical approaches to online intercultural language education. In: Thorne, S., & May, S. (Eds) *Language, education and technology. Encyclopedia of language and education.* Springer.

Kolb, D. A. (1984). *Experiential learning: Experience as the source of learning and development.* Prentice Hall.

Lave, J., & Wenger, E. (1991). *Situated learning: Legitimate peripheral participation.* Cambridge University Press.

Mollenhauer, R. (2023). Transcultural competence: Present-at-hand and ready-to-hand? A communication theory approach. In J. Baumann Montecinos, T. Grünfelder, & J. Wieland (Eds.), *A relational view on cultural complexity - Implications for theory and practice.* Springer International. https://doi.org/10.1007/978-3-031-27454-1

Paige, R. M. (2004). Instrumentation in intercultural training. In D. Landis, J. M. Bennett, & M. J. Bennett (Eds.), *Handbook of intercultural training* (3rd ed.). Sage.

O'Dowd, R., & Dooly, M. (2020). Intercultural communicative competence development through telecollaboration and virtual exchange. In J. Jackson (Ed.), *Routledge handbook of language and intercultural communication* (pp. 361–375). Taylor and Francis.

Schoel, J., Prouty, D., & Radcliffe, P. (1988). *Islands of healing: A guide to adventure-based counseling.* Project Adventure.

Smith, H. (2020). Transculturality in higher education: Supporting students' experiences through praxis. *Learning and Teaching, 13*(3), 41–60.

Spitzberg, B., & Changnon, G. (2009). Conceptualizing intercultural competence. In D. Deardorff (Ed.), *The SAGE handbook of intercultural competence* (pp. 2–52). Sage.

UNESCO (2021): *Reimagining our futures together: A new social contract for education.* United Nations Educational, Scientific and Cultural Organization.

Vande Berg, M., Paige, R. M., & Lou, K. H. (Eds.). (2012). *Student learning abroad: What our students are learning, what they're not, and what we can do about it.* Stylus.

Weick, K. E., & Roberts, K. H. (1993). Collective mind in organizations: Heedful interrelating on flight decks. *Administrative Science Quarterly, 38,* 357–381.

Welsch, W. (1999). Transculturality—the puzzling form of cultures today. In M. Featherstone & S. Lash (Eds.), *Spaces of culture: City, nation, world* (pp. 194–213). https://doi.org/10.4135/9781446218723.n11

Wenger, E. (1999). *Communities of practice: Learning, meaning and identity.* Cambridge University Press.

Wenger, E., McDermott, R., & Snyder, W. M. (2002). *Cultivating communities of practice: A guide to managing knowledge.* Harvard Business School Press.

Wenger, E., Fenton-O'Creevy, M., Kubiak, C., Hutchinson, S., & Wenger, B. (2015). *Learning in landscapes of practice: Boundaries, identity, and knowledgeability in practice-based learning.* Routledge.

Whitehead, A. N. (1929). *Aims of education and other essays.* The Macmillan Co.

Wilson, K., & Korn, J. H. (2007). Attention during lectures: Beyond ten minutes. *Teaching of Psychology, 34*(2), 85–89. https://doi.org/10.1080/00986280701291291

Wulf, C. (2010). Education as transcultural education: A global challenge. *Educational Studies in Japan: International Yearbook, 5,* 33–47.

Zohar, A., & Newhouse, D. R. (2019). Educating for a sustainable world. In *Intellectual, scientific, and educational influences on sustainability research* (pp. 121–137). https://doi.org/10.4018/978-1-5225-7302-9

Bios

Tobias Grünfelder is a research fellow at the chair of Institutional Economics and Transcultural Leadership at Zeppelin University in Germany and a project manager of the Transcultural Caravan Network, a platform for student research, global thinking, networking, and dialogue. As a lecturer, intercultural trainer, and magician, he is developing unique learning experiences for individuals, groups and organizations. Email: tobias.gruenfelder@zu.de

Julika Baumann Montecinos, PhD, is a professor of Transcultural Management at Hochschule Furtwangen University | HFU Business School and part of Zeppelin University's Transcultural Caravan Network. She focuses on research into the success factors of transcultural cooperation as well as on the development of related international and interdisciplinary teaching, training, research and networking projects. Email: julika.montecinos@hs-furtwangen.de

Heidi Smith is a lecturer in Outdoor and Environmental Education at the University of Edinburgh. She has a particular interest in researching transculturality in higher education, and the affordances of outdoor, indoor and online places and spaces, for developing authentic learning communities with diverse international student cohorts in a wide range of contexts. Email: Heidi.Smith@ed.ac.uk

Jessica Geraldo Schwengber is project manager of the Transcultural Caravan Network at Leadership Excellence Institute Zeppelin, a post-doc research fellow and lecturer at the chair of Institutional Economics and Transcultural Leadership at Zeppelin University. She graduated in Economics and Management from the University of Rome Tor Vergata. Her research focuses on organizational theory, relational economics and relational reconceptualization of organizational learning and transcultural learning. Email: Jessica.Schwengber@zu.de

---

1. The following elaborations are based in part on a 3-stage Delphi study that was conducted from 2020 to 2022 with a panel of around 50 experts from different countries and disciplines in order to better understand the concept of transcultural competence. The study questions specifically invited the experts to focus on (1) the determinants of people's perceptions of cultural diversity, (2) the role and creation of commonalities, (3) the competences to identify and develop commonalities, and (4) the formulation of corresponding conceptual conclusions as a point of departure for further research and practical application. The findings of the Delphi process are published in the International Journal of Intercultural Relations (Baumann Montecinos & Grünfelder, 2022) and the Springer book "A Relational View on Cultural Complexity" (Baumann Montecinos et al., 2023).

Chapter 6

Virtual Exchanges

Experiences with "Invisible Assumptions"

Yovana S. Veerasamy, PhD
Stony Brook University, United States of America

Emily Pelka, MA

ABSTRACT

Although a driver of intercultural learning, many socio-cultural assumptions undergird the development of Virtual Exchange/Collaborative Online Intercultural Learning (VE/COIL) programs as partners collaborate to implement these programs on campuses. Acknowledging that typologies of VE/COIL programs used within and across countries are plural in scope and lacking in uniformity, we employed a qualitative research design based on narratives from administrators and faculty members from the "Global South" to identify invisible socio-cultural assumptions they encountered when collaborating with the "Global North" especially with United States (U.S.) higher education institutions (HEIs) as VE/COIL proliferated during the pandemic. Using a power-based lens, this study highlights how a lack of intercultural awareness and one-sided assumptions create challenges for personnel from the "Global South" as they engaged with the U.S. to develop VE/COIL programs. We report our findings under six themes to share underrepresented voices of partners from the "Global South". Highlighting issues of importance to both higher education personnel and students, we offer five key recommendations to help optimize cultural responsiveness during North- South VE/COIL partnerships.

Keywords: COIL, critical intercultural communication, intercultural competence, virtual exchange, global south

INTRODUCTION

As we interact across cultures, we bring with us our own ways of being, knowing, and doing and inadvertently, we may assume that those we are interacting with are familiar with our ways. Additionally, history, economics, and power impact identities and relations between cultural groups as the groups interact (Halualani and Nakayama, 2010). It would therefore be remiss to overlook micro and macro processes that inform intercultural relations between Virtual Exchange/Collaborative Online Intercultural Learning (VE/COIL) Partners from the demarcations known as the "Global North " (North) and the "Global South" (South). The terms Global North and Global South loosely correspond to geographical locations, but more so they refer to countries based on socio-economic wealth (RGS, n.d.). As such, adopting a power-based lens to analyze socio-cultural assumptions during the development of VE/COIL partnerships between the North and the South enriches scholarship. Also, this approach helps unveil assumptions which undergird well-intentioned technology-based exchange programs as partners interact to develop them.

During the pandemic, technology-enabled activities surfaced rapidly at institutions in the U.S., a part of the "Global North," where issues of access to the internet and technological devices generally are a lesser problem than in the "Global South" (UNESCO, 2021). Such activities are broadly described as virtual exchanges, yet similar activities are known by different names around the globe. The nature or typology of internet-based cross-cultural activities remains evasive and non-uniform and some view them as inferior to physical mobility (UNESCO, 2022). One prominent technology-based activity which is sometimes used as a substitute for education abroad programs in the U.S. is Collaborative Online International Learning (COIL, n.d.). The U.S. has emerged as the dominant provider of such programs globally (Stevens Initiative 2021). Although an invaluable addition to campus intercultural learning activities, many socio-cultural assumptions undergird the development and implementation of COIL programs between nations. During the pandemic, Higher Education Institutions (HEIs) personnel fashioned such cross-cultural programs without prior training in intercultural competence. As a discipline, intercultural competence seeks to improve intercultural contact by building sensitivity and nurturing skills to shift human attitudes towards valuing other cultures, developing cultural awareness and encouraging self-awareness (Deardorff, 2009).

In this study, we employed a qualitative research design to explore socio-cultural assumptions in the experiences of higher education personnel from the South as they engaged in COIL partnerships with U.S. institutions during the pandemic. The following research question guided our study: What cultural challenges, if any, did you face when partnering with U.S. institutions to develop and implement VE/COIL programs? We categorized participant experiences under themes to amplify their voices. In part, their insights addressed linguistic and cultural translations needed to optimize cultural responsiveness particularly during North-South VE/COIL partnerships.

LITERATURE REVIEW

Campus internationalization programs are characterized by numerous activities which have typically taken place in person. In 2004, Knight identified two categories: Internationalization at Home (IaH) and Internationalization Abroad (IA). However, advancement in technology has given rise to a third category, Internationalization at a Distance (IaH) (Ramanau, 2016). This newest category is technology-based and exists within both IaH and IA activities. During the COVID-19 pandemic, technology-based internationalization activities became more prevalent due to international lockdowns and travel restrictions and helped maintain intercultural learning outcomes in higher education (Stevens Initiative, 2021). In the U.S., Collaborative Online International Learning (COIL, n.d.) became prominent and in other nations this type of technology-based activity is also known as Virtual Exchange (VE). We begin by providing a brief description of internet-based exchange programs to reduce confusion around names used to denote such exchanges worldwide.

Virtual Exchange/Collaborative Online International Learning

The word virtual refers to the use of the internet for learners and instructors to communicate during a learning experience, and the internet has become key for information and communication technology (ICT) (Stansfield et al. (2009). The word exchange denotes sharing knowledge across borders, and in the context of this discussion, entails use of ICTs to offer collaboration that enhances intercultural understanding. That said, Virtual Exchanges are not new to the higher education landscape (iEARN, 2007). Throughout their existence, this modality has been known under different names (See Appendix 1 for other names). Traditionally, Virtual Exchanges have taken place in fully ICT supported environments and/or as a complement to physical mobility (UNESCO, 2021).

In Europe, virtual mobility is the precursor to Erasmus+ (Ubachs & Brey, 2009). For the European Union the term Virtual Exchange (VE) describes:

a practice, supported by research, that consists of sustained, technology-enabled, people-to-people education programs or activities in which constructive communication and interaction take place between individuals or groups who are geographically separated and/or from different cultural backgrounds, with the support of educators or facilitators. Virtual Exchange combines the deep impact of intercultural dialogue and exchange with the broad reach of digital technology (Erasmus, n.d.)

In the U.S., the term Collaborative Online Intercultural Learning or its acronym COIL is used for similar experiences and describes:

an approach that brings students and professors together across cultures to learn, discuss and collaborate as part of their class. Professors partner to design the experience, and students partner to complete the activities designed. COIL becomes part of the class, enabling all students to have a significant intercultural experience within their course of study (COIL, n.d.).

In practice, in both Europe and the U.S. ("Global North"), the design and scope of VE/COIL programs vary. Practitioners in the field have asserted that along with differing terminology, aim, and scope, the quality of such programs remains largely undetermined (Stevens Initiative, 2021). During the pandemic, VE/COIL dominated international education offerings as a result of local and international lockdowns (Martel, 2020). Consequently, the quality and scope of VE/COIL programs drew attention, in part due to the ad hoc manner in which such programs were adopted by HEIs. The North was a dominant provider of VE/COIL programs on the global market. Between September 2020 and August 2021, 75% of programs originated in the U.S. and 11% originated in Europe (Stevens Initiative, 2021). In 2022, the U.S. was an "over-represented" player in the field, "whether as the country where the program originates or as the home country of a key partner in a virtual exchange program" (Stevens Initiative, 2021, p.12). This over-representation warrants attention from a critical lens given a general lack of familiarity by many educators with distance and online learning prior to the pandemic including interacting across cultures to develop programs (European Association of Distance Teaching Universities Report, 2020).

Power: "The Hidden and Destabilizing Aspects of Culture"

VE/COIL activities seek to develop intercultural awareness, and thus adopting a critical approach to intercultural communication helps unveil invisible assumptions, namely social and cultural norms which are not obvious to different groups as they interact. According to Halualani and Nakayama

(2010), "history, economics, and power have always positioned cultural group members and their identities disproportionately to one another within and across contexts" (p. 5). As such, a power-based approach to the study of North-South VE/COIL partnerships is important to scholarship to showcase how socio-cultural assumptions surfaced as partners collaborated across cultures.

Positioned within the context of critical internationalization, and leaning on critical intercultural communication studies, this study places VE/COIL partnerships within the macro context of politics, colonialism and hegemony to highlight "the hidden and destabilizing aspects of culture" as partners worked to adopt such programs across the globe (Nakayama & Halualani, p.2, 2010). Using critical perspectives helps highlight "the role of power and contextual constraints on communication" (Martin & Nakayama, p. 8, 2000). And acknowledging challenges that surface when collaborating across cultures, including issues of power, socio-economics, history, and coloniality, fosters equal and equitable mindsets to improve interactions in an interdependent world order.

RESEARCH METHOD

Using a qualitative research design, we collected and analyzed data from nine university personnel engaged with developing and implementing VE/COIL programs on their campuses. We collected data through semi-structured interviews. Using Braun & Clarke's (2006) *Thematic Analysis* framework, we analyzed raw data, and used lean coding to categorize the dataset (Creswell, 2013). We coded the data independently, compared and aligned our codes to allow for cross-verification, triangulation and validation of our data analysis. We classified our joint codes under six themes: (1) Language barrier; (2) Course design; (3) Infrastructure, Technology and Institutional Support; (4) Knowledge as an Assumption from "Global North"; (5) Context of Students in the "Global South"; (6) Politics, Sensitivity and Perspectives.

Participants

The 9 participants purposefully represented both faculty and administrative officers from institutions in the South. Two participants representing two distinct institutions were from Brazil. Two participants were from the same South African institution. Five participants were each from: Ecuador, India, Mexico, Niger and Venezuela.

RESULTS

We report our findings under six themes to reflect invisible socio-cultural assumptions made by partners from the North as they interacted with partners from the South.

Language barrier

When collaborating across cultures, participants shared that during VE/COIL programs, language was a barrier for non-native English speaking personnel and students. The dominant use of English by the North is often problematic because in the South: "not all faculty speak English, although most of our faculty members are fluent in English" (Participant 6). Use of English colloquialism and idioms pose more challenges. One participant shared that when U.S. personnel used the phrasing "dry run as opposed to rehearsal," faculty struggled. "[T]hey did not understand" which made them feel "I am not skillful enough, my English is not good enough" (Participant 4). Language barriers also lead to "fears of misunderstandings" and Participant 4 stated this "works for both sides" in the partnership. These misunderstandings can persist and "cause problems when negotiating for the project" at the outset of a collaboration (Participant 5). To circumvent this, participants reached out to colleagues for help: "we invited an English Professor to help us" (Participant 5).

Challenges relating to English also impacted students. In particular because: "We have diverse audiences, usually speaking English as a second language" (Participant 2). Participant 8 outlined the intersectional issues within diverse audiences: "We cannot ignore the digital divide that runs alongside or in parallel with the class divide, and also in South Africa the class divide runs alongside the racial divide." For another participant, "Language was a barrier, since the course material was in English and the students in KSA were not that familiar with the language" (Participant 1). In other words, low English proficiency "restricted levels of communication between students" (Participant 5). Yet, when VE/COIL partnerships were developed by the U.S. State Department, English was not a barrier, and Participant 3 explained why: "even though my students do not speak English, we did not face any problems because everything was simultaneously translated in French for them", illustrating that effective programs take language into account.

Course design

Given the global dominance of higher education by American and European norms, the impact of this power dynamic also surfaced during partnerships.

Although participants expected to be impacted by cultural differences, they did not always anticipate differences in course content, grading practices and syllabi. One faculty member noted that: "Cultural context is important; when we are not part of that, we don't know what the people are talking about" (Participant 4). For another "We faced cultural differences, and it was normal because it is a programme concerning all African Francophone countries" (Participant 3). Based on her experience in the Middle East another faculty partner stated:

One thing that was indeed daunting in business studies for us was translating the West-based business case studies to suit the local milieu... I had to give them [students] equivalent examples of local/Gulf based companies which they could relate to. So the content, case studies, and all illustrations in case of COIL need to be contextualized locally (Participant 1).

How VE/COIL programs are structured, namely whether they include graded or non-graded activities, influenced student attitude and level of participation in the North, which in turn affected students in the South:

In some programs you have different situations according to the school [in the North], students who have to participate in the activity because they will get credits and grades and those who don't, in that case you will have some of them more compromised than others which is not good for the program (Participant 2)

The way the courses are planned ahead, and the detailed nature of syllabi highlighted differences between educational practices between countries. To this point Participant 5 shared:

There is an aspect in Brazilian culture, we plan as we go, we are not used to planning one or two semesters ahead as some American professors require, and our syllabi are not as long and as detailed as Americans, this was a major problem in the very beginning of our COIL projects.

Infrastructure, Technology and Institutional Support

Socio- economic disparities between the North and the South also impacted cultural assumptions. For most participants, in-country infrastructural problems undermined their partnership experience. These issues were often unknown to partners in the North. Leading factors cited included power outages, poor internet connectivity, lack of institutional finance, and limited access to technology. Also, political instability can contribute to these issues. In the words of Participant 7:

structural violence, that is the struggles which are not visible but the human beings have to face every day, produces limitations, not cognitive limitations not intellectual limitations because the human capital is here...We struggle with all kinds of services in this country, the internet connection is weak, sometimes we don't have power, faculty salary is less than $20 a month which is a struggle...professors in the U.S. believe we are a functional democracy, this is also structural violence.

That said, it is important for students in the North to learn about these experiences: "students are sharing with other countries what we are facing. For example 'I could not do the joint assignment because I don't have internet or power or I did not eat today" (Participant 7).

Lack of financial support for HEIs in the public sector of some countries also drew attention. Participant 5 stated:

In Brazil, very few institutions will pay to enter a project like this. That's my experience with public institutions here. Some private institutions might, but it will depend on how involved they are with internationalization and VE/ COIL.

There is also an assumption about students' ability to use technology. Participant 3 highlighted: "The only problem I got came from my students that don't know much about IT; I spent time helping them use Zoom and Google Drive." For Participant 2, "Technology sometimes is an issue but now it is working very well, we use Zoom." This can put an additional burden on faculty in the South, but addressing these issues can be a learning opportunity.

Knowledge as an Assumption from the "Global North"

Participants noted several entrenched assumptions commonly made by partners in the North, such as an assumed familiarity with the U.S. higher education system and an expectation that partners would solve problems like Americans. Other assumptions included: having similar mindsets, that expectations and planning strategies coincide, and that all faculty operate within similar financial environments. A recurring statement by participants about a lack of interest in partner education systems is summarized by Participant 2:

Assuming that we know how COIL works in the U.S. or what to expect is a mistake, several meetings need to be organized before. The activities, schedule, contents, grades, etc. must be built together. It is also a good way to learn more about the educational systems of the participating institutions.

Another common challenge was "Assuming that peers will answer and solve the problems the same they do in the U.S." (Participant 6). Participant 4 stated: "we have different mindsets and that is something we cannot change but it is something we can learn about in order to be more understanding". Additionally, Participants 2 shared that "managing expectations is also very important. Being clear about what to expect." To work in partnership, those in the North need to know that:

In general, we are not good planners, but we are flexible and we don't need very strict schedules but need general information... For example, when we joined the partners their approach was - what exactly do you want me to do, the expectation from us was to have an initial conversation about the project,... we don't approach people that way, we want to discover things together (Participant 4).

Similarly, the effects of limited financial support for institutions in the South should be front of mind. Participant 5 stated:

At the institutional level, I would like some focus on the financial aspect. I know colleges and universities in the U.S. are going through a rough patch, but they have no idea what it is like to work in a country where more than 50% of the population has more debt than property. It is not just money, there is a lot missing in terms of structure, vision for the future. I would like U.S. institutions to look at VE/COIL projects and try to be more inclusive, especially of those who face financial challenges... Money is always an issue. I would expect not only American but also European institutions to look at this in a different way.

Moreover, partners were urged to show sensitivity to the local political contexts in the South:

It is a whole system of limitations that we have to face even though we are able to do COIL and we are responding. My responsibility is to teach others - what is taken for granted by you in the U.S. What is easy for you is not as easy for us. To be here with you I have to overcome all sorts of struggles. COIL is a practice in democracy. The positive thing about VE is we can tell our story to the world otherwise we will be invisible (Participant 7).

Context of Students in the "Global South"

Calling for cultural sensitivity, participants also asked their partners to upscale their understanding of their students' contexts, be flexible, interpret student behavior charitably and be responsive to students' technology preferences. Although one Participant stated that: "The U.S. Department through the

Embassy in Niamey already knew everything about our culture, the educational system, the barriers, so there was no need to tell them anything" (Participant 3); most participants called for clarification on the process of engagement because "sometimes the structures were not clear, some of the members from our university thought they meant something different, there needs to be a cultural translation of the content not only the language translation" (Participant 4). Additionally, Participant 6 urged "U.S. institution colleagues to develop intercultural sensitivity for the Mexican students". With student interest in mind, Participant 6 further stated that:

The majority of the interactions are conducted in English, therefore, Mexican students are doing a double effort in the project. U.S. institutions (admin, faculty & students) must be aware of that and be sensitive to that.

Also, Participants called for sensitive interpretations of student behavior because numerous factors underscore why students from the South do not participate in class; in other words, don't assume they are "lazy". Participant 8 explained why:

Students who are from the Global North, the U.S. or Western Europe, don't understand the context in which our students are operating. This is not the fault of the students in the Global North. For example we have load shedding [regular power outages undertaken by the South African government to manage energy demands]. Our students are not communicative about their challenges, they are shy to talk about the fact that they don't have electricity or they don't have access to equipment or data or Wi-Fi. The result of that is our students have been branded as lazy and noncommittal to the COIL project.

Irrespective of cultural differences, Participant 5 stated that in general students from the Global South

felt they knew a lot about American culture based on American TV series and films and sometimes they are shocked to find out that this is not reality. In contrast, American students don't know much about Brazilian culture...Some American students get very frustrated with the chit chat we have at the start. Brazilian students like to make friends, and in general American students are interested in finishing the task (Participant 5).

When communicating via technology, Participant 2 called for flexibility, stating that:

"Time zones are a problem when you have people from diverse countries and continents... use other tools to keep the communication outside the virtual classroom". Also, amidst the swath of available technologies, the existing technology preferences of students from the South need consideration. Participants pointed out that: "the technological tools used to do COIL, for example for Mexican students, the use of WhatsApp as a communication tool is very easy and obvious and it does not represent the same for U.S. students or faculty members" (Participant 6). This observation was echoed by Participant 7: "The problem is Americans prefer Facebook, here in Brazil students use another social media, also Brazilian students use WhatsApp a lot and American students do not use it as much - this poses a brief problem."

Politics, Sensitivity and Perspectives

Cultural responsiveness relies on intercultural sensitivity and competence, and a good starting point along this journey is understanding the history of countries and peoples we interact with. Partners from the North are urged to educate themselves about the history and politics of partnering countries. For example, Participant 5 mentioned a meeting in which a student from the U.S. had a Trump flag behind them, which was offensive to some students. This can also happen in other ways, such as in the following example from Participant 7:

In one of the collaborations we were creating a padlet and one of the faculty put the background with a red fist thinking that it was a symbol of freedom. I had to mention to that faculty that we could not have that there because my students will get very very offended because that red fist is what the dictatorship used to get into power, so for us that is the symbol of oppression.

Participant 9, drew attention to colonial lenses which undergird academia in the South. Although he refers to Africa, similar propositions were made by participants from Latin America:

A lot of Global South is not progressive, a lot of Global South has been trained and educated in or by the Global North or through scholarship in the Global North... in South Africa, academia is not progressive, it is very much white, very much Eurocentric ... scholarship on international research collaborations by South African HEIs .. is very much still similar to the time under apartheid; trends and patterns of where South Africa was with the Global North is still like in 1994. Academics in South Africa seek connections with the Global North; there is hardly any collaboration with the African continent... When looking at course content, reading lists are from the Global North, the Global South is not there.

The challenge of being open to collaboration with the North after times of political isolation can continue long after things appear open, as Participant 5 noted:

Brazilians are very interested in international things, we had the military coup that lasted between 1964-5 and we were shunned from the world for a while. After the coup, people started to be more welcoming to international things and people.

Most participants in this study started their VE/COIL programs through the State University of New York (SUNY) in the U.S. Participant 8 summarizes the perspectives that this brought to her classrooms:

Our COIL journey started with the "Global North" with SUNY, the global network that we accessed through SUNY is why we still think it is important to interact with the North. Our partners in the North are those that have values and ethos similar to our own in terms of broader internationalization and that gives us access to even more universities in the Global South and in the Global North, and it adds to diversity in our classrooms, diversity of our curriculum and diversity of perspectives.

DISCUSSION AND CONCLUSIONS

Our findings show that interactions across cultures are influenced by socio-cultural assumptions and power dynamics. At the micro level, targeted training can help improve such interactions. Personnel from the North are invited to assess their invisible assumptions by being more open minded and flexible and training in intercultural competence (Deardorff , 2009) is likely to help in this regard. To better understand the context and needs of partners from the Global South, and the impact of power dynamics, partners from the North need to be culturally responsive. Intercultural competence skills can help partners from the North adjust their attitudes and behavior to pay attention to:

- linguistic differences;

- inclusive course content;

- student context and technology preferences; and

- in-country structural challenges and histories.

Power dynamics as played out through linguistic dominance reveal a need to invest in communication in both English and partner country languages during collaborations. Such investments would display respect for both staff and students and is a step away from cultural dominance. Also, communicating solely in English places an unfair burden on the South. And equality in cross-cultural interactions calls for the North to familiarize themselves with partner country languages. In turn, this will promote intercultural awareness on U.S. campuses by exposing U.S. students to world languages. More so, participants shared that aspects of culture remained mostly invisible during interactions. Bringing visibility to cultural contexts requires moving away from self-centeredness, Eurocentrism, and cultural superiority mindsets to embrace reciprocity.

Also, equity requires course content to reflect Southern contexts, a move which calls for the North to understand the diverse contexts of partners and their students. This intentionality may foster deeper conversations about ongoing infrastructural deficits and challenges while raising awareness on access to technology and resource allocations in the world. Or, it may include simpler accommodations such as using technology which is prevalent and preferred in the South. Additionally, VE/COIL programs designed with students and their local contexts in mind are poised to improve student participation and satisfaction with COIL partnerships. Because in-country infrastructural deficits are challenging, being aware and mindful of its effects on learners is an inclusive approach that can shift power dynamics to encourage equality through education.

Partners from the North are invited to accommodate and use local professor expertise to better understand in-country contexts. It remains incumbent upon Northern partners to learn from their peers about cultural or institutional practices that relate to course design to avoid imposing their structures on the South. Finally, sensitivity to political issues and the gamut of perspectives that may fill a VE/COIL classroom must be front of mind. This requires accessing readily available knowledge of the history and politics of partnering countries including their colonial pasts and present relationships with the North, to attenuate perceived neo-colonial approaches.

IMPLICATIONS

Broadly speaking, the Global South values the exchanges enough to work through the invisible assumptions; it is therefore necessary for Northern partners to act proactively to mitigate challenges to improve North-South VE/COIL partnerships. To this end, we offer five key recommendations to reach more equitable and culturally responsive partnerships between the North and the South.

Figure 1: Towards Equitable North- South VE/COIL Partnerships

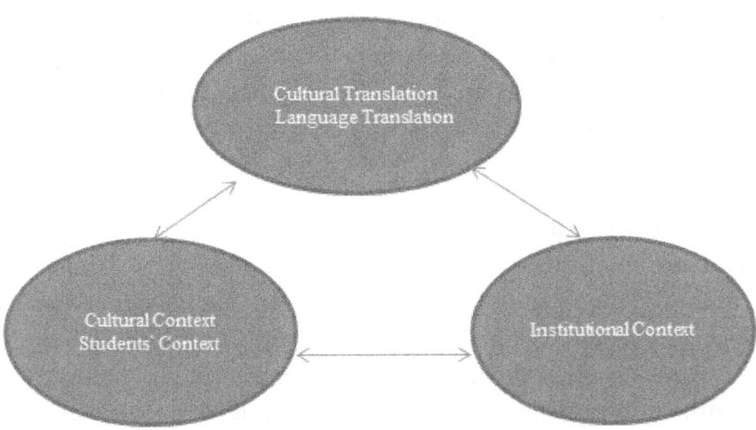

Acknowledging intercultural complexity between stakeholders, it is important for partners from the North and South to engage through reciprocity and increased awareness of the local context (Van Cleave & Cartwright, 2017). To achieve this, first, engage in cultural translation. A starting point is remembering that culture matters; therefore, listen for understanding across cultures and treat partners from the South as experts on their own cultural contexts. This can start with adopting practices that allow partners to feel part of the preparation process and show interest in their needs. Second, advocate for language translation. Mitigate the effects of language barriers for both personnel and students by providing translations and learning the language of partnering countries. Third, be aware of the cultural Context. Start by diversifying your content to make it relatable to students in the South. Go beyond familiar texts, case studies, or general course materials to foster inclusivity and to broaden perspectives. Fourth, familiarize yourself with your students' context: know the students' academic, economic, socio-cultural and political environment. Lastly, remember that institutional context requires a deeper understanding of in-country politics including media rhetoric on issues in the partnering country, understanding education systems and institutional financial realities, including approaches to intercultural learning which emanate from the South (Heleta & Chasi, 2022). Overall, work to challenge invisible assumptions.

This chapter shared underrepresented voices of partners from the "Global South", bringing visibility to socio-cultural assumptions they encountered during VE/COIL partnerships with the " Global North". Limited by the voices of nine personnel, the insights exposed lived experiences that encourage future discussions around invisible assumptions to optimize cultural responsiveness during North-South VE/COIL partnerships: We recommend considering:

1. What steps can partners in the Global North take to optimize cultural responsiveness during VE/COIL partnerships in general and with the Global South in particular?

2. Should all HEI personnel be trained in intercultural competence to meet challenges posed by invisible assumptions?

REFERENCES

Barbosa, Marcelo & Ferreira-Lopes, Luana. (2021). Emerging trends in telecollaboration and virtual exchange: a bibliometric study. *Educational Review.* https://doi.org/10.1080/00131911.2021.1907314

Bellz, J. A. (2003). Linguistic perspectives on the development of intercultural competence in telecollaboration. *Language Learning & Technology, 7*(2), 68-117.

Braun, V. & Clarke, V. (2006) Using thematic analysis in psychology. *Qualitative Research in Psychology, 3*(2). 77-101.

COIL Center, State University New York, (n.d.). https://coil.suny.edu/

Creswell, J. W. (2013). *Qualitative enquiry and research design: Choosing among five approaches* (3rd ed.). Sage.

Deardorff, D. K. (2009). *The SAGE handbook of intercultural competence.* Sage. https://doi.org/10.4135/9781071872987

Erasmus (n.d.). *What is virtual exchange?* https://evolve-erasmus.eu/about-evolve/what-is-virtual-exchange/

European Association of Distance Teaching Universities Report, (2020). *Report Covid-19 responses by Higher education in Europe.* https://empower.eadtu.eu/images/EADTU_Report_Covid_responses_by_Higher_education_in_Europe.pdf

Geographical Royal Society. (n.d.). *A 60 SECOND GUIDE TO the Global North/South divide.* https://www.rgs.org/CMSPages/GetFile.aspx?nodeguid=9c1ce781-9117-4741-af0a-a6a8b75f32b4&lang=en-GB

Heleta, S. & Chasi, S. (2022) Rethinking and redefining internationalisation of higher education in South Africa using a decolonial lens. *Journal of Higher Education Policy and Management, 45*(3), 261–275. https://doi.org/10.1080/1360080x.2022.2146566

iEARN. (2007). *The New York State – Moscow Schools Telecommunications Project: The founding project of iEARN.* https://iearn.org/assets/general/iEARN_NY-Moscow_Evaluation.pdf

Knight, J. (2004). Knight, J. (2004). Internationalization remodeled: Definition, approaches, and rationales. *Journal of Studies in International Education, 8*(1), 5-31.

King, R., Findlay, A., & Ahrens, J. (2010). *International student mobility literature review.* HEFCE. http://www.hefce.ac.uk/media/hefce/content/pubs/2010/rd2010/rd20_10.pdf

Martel, M. (2020). *COVID-19 effects on U.S. higher education campuses.* https://www.iie.org/en/Research-and-Insights/Publications/COVID-19-Effects-on-US-Higher-Education-Campuses-Report-2

Maznevski, M. L., & Chudoba, K. M. (2000). Bridging space over time: Global virtual team dynamics and effectiveness. *Organization Science, 11*(5), 473–492.

Jackson, J. (2012). *The Routledge handbook of language and intercultural communication.* Routledge.

Martin, J. N., & Nakayama, T. K. (2000). *Intercultural communication in contexts, 2nd edition.* Mayfield.

Nakayama, Thomas & Halualani, Rona Tamiko. (Eds.). (2010). *The handbook of critical intercultural communication.* Blackwell Publishing Ltd.

O'Dowd, Robert. (2021) Virtual exchange: moving forward into the next decade. *Computer Assisted Language Learning, 34*(3), 209-224.

Ramanau, R. (2016). Internationalization at a distance: A study of the online management curriculum. *Journal of Management Education, 40*(5), 545–575. https://doi.org/10.1177/1052562916647984

Royal Geographical Society (n.d.). *A 60 second guide to the Global North/South divide.* https://www.rgs.org/CMSPages/GetFile.aspx?nodeguid=9c1ce781-9117-4741-af0a-a6a8b75f32b4&lang=en-GB

Stansfield, M., & Connolly, T. (Eds.). (2009). *Institutional transformation through best practices in virtual campus development: advancing e-learning policies.* Information Science Reference.

Stevens Initiative (2021). *Survey of the virtual exchange field report.* https://www.stevensinitiative.org/resource/2021-survey-of-the-virtual-exchange-field-report-stevens-initiative/

Ubachs, G., & Brey, C. (2009). From virtual mobility to Virtual Erasmus: Offering students courses and services without boundaries. In Stansfield, M., & Thomas Connolly, T. (Eds.), *Institutional transformation through best practices in virtual campus development: Advancing e-learning policies.* Information Science Reference.

UNESCO (2021). *About virtual student mobility in higher education.* https://www.iesalc.unesco.org/en/2021/01/20/about-virtual-student-mobility-in-higher-education/

Van Cleave, T., Cartwright, C. T. (2017). Intercultural competence as a cornerstone for transformation in service learning. In Dolgon, C., Mitchell, T. D., & Eatman, T. K. (2017). *The Cambridge handbook of service learning and community engagement.* (pp. 204-218). Cambridge: Cambridge University Press. https://doi.org/10.1017/9781316650011

Acknowledgment

We thank all participants and our colleagues at the American Council of Education and the Inter-agency Network for Education in Emergencies for connecting us with professionals around the globe.

Bios

Yovana S.Veerasamy, PhD, is a Researcher in International Education. Her publications cover U.S. and comparative internationalization policy, international student services in the virtual context, intercultural competence and VE/COIL. Email:yovanas@mail.com

Emily Pelka, MEd, is an intercultural educator. In addition to her experience overseeing implementation of virtual exchange programs at the university level, she served as coordinator of Virtual ICC Working Group for the World Council on Intercultural and Global Competence. Email:e.pelka@fulbrightmail.org

Developing Intercultural Skills to Advance the United Nations' Sustainable Development Goals

Shabnam (Shay) Ivković
University of Waterloo, Canada

Alessio Surian
University of Padova, Italy

Joris Boonen
Maastricht University | Zuyd University of Applied Sciences, Netherlands

Julika Baumann Montecinos
Furtwangen University | HFU Business School, Germany

Maura Di Mauro
Intercultural & DEI Expert Trainer & Consultant, Italy

Xiuying Sophy Cai
Xiamen University, China

ABSTRACT

The United Nations' Sustainable Development Goals (UN's SDGs) articulate urgent global challenges that will require global solutions. For these solutions to be discovered, designed and implemented, a key construct is having well-honed intercultural skills. For problems as complex, solutions require a systematic and logical approach. This chapter presents the application of STEM design methods, such as design thinking and systems thinking, to a people-based challenge. Given the widely-understood definitions of systems thinking and design thinking methods, from a systems thinking synthesis perspective, global challenges are a system wide set of planetary problems that require urgent solutions at a global level. From a design thinking analysis perspective, the critical need is to grow intercultural effectiveness through study, work, co-curricular and extra-curricular experiences. Through several global case studies, this chapter will demonstrate how intentional inclusion of intercultural skills education builds individuals who are better prepared to engage with global challenges.

Keywords: United Nations' Sustainable Development Goals (UN's SDGs); intercultural skills; STEM design methods; design thinking; systems thinking; intercultural effectiveness through study, work, co-curricular and extra-curricular experiences; global case studies

INTRODUCTION

In an increasingly complex world, more and more people, like students, practitioners, policy makers, etc. need to understand the critical challenges facing our planet that are well defined by the United Nations' Sustainable Development Goals (UN's SDGs) (United Nations, n.d.), a comprehensive and compelling taxonomy to understand global challenges. Additionally, those in the solutions space must be interculturally effective to work across boundaries, diverse workplaces and multicultural teams if they are to design and deliver culturally-sensitive solutions that address these complex challenges. The interconnection of global competence or intercultural competence with the UN's SDGs comes up over and over again. In a highly-interconnected era, global collaborations are becoming the norm, even if working remotely, which requires enhanced capabilities of navigating complex and nuanced intercultural encounters. At the same time, in view of critical and coexisting local and global problems that may need international experts, multi-cultural teams, and effective international diplomacy in an increasingly complex geopolitical landscape, diverse perspectives, knowledge, talents, and strategies are required, including a deep awareness of the big challenges facing our planet (United Nations, 2014, Matsumoto & Hwang, 2013, McRae and Ramji, 2017, Bennet, 1986, Deardorff, 2006, Javidan et al., 2007, Earley & Ang, 2003, Hofstede 1982, 2001). The UN's SDGs are developmental challenges pervasive across the globe, which will require the coming together of field experts, funders, local mobilisers, academics, policy makers, politicians and diplomats in addition to the various populations in local regions requiring support. As has been shown time and time again through various case studies, reports and opinion pieces from organizations such as CIDA (n.d.) and CAIDP (n.d.), those tackling solutions to a given developmental issue should have a deep understanding of the mores of a local region, be able to read the environment, situate oneself authentically within it, and then build ways to navigate the environment respectfully, ethically and effectively (Dingwall, et al, 2018).

Organizations and systems call upon the education of intercultural competence in youth as a key construct (Kaplan, 2001, Livermore, 2013) for developing change agent mentality in advancing the UN's SDG agenda. The Worldwide Educating for the Future Index suggests that in this age of unpredictability in social and geo-political ideologies, future-oriented skills such as intercultural competency (Deardoff, 2006) are critical (WEFI, 2019, GUNi, 2019). Against these backdrops, Andreas Schleicher, from the Organization for Economic Co-operation and Development (OECD) said that the extent to which the UN's 2030 vision for the SDGs will become a reality depends on today's educators and classrooms. This is the inspiration behind the OECD Programme for International Student Assessment (PISA) (OECD PISA, 2018, 2015). The United Nations' Office of the Secretary-General's Envoy on Youth claims that global competence in youth is critical to achieve the UN's SDGs (Hunter, n.d.). For this chapter, we consider global competence and intercultural competence as presented within the definition of Intercultural Competence (Deardoff, 2006).

For challenges rooted in the multi-axes complexity of regional mores, local attitudes and leanings, influence of global experts and funders, insights from academics, policy makers and governments across multiple economic and political systems, the solutions space can be a quagmire if not approached in a systematic and logical manner. This chapter presents an attempt to apply STEM design methods to a people-based challenge. The design thinking methodology addresses biases and behaviors that hamper constructive problem solving and ideation (Liedtka, 2018). Systems thinking makes sense of complexity by looking at it holistically in terms of relationships (Arnold & Wade, 2015). The philosophy of systems thinking is rooted in being sensitive to the circular nature of the world where there are known and unknown consequences of our actions that impact the conditions we live in. This approach requires the willingness to see a situation as completely as possible, to recognize inter-relations, and to understand that sometimes multiple solutions are needed to solve a problem. Systems thinking is best applied if an issue is important, a problem chronic, and / or previous approaches have not worked as well as desired. The big advantage of systems thinking is that it broadens perspectives and allows us to make informed choices under the acute realization that whatever choice we make will impact other parts of the system, and therefore, our design choices should be mindful of optimizing the impact we want to have on a system (Goodman, 2018). As a solution design method, design thinking is one that is human centered at its core. It focuses solutions on the people who need them more than product, service, and process efficiencies. Desirability, feasibility and viability are the key constructs of design thinking - what makes most sense from a people perspective; what is possible within the foreseeable future; and what is sustainable over the long term. Simply stated, design thinking requires gathering info on what people need, framing a question that empathizes with a people's need, solutions ideation towards breakthrough ideas, tangibility of design through prototyping, testing to learn, and sharing the outcomes (IDEOU, n.d.). So, where systems thinking is a wide-spectrum approach that analyzes a system by breaking it down into separate elements to understand how they come together to work collectively, design thinking is a narrow focus approach about synthesizing a solution with focus on creating and building.

Combining these two approaches is an ideal way to better understand the urgent need and incredible potential of developing intercultural skills for solving global problems as defined by the UN's SDGs. Essentially, from a systems thinking perspective, global challenges are a system wide set of planetary problems that require urgent solutions at a global level. This means that people from various cultures will need to work together to design solutions at individual, team-based, organizational, community and societal levels. A key construct of people from different cultures working together is the need for a high level of intercultural effectiveness in communication, teamwork, identity understanding and development, and so on. From a design thinking paradigm perspective, the critical need is to grow intercultural effectiveness skills through study, work, co-curricular and extra-curricular experiences. Through several case studies situated globally, this chapter will demonstrate how intentional inclusion of intercultural skills, education and perspectives, especially within formal educational programs, builds individuals who are better prepared to address global challenges as defined by the UN's SDGs in more effective ways.

CASE STUDIES

Case study 1: Reflecting on global competence using the Global Mind Monitor (Netherlands)

Systems-level synthesis

Young professionals who aim to contribute to solutions for complex 21ˢᵗ century challenges need the intercultural knowledge, skills and attitudes to collaborate effectively in interdisciplinary and often international teams. Employers often explicitly ask for intercultural skills or experience in working with internationally composed teams (Trilling & Fadel, 2009). As a result, higher education institutes try to simulate these environments to allow their students to develop these skills within and outside of school buildings, through (virtual) international collaborations projects, international internships, study abroad periods, etc. However, as is the case for employees, it is very challenging for both teachers and students to make this competency tangible. Illustrative for this challenge are the many conceptualizations and frameworks that are used, such as intercultural skills, global competence, global citizenship, etc. Understanding how to design meaningful assessment for intercultural learning is therefore a known and ongoing challenge that many internationally-oriented higher education institutes struggle with (Deardorff, 2006).

Design thinking-based analysis & outcomes:

At Zuyd University of Applied Sciences in the Netherlands, the Global Mind @ Work research centre designed the 'Global Mind Monitor' (GMM) (Globalmind, n.d.), an online intercultural reflection instrument that was designed to map different aspects of students' intercultural competencies. It uses validated measurement scales such as the Multicultural Personality Questionnaire (van der Zee & van Oudenhoven, 2000) and Cultural Intelligence (Ang *et al.*, 2007) to provide students with personalized insights regarding a variety of cultural knowledge, skills and attitude. From 2023 onwards, the tool also includes a recently developed measurement instrument on engagement and disengagement with sustainability (Moreira et al.,2021), to account for the important intersection between sustainability and global competence.

The GMM is designed as an online learning environment in which students regularly fill out a questionnaire in which the above-mentioned constructs are the main variables. However, the GMM is not designed as an assessment tool. In the first place, it is a self-assessment instrument that is used to start a meaningful conversation about intercultural competence development between students and their coaches, at multiple occasions throughout their curriculum. When we look at how the tool is used in educational practice since 2017, we can observe a variety of applications. In some programs, the GMM is used as a single measure, for instance related to a reflective exercise within a specific module or project. In most programs, it is used as a pre- and post self-assessment, where students for example fill out the monitor before and after a study abroad experience, interpret differences and compare themselves with the rest of the (anonymized) sample. Usually, these comparisons provide insights for reflective reports or mentor meetings. In some exceptional cases, students fill out the monitor yearly, and even after graduation, to get a view on their development from freshman to junior professional (Boonen, et al, 2019, 2021).

Case study 2: Exploring and enhancing multi-cultural identity to develop interculturally competent and global citizens (Italy)

Systems-level synthesis:

For different reasons the current age is characterized by the increase of human mobility and fluidity, particularly for certain categories of people, such as migrants, international assignees, self-initiated expatriates and students (OECD, 2019). Living in more than one country givesa growing cohort of people the opportunity to develop a multicultural identity, by learning more languages and by absorbing different cultural customs and values. However, not all people with a multicultural identity are aware of their acquired cultures or of who they are, neither they necessary possess intercultural or global skills. Indeed, some of the risks that people with multicultural and fluid belonging may face are: the ambivalence of positioning oneself along continuing moving and uncertain boundaries; the difficulty of structuring an integrated and consistent self-identity based on the awareness of a sense of belonging to different and multiple cultural groups as life choice, or to a broader human kind (Di Mauro & Gehrke, 2019); socially and professionally exhibited behaviors that are contrary of feeling and of acting as an aware and responsible *global citizen* (Di Mauro & Bolzani, 2020). Education can play an important role, in accompanying the process of awareness of one's multicultural identity, determining identity building choices, and developing intercultural and global skills (Barrett, 2018).

Design thinking-based analysis & outcomes:

This case study is based on: the use of the photo book *Feeling Italian* (Di Mauro and Gehrke, 2019) in several university courses, particularly of intercultural management; and on the use of the self-reflection exercise "Developing (Multi)

Cultural Identity and Global Citizenship" (Di Mauro, 2021) as a didactic tool to enhance (local and international) students' awareness about the development of their multicultural identity, and on their personal starting development journey of their intercultural and global citizens' skills. The *Feeling Italian* book is used to initiate an inner dialogue within the readers about their multicultural identity, independently from where students are based, or whatever their origins or family background are. The written self-reflection exercise helps students to explore and increase their awareness on their own multi-cultural identity; to activate them to look for diversity intentionally; to learn them to live on the "borders" as potential, for personal growth as global citizens. The book can also help the reader to become aware of SDGs, particularly the ones connected with "social" sustainability, while developing their commitment as global citizens.

Within the European WeLcarn project, both Italian and international students' feedback said that reading the book and the self-reflection exercise helped them to learn about internal cultural variability, within every country, and that they had the possibility to think about themselves, and to start to commit to who they wanted to become, and how they wanted to contribute to SDGs achievement.

Case study 3: ICC in teaching and learning with sustainability perspectives (Europe-Brazil)

Systems-level synthesis:

Knowledge co-production provides a research approach that promotes a more inclusive, socially robust, and deliberative scientific process that is concerned with transformative learning. This is particularly relevant to address sustainability issues (Verwoerd et al., 2022) and it requires to acknowledge the relations between re-framing human choices in front of ecological crises and the necessary conceptual and affective negotiations implied by an ecology of knowledge. Consistent with this knowledge co-production perspective, this case study (Yin, 2018) is based on collective writing experiences that enhance specific attention for situated learning and place-based pedagogies inspired by participatory action-research and by listening to the contingencies, the contexts, and the indigenous knowledge of the places where the co-writing actors are living and operating. Specific attention is given to the relationship between the life system of an indigenous community, issues related to "development", and the ways the latter are addressed in higher education.

Design thinking-based analysis & outcomes:

The case study is structured around a core narrative provided by a Terena indigenous leader in Mato Grosso do Sul (Brazil) and how this has been an opportunity for involving both local people and foreign students to understand its claims and insights and to elaborate on the oral speech's intuitive dimension and ancestral wisdom relating to specific indigenous worldview concerning agriculture, community, and education (Maciel, de Campos, et al., 2019).

The meeting between the Terena "Mãe Terra" (Mother Earth) village people and international students was an initiative of a joint group of four Universities within the Sustainable Territorial Development (STEDE) Erasmus Master Mundus programme, i.e. the University of Padua (Italy), the University of Paris I Panthéon-Sorbonne (France), the Catholic University of Leuven (Belgium), and the Catholic University Dom Bosco in Campo Grande (Brazil). During the visit, Leosmar Antonio Terena delivered a welcome speech that introduced students to the importance of the spiritual and ancestral dimension in sustainability studies. The speech was recorded and transcribed with the consensus of Leosmar, and since it was the source of in-depth reflection by students it generated a process of co-authorship involving four other contributors. Students appreciated Terena communities' capacity for improvisation and negotiation in adverse conditions based on their specific relationship with the local territory and their fluidity concerning the relation to the environment and to land tenure, despite having faced significant forms of violence and attempts to restrict Terenas' access to their ancestral lands and to impose the confinement in small and fragmented reservations. In "Mãe Terra" students could experience Terenas' efforts to move beyond these restrictions. They were specifically intrigued by the fact that Terena young people went away to study and then came back to live and work in the community while there is a tendency worldwide of young professionals leaving the countryside to live and work in the big cities. The Terena attitude is rooted in spirituality, i.e. the connection that is felt to ancient roots, common origins, the realization of being only a part of the whole living system, and that we all have to contribute to trying to conceive what makes it possible to continue existing in a sustainable way.

Case study 4: Intercultural effectiveness and SDGs as components of quality work-integrated learning (Canada)

Systems-level synthesis:

Climate change, globalization, technological disruption, shifting economic and political landscapes, and other challenges have made our world volatile, uncertain, complex and ambiguous (VUCA). Industry and labour markets globally are at the receiving end of critical challenges that are well-identified within the UN's SDGs. The world of work is in a state of constant change – most recently, that of moving to Industry 5.0 – which has amplified previously existing VUCA conditions. Preparing for this shift is critical. Post-secondary institutions (PSI) globally have a deeper mission imperative to graduate individuals as change agents for creating a sustainable world. While not a silver bullet, work integrated learning (WIL) has been identified as an effective strategy to develop this type of talent (RBC, 2018). WIL is a curricular form of experiential education involving a partnership between student, PSI, and community/industry partners.

Design thinking-based analysis & outcomes:

At the University of Waterloo, one of the key constructs of excellence in quality WIL is the Future Ready Talent Framework (FRTF, n.d.) with key competencies needed to navigate the future of work and learning. The FRTF profiles 4 clusters of 12 competencies (specifically lists 'Intercultural Effectiveness') that are expected to be in demand in the emerging global workplace.

In concert with the Canadian HQ of the Sustainable Development Solutions Network (SDSN) situated at Waterloo, the Co-operative & Experiential Education (CEE) unit is ideally situated to increase SDG awareness of interns and employers, and to motivate them to be more effective agents of change for advancing the UN's SDG agenda. This is of strategic pedagogical importance as higher education institutions develop effective programming to create change agents who will advocate for and drive the SDGs forward. CEE has put in place an SDG awareness-building and engagement activity during co-op work terms, using international work terms as a pilot. Interns and supervisors are provided a quality framework of questions to begin a conversation about the company's sustainability direction and contributions, and opportunities for the intern to engage (Ivkovic & McRae, 2021). Early survey results show that both interns and employer supervisors increase their awareness of SDGs and motivation to engage post activity significantly. Interns identified the highest benefit of the activity being increased knowledge of the SDGs, which led to many indicating a desire to apply SDGs in their future coursework, engage in campus activities, and seek future SDG-related internships. For the employer supervisors, the top outcomes were the learning value of the activity, deeper intern engagement, and developing future SDG best practices for their own organizations.

The FRTF competency development tool in concert with the internship SDG activity is one approach to develop intercultural effectiveness in students while developing greater awareness of the SDGs and driving motivation to engage via WIL experiences.

Case study 5: A bottom-up subsistence marketplace approach to addressing SDGs and developing ICC (USA – India; global)

Systems-level synthesis:

The big question facing those of us in the field is how to cultivate, pedagogically and programmatically, key competencies for sustainability (UNESCO, 2017) among students in higher education institutions as we strive to educate next generation of global citizens to achieve SDGs? While mainstream "banking" model of education and teaching to the test have been criticized among progressive education researchers as least effective and even denounced as "oppressive" pedagogy (Freire, 2000 [1970]), alternative educational models, even those identified as experiential education, have been mostly "top-down," i.e. to "experience" and "educate" in resource-rich and high literacy communities in order to design solutions and then apply them to low-income and low literacy communities. However, the majority of the humanity facing the problems of unsustainable development are still living in impoverished communities. Thus, a bottom-up approach to addressing SDGs is emerging (Viswanathan & Gau, 2018), that is, learning from actual ground level reality in subsistence communities, which requires a wholly different set of intercultural skills than what university students might have due to social, geographic and economic differences.

Design thinking-based analysis & outcomes:

The Subsistence Marketplace Initiative (SMI), first started at the University of Illinois at Urbana-Champaign by Professor M Viswanathan, is a bottom-up approach to SDGs. Built upon research and outreach to low-income, low-literacy communities, the SMI initiative provides "education for subsistence" (teaching marketplace literacy to low-income persons in local communities in the U.S, India, Tanzania, Uganda, Argentina, etc.) and "education about subsistence" (various teaching initiatives at the university for students to learn about subsistence marketplaces). The focus here is on the pedagogical impact of intercultural development among university students as they learn to design sustainable solutions to address global poverty and other SDGs in subsistence contexts around the world.

In both forms of education, the "bottom-up" approach has been the center of the teaching pedagogy (Viswanathan, 2016): 1) the educational program was based on research on micro-level life circumstances of consumers and entrepreneurs in subsistence communities; 2) when conducting educational programs for people living in subsistence, they start from the life circumstances of the participants; 3) when teaching about subsistence at the university, they start from the life circumstances of the students and the people living in poverty, instead of starting from macro-statistics or business strategies such as the Bottom-of-the-Pyramid (BoP) approach (Prahalad, 2005). Taken as an example, a yearlong course (henceforth SMC) was designed to provide an integrative learning experience about subsistence marketplaces to graduate and advanced undergraduate students. By emphasizing the roles of business and engineering in poverty contexts, it seeks to design solutions to lead subsistence marketplaces to ecologically, socially, and economically sustainable marketplaces. The students form interdisciplinary groups to take on issues in subsistence, such as sanitation, water quality, open defecation, and clean cooking, to conduct market research and design sustainable solutions such as product development, business plan, service or educational programs, to address these issues.

With the innovative curricular and a "bottom-up" pedagogy, students consistently concluded that they learned a lot about technical knowledge in business plans, product design, and most importantly, perspectives of business and engineering in different contexts in rural and urban low-income communities for different segments of consumers. Many students talked about how this experience made them think about their own personal and professional lives and rethink their positionality in the world, wherein their intercultural competence was expanded into a moral universe within which they can make positive change (Cai, 2020).

Case study 6: Transcultural learning by cooperating within the Transcultural Caravan Network (Brazil, Germany, Poland, South Africa, Vietnam)

Systems-level synthesis:

As a platform of transcultural teaching formats, the Transcultural Caravan Network (Transcultural Caravan, n.d.), initiated by Zeppelin University's Leadership Excellence Institute, aims to provide students with relational, experiential learning opportunities. In Transcultural Student Research Groups (TSRGs) with participants from different countries and disciplines, students experience first-hand what it means to learn from and with each other by cooperating over a longer term in a culturally complex constellation. The SDGs offer this project an opportunity to apply a transcultural approach not only as a didactic method, but also to make the SDGs the subject of such student research projects. Accordingly, the SDGs are considered to stand for a mutually enhancing coexistence between commonality of goals and diversity in local implementations, which characterizes the transcultural concept (Baumann Montecinos, 2022: 195f., Wieland & Baumann Montecinos, 2019). Likewise, the diversity of sectoral perspectives is explicitly recognized in its relevance when SDG 17 calls for a global pact between actors from politics, business, and civil society to address the common challenges, requiring "an unprecedented level of cooperation and collaboration" (Stibbe et al., 2018: 6). To focus on the SDGs, especially on Goal 17, is therefore a promising avenue for the Transcultural Caravan Network and its projects of collaborative learning.

Design thinking-based analysis & outcomes:

Aiming to offer students real-life transcultural cooperation and learning experiences, the format of the TSRGs has continuously evolved since the first project in 2017 and has now given rise to a network of seven universities that jointly implement these formats (Baumann Montecinos et al, 2021). In the TSRGs, approximately 15 to 20 students work together on common research questions, building thematic subgroups who contribute a specific perspective to the overall picture, thus co-creating shared meaning in a moderated process of dialogue, cooperation, and reflection. In concrete terms, this involves the Transcultural Learning Cycle which the student groups go through together over a period of more than a year, consisting of a topic-setting conference, a group-building preparation phase, a field research trip, a data evaluation and analysis phase, a Winter School, and a joint book publication. These formats focus on cultivating communities of practice of the participating students, educators and cooperation partners. Their design reflects a transcultural approach, in which the recognition of cultural diversity, the awareness of one's own culture, position and biases and adopting a non-normative attitude build the foundations for finding existing commonalities and developing new ones out of collaborative practice and experience. Placing the thematic scope of these groups on SDG-related topics has proven to be a highly appropriate approach in many respects. To name these indicative experiences, such transcultural formats were used in a student research project on the women's empowerment social enterprise Hope Development Initiative in Uganda, in a project on traditional communities in the Brazilian Amazon, in a project on the social start-up Insolar in Rio de Janeiro, Brazil, and in a project on partnerships for the SDGs in Southeast Asia. In all these projects, the SDGs have provided very valuable learning experiences for all involved, due to the relevance, global and intersectoral reach and complexity of their concerns and implications. *{Also see concepts of transcultural education in higher education by Grünfelder et al. in this book}*

DISCUSSION AND CONCLUSIONS

Global challenges, as defined by the UN's SDGs, need global solutions, with contributions at all levels – individual, team, organizational, community, societal. Thes contributions will come from teams of solutions providers based in and exposed to different regions of the world. As mentioned in the introduction, success of these types of global engagement will rely on high intercultural effectiveness of the people in these solutions teams. Collective experience suggests that designing the right approach for developing intercultural skills is greatly dependent on learning from the experiences of peers in the field. With greater understanding of the need of intercultural competence in addressing global challenges, there is also a heightened awareness of the need to develop this skill during formative educational years in future champions of change.

Systems thinking is a wide-spectrum approach that analyzes a system by breaking it down into separate elements to understand how they come together to work collectively, and design thinking is a narrow focus approach about synthesizing a solution with focus on creating and building. Applying what are classically considered STEM approaches to the problem of intercultural skills education is one way to approach intercultural skills development. The case studies in this chapter are presented to illustrate intentional intercultural skills education towards priming individuals who are better prepared to address global challenges as defined by the SDGs in more effective ways. These case studies provide a systems level synthesis of an issue related to intercultural competence development, then present the solution to that issue built on an analysis based in design thinking principles, and then share the outcomes of designing the solution to intercultural competence development in this manner. The collective goal of all the case studies is to prepare future graduates to be ready to engage with global problem solving in respectful, ethical and effective ways that truly situate oneself authentically within local or regional perspectives.

The contributions of this chapter present one way to approach the complex task of intercultural competency development in graduates who will be the solution makers of the future. What was very reassuring to the authors of this chapter is that each individual case study could be easily put into the mould of defining the problem through a systems thinking lens and presenting the solution via design thinking methods. This suggests that the application of STEM approach to a people-based challenge could be a reliable method to analyze how intercultural competence development for addressing global challenges (as defined by the UN's SDGs) can be approached at a program level. The authors do not suggest that this is the best way to impart intercultural competence education, but it is one that should be taken into account when designing a skills development program. Effective intercultural competence development and application remains an ongoing challenge, even beyond the space of advancing the UN's SDGs. This chapter is a humble contribution to global dialog and peer support in discovering new ways and means to integrate the narratives of intercultural competency development and its critical place in addressing complex global challenges.

The authors thank Bettina Wahl, University of Waterloo, for her work formatting the content and citations.

REFERENCES

Arnold, R. D. and Wade, J. P. (2015). A definition of systems thinking: A systems approach. *Procedia Computer Science, 44*, 669–678. https://doi.org/10.1016/j.procs.2015.03.050

Barrett, M. (2018). How schools can promote the intercultural competence of young people. *European Psychologist, 23*(1), 93–104

Baumann Montecinos, J. (2022). Transcultural cooperation in global networks. A contribution to the research program of relational economics. In L. Biggiero, et al. (Eds.), *The relational view of economics* (pp. 193–212). Springer.

Baumann Montecinos, J., Schwengber, J. G., & Grünfelder, T. (2021). Transcultural education - The transcultural caravan as a relational learning journey. In J. Baumann Montecinos, et. Al. (Eds.), *Kooperation, Governance, Wertschöpfung. Perspektiven auf eine Relationale Ökonomie* (pp. 227–262). Metropolis

Bennet, M. J. (1986). A developmental approach to training for intercultural sensitivity. *International Journal of Intercultural Relations, 10*(2), 179-196

Boonen, J., Hoefnagels, A., & Pluymaekers, M. (2019). The development of intercultural competencies during a stay abroad: Does cultural distance matter? In R. M. O. Pritchard, et al. (Eds.), *The three Cs of higher education: Competition, collaboration and complementarity* (pp. 185-204). CEU Press.

Boonen, J., Hoefnagels, A., Pluymaekers, M., & Odekerken, A. (2021). Promoting international learning outcomes during a study abroad: The moderating role of internationalisation at home. *International Journal of Educational Management, 35*(7), 1431-1444.

CAIDP. (n.d.) Canadian Association of International Development Professionals. https://www.caidp-rpcdi.ca/caidp-programming

CIDA. (n.d.) Canadian International Development Agency. https://www.international.gc.ca/world-monde/funding-financement/funding _development_projects-financement_projets_developpement.aspx?lang=eng

Deardorff, D. K. (2006). Identification and assessment of intercultural competence as a student outcome of internationalization. *Journal of Studies in International Education, 10*(3), 241-266.

Dewey, J. (1934). *Art as experience.* In the collected works of John Dewey, 1882-1953. Later works, vol 10 (LW10). Southern Illinois University Press.

Di Mauro, M. & Bolzani, D. (2020). *"Neighbourness" competences: A literature review.* http://welearn-project.eu/files/IO1_Report_WeLearn.pdf

Di Mauro, M. (2021). *Developing (multi)cultural identity and global citizenship.* https://centerforinterculturaldialogue.files.wordpress.com/2021/02/icd-exercis e-2-di-mauro.pdf

Di Mauro, M., & Gehrke, B. (2019). Feeling Italian. SIETAR Italia.

Dingwall, JR., Labrie, C., McLennon, T. & Underwood, L. (2018). *Cross-cultural communication.* OER developed for Olds College.

https://ecampusontario.pressbooks.pub/profcommsontario/chapter/cross-cultural-communication/

Earley, P. C. & Ang, S. (2003). *Cultural intelligence: Individual interactions across cultures.* Stanford University Press.

FRTF (n.d.) *University of Waterloo's Future-Ready Talent Framework.* https://uwaterloo.ca/future-ready-talent-framework/

Globalmind (n.d.) *Global Mind Monitor.* https://globalmind.info/

Goodman, M. (2018). The Systems Thinker. https://thesystemsthinker.com/systems-thinking-what-why-when-where-and-how/

GUNi. (2019). *Implementing the 2030 agenda at higher education institutions: Challenges and responses.* GUNi Network.

Hofstede, G. (1982). *Culture's consequences (2nd ed.).* Sage.

Hofstede, G. (2001). *Culture's consequences: Comparing values, behaviors, institutions, and organizations across nations (2nd ed.).* Sage.

Hunter, B. (n.d.). Global competence amongst youth is critical to achieve sustainable development goals. https://www.un.org/youthenvoy/2015/07/global-competence-amongst-youth-critical-achieve-sustainable-development-goals/

IDEOU (n.d.) *What is design* https://www.ideou.com/blogs/inspiration/what-is-design-thinking

Ivković, S., & McRae, N. (2021). Improving engagement of interns and employers with the United Nations' Sustainable Development Goals. *International Journal of Work-Integrated Learning, 22*(3), 345-356.

Javidan, M., Steers, R., & Hitt, M. (Eds.) (2007). The global mindset (Vol. 19). San Diego, CA: Elsevier

Kaplan, R. (2001). Cultural thought patterns in intercultural education. In P. Kei Matsuda & T. Silva (Eds.) *Landmark essays on ESL writing.* Hermagoras Press.

Liedtka, J. (2018). *Why design thinking works.* Harvard Business Review. https://hbr.org/2018/09/why-design-thinking-works

Livermore, D. (2013). *Expand your borders: Discover 10 cultural clusters.* Cultural Intelligence Centre.

Maciel, de Campos, J., Surian, A., Brahmllari, E., Ferreira Tarasconi, B., & Leosmar, A. (2019). Terena agriculture and life-system: A speech and beyond. *Interações (Campo Grande), 20*(3), 861-877.

Matsumoto, D., & Hwang, H. C. (2013). Assessing cross-cultural competence: A review of available tests. *Journal of Cross-Cultural Psychology, 44.*

McRae, N., & Ramji, K. (2017). Intercultural competency development curriculum: A strategy for internationalizing work integrated learning for the 21st century global village. (M. Drysdale & T. Bowen, Eds.), *Work-integrated learning for the 21st century global village: International perspectives on education and society* (pp. 129-143). Emerald.

Moreira, P. A. S., Ramalho, S., & Inman, R. A. (2021). The engagement/disengagement in sustainable development inventory (EDiSDI): Psychometric properties and validity-based studies. *European Journal of Psychological Assessment, 37*(5), 344–356.

OECD PISA. (2018). *Preparing our youth for an inclusive and sustainable world: The OECD PISA global competence framework.* https://www.oecd.org/education/Global-competency-for-an-inclusive-world.pdf

OECD. (2015). *OECD innovation strategy 2015: An agenda for policy action.* https://www.oecd.org/sti/OECD-Innovation-Strategy-2015-CMIN2015-7.pdf

OECD. (2019). *International migration and displacement: Trends and policies report to the G20.* https://www.oecd.org/migration/mig/G20-migration-and-displacement-trends-and-policies-report2019.pdf

Prahalad, C. K. (2005). *The fortune at the bottom of the pyramid: Eradicating poverty through profits.* Wharton School Publishing.

RBC (2018). *Humans wanted: How Canadian youth can thrive in the age of disruption.* https://www.rbc.com/dms/enterprise/futurelaunch/_assets-custom/pdf/RBC-Future-Skills-Report-FINAL-Singles.pdf

Stibbe, F. T., Reid, S., & Gilbert, J. (2018).*Maximising the impact of partnerships for the SDGs: A practical guide to partnership value creation.* The Partnering Initiative and UNDESA.

Transcultural Caravan (n.d.). http://www.transcultural-caravan.org/

Trilling, B., & Fadel, C. (2009). *21st century skills: Learning for life in our times.* Wiley & Sons.

UNESCO (2017). *Education for sustainable development goals: Learning objectives.* https://www.unesco.de/sites/default/files/2018-08/unesco_education_for_sust ainable_development_goals.pdf

United Nations (2014). *The road to dignity by 2030: Ending poverty, transforming all lives and protecting the planet. Synthesis report of the Secretary-General on the Post-2015 Agenda.* United Nations. http://www.un.org/disabilities/documents/reports/SG_Synthesis_Report_Ro ad_to_Dignity_by_2030.pdf

United Nations. (n.d.). *Sustainable development goals.* https://sustainabledevelopment.un.org/?menu=1300

Verwoerd, L., Brouwers, H., Kunseler, E., Regeer, B., & de Hoop, E. (2022). Negotiating space for knowledge co-production. *Science and Public Policy, 50*(1), 59–71. https://doi.org/10.1093/scipol/scac045

WEFI. (2019). *Worldwide Educating for the Future Index 2019* https://educatingforthefuture.economist.com/the-worldwide-educating-for-th e-future-index-2019/

Wieland, J., & Baumann Montecinos, J. (2019). A competence-based approach to transcultural leadership – Introduction to a research program. In J. Wieland & J. Baumann Montecinos (Eds.). *Transcultural leadership and transcultural cooperation* (pp. 11-20). Metropolis Publisher.

Yin, R. K. (2018). *Case study research and applications: Design and methods* (Sixth ed.). Sage.

Bios

SHABNAM (SHAY) IVKOVIĆ is the Director of International Strategic Initiatives, Co-operative & Experiential Education at the University of Waterloo, Canada. Her major practitioner and research interests lie in the various areas of international work-integrated learning (IWIL), such as intercultural effectiveness skills, advancing the UN's SDGs through IWIL, risk management of mobility, etc. Email: sivkovic@uwaterloo.ca

ALESSIO SURIAN, PhD, is an Associate Professor and the Director of the Centre for Intercultural and Migration Studies (CIRSIM) at the University of Padova. His research focuses on intercultural and social competences, peer learning and feedback and on participatory decision making approaches, especially in sustainability planning. Email: alessio.surian@unipd.it

JORIS BOONEN, PhD, is a Senior researcher at Zuyd University of Applied Sciences and a senior teacher at the B.Sc. Global Studies at Maastricht University. His research focuses on the effects of different educational interventions (at home and abroad) on the development of students' global competence. Email:joris.boonen@zuyd.nl

JULIKA BAUMANN MONTECINOS, PhD, is a professor of Transcultural Management at Hochschule Furtwangen University | HFU Business School and part of Zeppelin University's Transcultural Caravan Network. She focuses on research into the success factors of transcultural cooperation as well as on the development of related international and interdisciplinary teaching, training, research and networking projects. Email: julika.montecinos@hs-furtwangen.de

MAURA DI MAURO works as an independent Intercultural and DEI Trainer & Consultant. She is Lecturer of Intercultural Management at Università Cattolica del Sacro Cuore, in Italy and for other universities. She wrote several publications and developed several didactic tools to enhance the development of Intercultural and Global skills and of Diversity & Inclusion strategies. Email: maura.dimauro@unicatt.it

XIUYING SOPHY CAI, Ph.D., is assistant professor in the Institute of Education at Xiamen University, China. Her research and teaching interests include globalization and education, education for Sustainable Development Goals, global poverty and international development education, experiential education and intercultural pedagogy. Email: sophycxy@xmu.edu.cn

Chapter 8

Challenges Health Care Educators Face Facilitating Intercultural Competence

Susan Schärli-Lim
Zurich University of Applied Sciences, Switzerland

Elena de Lorenzo
Servicio Vasco de Salud Osakidetza, Spain

Mette Bønløkke
VIA University College, Denmark

ABSTRACT

This chapter focuses on the importance of intercultural competences in health care and four different challenges we face when developing these competences in educators and students. The challenges are 1. Misconceptions about the concept of culture and facilitation of intercultural competence, 2. Intercultural development can be threatening and cause anxiety, 3. An ethnocentric world view and Resistance and 4. Educators and institutions require adequate preparation to develop intercultural competence. You will also learn about the complex role of an interculturally competent educator and the knowledge, attitude, values, and skills it demands.

Keywords: Culture, Competences, Educator, Ethnocentrism, Intercultural competence, Health, Professional Role, Teacher training

INTRODUCTION

Recent years have witnessed a growing academic interest in developing intercultural and global competence to ensure peaceful societies. The UNESCO Future of Education Initiative examined the future of education towards 2050, indicating the crucial role intercultural and global competence play (Arvanitis et. al., 2021). In addition, PISA - Programme for International Student Assessment has also recognised the importance of global competence and commenced measuring it in 2018 (OECD, 2020).

In this chapter, the definition of intercultural competence used, is based on worldwide expert opinion consented through a Delphi method (Deardorff, 2006, p. 247-248). This definition of intercultural competence is "the ability to communicate effectively and appropriately in intercultural situations based on one's intercultural knowledge, skills, and attitudes".

Intercultural competence is vital in health care. Napier et al. (2014, p. 1610) indicate that "the systematic neglect of culture in health care is the single biggest barrier to the advancement of the highest standard of health worldwide". This barrier has contributed to widening health care disparities leading to increased medical errors, prolonged lengths of stay, avoidable hospitalizations, and the over- and under-utilization of procedures (Smallwood, 2018). LaVeist et.al (2011) determined that in the USA, between 2003 and 2006, the combined direct and indirect costs of health disparities due to cultural diversity was 1.24 trillion dollars.

The lack of intercultural competence has a direct impact on patient-centred care, one of the most important interventions in terms of positive health-related outcomes (College of Nurses of Ontario, 2022). Poitras et al, (2018), indicates that providing a patient-centred approach influences diagnosis, adverse drug events, clinical outcomes, health status, treatment adherence, and patient satisfaction. This approach requires a true partnership between individuals and their health care professionals.

Results of the intercultural sensitivity of nurses, physiotherapists, physician assistants and pharmacy students indicate an ethnocentric world view of minimisation according to the Intercultural Development Inventory- IDI (DiBiasio, Vallabhalosuja & Eigsti, 2022; Huckabee & Matkin, 2012; Kirby, Earle, Calahan & Karagory, 2021; Schellhase, Hassan, Hendricks & Miller, 2021; Zazzi, 2020). This means that these professionals view the world from their own cultural perspectives and fail to recognize the complexity of cultural others.

Intercultural training of health professionals has an impact on the effective use of health and social resources (Majumdar et al., 2004), on patients' satisfaction (Beach et al., 2005; Truong et al., 2014), on improved patient perceptions of health professionals (Vella, White & Livingston, 2022), on patients' adherence to the therapeutic regimen, (Beach et al., 2005; Truong et al., 2014) on patients' quality of life (Patel et al., 2019) on patients health outcomes (Beach et al., 2005; Horvat et al., 2014; Truong et al., 2014) and in the reduction of related hospitalizations (Vella, White & Livingston, 2022). Therefore, there is an urgent need to train future health care professionals. The role of the educator is pivotal in the facilitation of intercultural competence. (Paige & Vande Berg, 2012).

Educators need to be trained and equipped to develop their students' intercultural competence. In the next section four challenges associated with the development of intercultural competence will be highlighted:

- misconceptions about the concept of culture and facilitation of intercultural competence

- intercultural development can be threatening and cause anxiety

- an ethnocentric world view and resistance

- educators and institutions are inadequately prepared to develop intercultural competence.

CHALLENGE 1: MISCONCEPTIONS ABOUT THE CONCEPT OF CULTURE AND FACILITATION OF INTERCULTURAL COMPETENCE

One of the misconceptions is to conceive culture based on a narrow and essentialized definition, focusing on knowledge of the practices and customs of people of other ethnicities and nationalities, supposing to have a high degree of homogeneity (M.J. Bennett, 2013). A growing body of literature shows this essentialized definition of culture influences the way educators approach training intercultural competence and undermines its development.

If culture is considered as a thing and equated with ethnicity, nationality, and language, training intercultural competence would consist of the accumulation of knowledge of the specific culture of different countries (Napier, 2014). Therefore, it can be satisfied using a checklist – do this, not that. However, this approach of the concept of culture is problematic. Taras et. al. (2016), in their meta-analysis of 558 studies indicate that "there is far more variation in cultures within countries than between countries" (p. 479). Therefore, a broader definition of culture that introduces the diversity all around us is needed.

Another misconception is the belief that intercultural competence can be developed by intellectually understanding cultural concepts (Schärli, 2017). Consequently, educators are reduced to lecturing theory leading to fragmented programs that cannot facilitate the development of intercultural competence, because the complexity of intercultural development goes beyond intellectual understanding.

Intercultural competence as an end state is yet another misconception. Some researchers studied the effectiveness of short programs (one hour to half a day) claiming that they had improved cultural competency of their students (Liaw et. al., 2015; Patel et. al., 2019). This type of studies reveals a naive concept of the development of cultural competence and its measurement. Many research studies, evaluate intercultural competence using self-administered questionnaires reporting attitudes and behaviour, which may be subject to social desirability bias. Consequently, some studies claimed that development after a course take place. However, intercultural competence growth is a complex developmental process (M.J. Bennett, 2013) and implies profound changes including frame of reference.

Schärli-Lim (2020) states that a further misconception is the idea that intercultural competence is about a positive attitude, open-mindedness, common sense, and these elements can solve intercultural misunderstanding. Florczak proposes; instead of coming to a relationship with any preconceived notions of cultural differences, you should come to each person with an open mind and simply ask about their values (2014).

In internationalization, there is a misconception that students become interculturally competent simply through sending students for longer exchanges, improving second language proficiency, maximizing contact with host nationals, enrolling in host classes, doing internships, and home stays. Research indicates that these practices have limited or no impact on intercultural learning unless guided by interculturally trained educators (Paige & Vande Berg, 2012). Findings from the CIEE (Council on International Educational Exchange) indicate that "effective cultural mentoring means engaging learners in ongoing discourse about their experiences, helping them better understand the intercultural nature of those encounters, and providing them with feedback relevant to their level of intercultural development" (Paige & Vande Berg, 2012, p. 53). Ongoing reflection is essential to make meaning out of their intercultural interactions and to start challenging their own cultural assumptions.

According to Vande Berg, Quinn and Menyhart (2012), there are four core intercultural competences that are essential to help students interact effectively and appropriately in intercultural interactions. These core competences include increasing your own cultural and personal self-awareness through reflecting on your experiences; increasing your awareness of others within their cultural and personal contexts; managing emotions in the face of ambiguity and learning to bridge cultural gaps - by shifting frames and adapting behaviour to other cultural contexts. This clearly indicates that the process of intercultural development must include not only knowledge, but also requires developing attitudes, values, and skills. Hence, students need to be exposed to experiential or transformative pedagogical strategies that are active and innovative, intellectually stimulating, emotionally rewarding and adequate to develop intercultural competence (De Lorenzo, 2018).

CHALLENGE 2: INTERCULTURAL DEVELOPMENT CAN BE THREATENING AND CAUSE ANXIETY

It is imperative to remember that intercultural development is *"potentially threatening to the learner because it challenges existing and preferred beliefs, values and patterns of behaviour"* (Paige & Martin, 1996, p. 46) and may lead to anxiety. A high level of stress has been identified as a barrier to the development of intercultural competence (De Lorenzo, 2018; Duffy et al., 2005). A low level of cultural stress in cultural encounters is also not conducive to the development of intercultural competence. Adler (1975) points out the necessity to experience critical moments of medium - high but controlled intensity. Hence the importance to create and maintain a safe and non-threatening environment that is conducive to develop intercultural competence (Dimitrov & Haque, 2016; Paige & Martin, 1996).

Balancing Challenge and Support

One important element to reduce resistance is to assess the readiness level of the participants and to sequence interventions appropriately (J.M. Bennett, 2013). To learn, one must leave the comfort zone and be challenged to start learning. The educator must avoid the learner entering the panic zone and retreating from learning. Sequencing is defined as "the developmental patterns we use to order the content and process in our instructional design" (p. 52). Typically, moving from low-risk content and activities to higher risk, from cognitive frameworks to subjective applications, from support to challenge and from culture general to culture specific.

The following content increasingly provides challenge; culture, interpersonal perception, language use, cultural stereotypes, nonverbal communication, communication styles, values, problem solving, gender, intercultural adaptation, cultural privilege and race, contexts of power and sexual orientation (J. M. Bennett & M. J. Bennett, 2013, p. 53).   Study after study "demonstrates the importance of providing learners with such cultural content" (Paige & Vande Berg, 2012, p. 54). M.J. Bennett (2013) also supports this, stating that to acquire general intercultural competence, it is essential "to have learned some "etic", or culture-general, categories for recognizing and dealing with a wide range of cultural differences" (p. 114).   These culture-general frameworks can be used for *"identifying relevant cultural differences and for predicting misunderstanding related to those differences"* (p. 128), they serve as a foundation for reflection and learning.

It is also important to consider process challenge to enhance learning skills or knowledge. Process challenge focuses on teaching methods in order of increasing complexity and involvement. Starting from lectures to film, reading, instruments, critical incidents, case study, fishbowl, role-play to finally a simulation (J.M. Bennett, 2013, p. 58). A combination of content and process challenge can be used to address issues of resistance. In Figure 1 a schematic structure shows what happens to the student depending on balancing content and process challenges.

Ideally educators assess the students to plan adequate challenging learning opportunities, are aware of the level of anxiety of the students and incorporate strategies to reduce its impact. This entails an in-depth student analysis of personality traits, cultural background of the student, previous cultural experiences, differences in physical traits, communication style, cultural values orientations, expectations, cultural allegiances, preferred learning styles, cognitive styles, and the developmental stage according to the Developmental Model of Intercultural Sensitivity (will be discussed in detail further on).

Other factors that require consideration related to anxiety include factors such as risk of personal disclosure, risk of failure, the risk of embarrassment, risk of threat to one's own cultural identity, risk of becoming culturally marginal and culturally alienated, and the risk of self-awareness (Paige & Martin, 1996).

Figure 1: Content and process: balancing challenge (Bennett, 2013, p. 59)

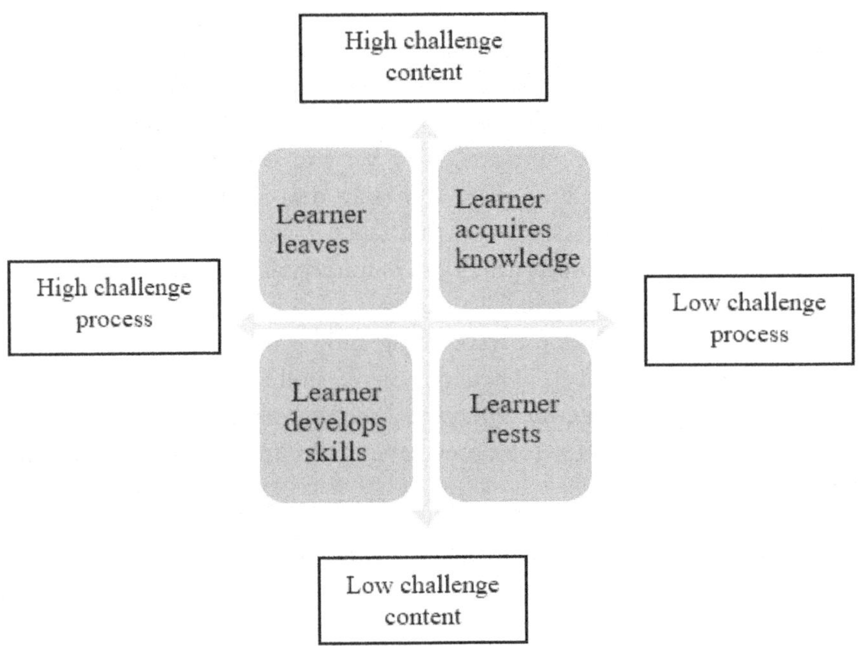

Research indicates that certain coping strategies are helpful in controlling levels of stress, such as managing hostile feelings, positive thinking reconstruction, using a problem-based approach, rest, and search for support (De Lorenzo, 2018). Relationship building and a positive classroom contact can also alleviate anxiety over interacting with outgroup members (Pettigrew, Tropp, Wagner & Christ, 2011). This also leads to enhanced empathy for the outgroup and perspective taking. Furthermore, it reduces prejudice. It seems that it is essential for intercultural development to focus on building relationships, fostering friendship and creating a sense of community (Houge MacKenzie, Son, & Hollenhorst, 2014).

Therefore, a safe environment and sufficient challenge to encourage intercultural learning is essential – this requires an educator with the skill to nudge the student enough to ensure learning takes place.

CHALLENGE 3: ETHNOCENTRIC WORLD VIEW AND RESISTANCE

As mentioned before most students have an ethnocentric worldview, this means that they are not interculturally competent (Kirby, Earle, Calahan & Karagory, 2021, Zazzi, 2020). Ethnocentrism is *"the experience of one's own culture as "central to reality"* (M.J. Bennett, 2021, p.1). This can lead to cultural others feeling ignored, uncomfortable or excluded. To facilitate intercultural learning, it is important that the students' worldview is known to tailor a developmental program. Attempting to develop students before they are ready for the next developmental stage may create resistance. Bennett' Developmental Model of Intercultural Sensitivity - DMIS is a model that is used internationally to guide the design and assessment of training programs in intercultural competence. The advantage of the DMIS is that educational interventions can be tailored to facilitate development along the continuum based on the students' developmental position. Development along the DMIS continuum moves from ethnocentrism *"the experience of one's own culture as "central to reality"* to ethnorelativism, *the experience of one's own and other cultures as "relative to context"* (p.1). See Figure 2. Appropriately designed programs will further develop the students toward ethnorelativism.

Figure 2 Developmental Model of Intercultural Sensitivity (M. J. Bennett, 2021)

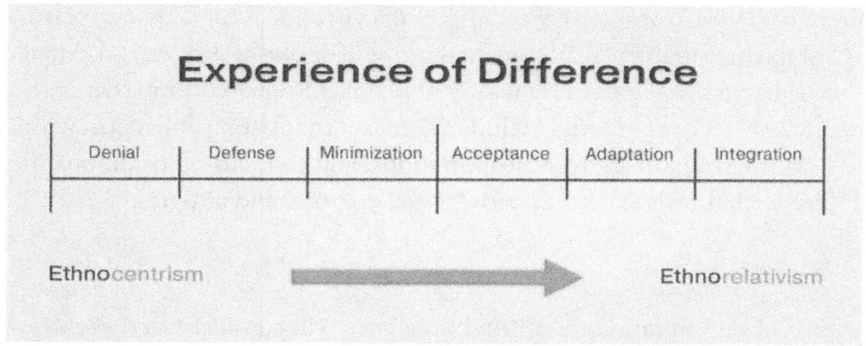

DMIS Orientations

This section will discuss the continuum of the DMIS and an educational focus for each developmental orientation (Bennett, 2013, p. 100).

Denial

A person in denial of cultural difference experiences their own culture as the only real one (M.J. Bennett, 2013). They have limited experience with cultural others and are generally not interested and prefer to avoid contact. Cultural difference is understood in broad, often stereotypical categories like "people from Africa" failing to recognize that the continent of Africa contains 54 countries. Typical statements of this orientation include "Usually when we get foreign patients, I ask my colleagues to take care of them" thus continuing to avoid them or "If they just spoke our language, all would be OK", failing to recognize that many aspects of culture influence intercultural interaction, and this will not be remedied by speaking the same language. Diverse persons may feel ignored. The developmental task for persons in denial is recognizing cultural differences (Bennett & Bennett, 2013). Strategies to encourage development include arousing their curiosity about cultural difference and embedding cultural differences in non-threatening contexts. Content could include objective culture in the form of art, music, film, or an international dinner.

Defense

In the defense of cultural difference position, there is a discrimination between "us and them" (M.J. Bennett, 2013). In general, they are often overly critical of other cultures und uncritical towards one's own cultural values and practices. Statements of someone in this position include "We know the best way to treat their symptoms, but they never listen to our good advice". This position can also be turned around in "reversal". One statement reflecting a "Reversal" position is "Family values are stronger in other cultures than in our culture". Diverse persons may feel uncomfortable. Developmental movement out of defense is facilitated by "recognizing the common humanity of people of other cultures (Bennett & Bennett, 2013). Content could include a focus on the existing differences within their own in-group, to address their emotions, and to focus on commonalities including shared goals and needs between the in-group and out-group.

Minimization

A person in minimization of cultural difference will consider their worldview as universal and highlight commonalities (M.J. Bennett, 2013). Often dominant group members lack cultural awareness especially regarding power and privilege, non-dominant group members may use this as a strategy to adopt to the dominant group members. For example, a nurse caring for a Muslim patient who did not wish a male staff member to shower said: "I don't like being washed by a man either, but I allow it too". In this example sameness is considered, but the nurse doesn't realize the difference gender means in her context and the context of the patient. The nurse is using her own cultural lens and applies this to the patient who is culturally different, thus still maintaining an ethnocentric worldview. Other typical statements for this worldview are "Deep down we are all the same" (Bennett & Bennett, 2013). Deeper cultural differences are not recognized, and diverse persons may feel ignored. Minimization is a transitory position moving towards ethnorelativity. To continue development the person must develop a deeper cultural self-awareness. Content includes definitions of culture, stereotypes, communication styles, and categories and frameworks to understand one's own culture including values and beliefs.

Acceptance

Acceptance of cultural difference is the state in which one's own culture is experienced as just one of many equally complex worldviews. Cultural differences in behaviour and values are recognized and valued (Bennett & Bennett, 2013). A person may state *"I can understand how important their large family is, I just don't know how to introduce that successfully in their treatment plan"*. Diverse persons feel understood. Development continues by improving cultural contrasts. Content includes cultural values analysis, correctly using culture general and culture specific categories.

Adaptation

Adaptation to cultural difference is the state in which the experience of another culture yields a perception and behaviour appropriate to that culture (Bennett & Bennett, 2013). They can change their own cultural approach to adapt to context. One staff member said: *"I can change my communication style, depending on whom I have in front of me"*. One's worldview is expanded to include constructs from other worldviews. People in adaptation are able to look at the world «through different eyes» and may intentionally change behaviour to communicate more effectively in another culture. Diverse persons feel valued and involved. Further development includes developing frame-of-reference shifting skills. Content here includes culture shock and cultural adaptation, advancing cultural empathy and a focus on cultural identity development.

Integration

In "integration of cultural difference" one's experience of self is expanded to include the movement in and out of different cultural worldviews (Bennett & Bennett, 2013). Statements here include *"Whatever the situation, I can usually look at it from a variety of cultural points of view"*. In this position they become bicultural or multicultural and further development is focused on accepting their multicultural identity and learning how to leverage their contributions.

The assessment of students provides an ideal base to tailor an effective program along the continuum of the DMIS and reduces resistance in students. The Intercultural Development Inventory assess these stages based on DMIS and has demonstrated nonsignificant associations with social desirability "suggesting the IDI is not 'transparent' to participants" (Jankowski, 2019).

CHALLENGE 4: EDUCATORS AND INSTITUTIONS REQUIRE ADEQUATE PREPARATION TO DEVELOP INTERCULTURAL COMPETENCE

The intercultural educator plays a pivotal role in the development of intercultural competence (Paige & Vande Berg, 2012) There is a paucity of publication focused on faculty's level of intercultural competence. Three studies indicate that educators have moderate levels of intercultural competence (Baghdadi & Ismaile',2018; Burns, 2020; Marzilli, 2016). Some other studies found that educators are in minimization according to the IDI (Kruse et al., 2014). This difference in results in these few studies may be due to a lack of control for social desirability, as few assessments instruments control for this in comparison to the IDI. An educators' effectiveness in facilitating intercultural learning correlates to their own developmental worldview (Vande Berg, Quinn & Menyhart, 2012). Therefore, to be effective, intercultural educators should be ethnorelative, and at least one stage ahead of the developmental aim of the students.

The role of the intercultural educator is complex, not any educator can guide intercultural development processes, educators require academic preparation. Unfortunately, few educators possess the intercultural skills, attitudes, and knowledge necessary to teach intercultural competence (Farber, 2019; OECD, 2020). These studies clearly indicate that it is crucial to generate validated programs for intercultural educators to develop the capacity to train intercultural competence to the future generation of health care professionals.

To generate effective educational programmes, it is imperative to have a clear idea of the competences needed by intercultural educators. Due to the lack of a profile for an intercultural educator, the international TraINErs-project (Training Intercultural Nursing Educators and Students) financed by Erasmus + and Movetia (Schärli-Lim et. al., 2020) performed a Delphi method to develop the profile of an intercultural nurse educator. Even though it was initially developed for nursing educators, it is convertible to other professions.

This profile classifies the competences of the intercultural educator in three dimensions: The Personal, the Professional and the Pedagogical. Each dimension of the profile builds on the others, relying on previous knowledge, attitudes, and skills.

Table 1 Dimensions and content of the profile of an intercultural educator

The Personal Dimension	The Professional Dimension	The Pedagogic Dimension: Intercultural competent educator	The Pedagogic Dimension: Educator for intercultural competence
Knowledge	**Knowledge**	**Knowledge**	**Knowledge**
Culture and diversity	Ethnocentrism to ethnorelativism	Role expectation and culture	Conceptual framework of intercultural development
Intercultural communication	Ethical dilemmas	Learning styles and culture	Didactic training strategies for intercultural learning
Influence of culture on perception	Cultural shock, migration & acculturation	Teaching styles and culture	Risk factors in a cultural learning process
Intercultural conflict styles	Cultural issues relevant for the profession	Ethical codes related to the profession	Facilitation of intercultural development
Migration and acculturation	Equity and equality	Inclusive classroom Teaching a diverse group	Tools to evaluate intercultural development
Health and culture			Reflective strategies
Attitudes & Values	**Attitudes & Values**	**Attitudes & Values**	**Attitudes & Values**
Respect, openness Curiosity for cultural others	Cultural empathy & humility	Create a safe environment	Commitment to individualise students' learning process
Tolerance for ambiguity	Cultural curiosity and desire	Motivation for including cultural differences	Sensitivity towards students' learning process
Human dignity, diversity and global mindset	Awareness of own professional culture	Promoting ethical behaviours of respect and tolerance	Commitment to lifelong learning about intercultural competence
Skills	**Skills**	**Skills**	**Skills**
Challenge own cultural assumptions	Intercultural communication	Manage a diverse group	Appropriate methods in students' intercultural development process
Embrace differences Practice cultural bridging	Assessment tools sensitive to culture	Pedagogic interventions adapted to cultural diversity	Reflection in intercultural differences and commonalities
Cultural self- and other awareness	Apply social equity Manage prejudice	Include cultural diversity in any subject taught	Facilitate the students' own awareness of cultural construction
Suspend automatic pilot to examine multiple perspectives	Manage intercultural interactions	Create opportunities for peer learning and inclusion	Help learners to suspend judgement long enough to examine multiple perspectives
Differentiate between cultural stereotyping	Diverse team	Model and encourage perspective shifts	Foster reflection on intercultural differences and commonality

The Personal Dimension presents intercultural aspects that are necessary to operate appropriately and effectively in cross-cultural situations. Ideally, the person should be ethnorelative. The professional dimension focuses on the application in a professional context and is a prerequisite for an intercultural competent educator. The pedagogic dimension consists of two subdimensions: the intercultural competent educator and the educator to develop intercultural competence. The first describes competences of an educator teaching a culturally diverse group in an interculturally competent manner, the latter focuses on the competences to teach, facilitate, and foster the development of students' intercultural competence.

This comprehensive profile contains 127 items. Table 1 shows the profile in a condensed version. The complete profile is available online (TraINErs, 2023).

Frequently the development of intercultural competence of future professionals falls on the responsibility of educators and is taught in separate subjects. However, the educational institutions should also be prepared and committed. The organisations need to be aware about their own developmental stage of intercultural sensitivity, reflecting about their policies, and the way to function.

Due to the complexity of the training, they should create integrated curricular programs. In these programs, the objectives, and experiential pedagogical strategies, oriented to all dimensions of intercultural competence (cognitive, affective-attitudinal, and behavioural), should be progressively incorporated into the different subjects and years of the educational programs. For example, the American Association of Medical Schools approved a Plan for the integration of cultural competence in its curriculum (BICCC) (Cuéllar et al, 2008). The evaluation of this curricular plan identified an improvement in the organization, the content approach, and the integration of creative learning strategies by all the teachers of the faculty. Schroeder (2012) states that this type of approach is difficult to implement, since it requires the cooperation and training of all teaching staff and careful evaluations in all the courses of the training program to ensure that expectations are being met.

Higher education institutions should also generate appropriate learning resources and opportunities for students (internationalisation strategies, exchanges ...) These opportunities and resources should also be available for educators so they can become interculturally competent and increase their ability to facilitate intercultural learning of their students.

To summarize, intercultural competence is vital in health care – the lack of it, leads to increased health care costs as well as suffering for patients and their families. Assessment of health care professionals using the IDI, where social desirability cannot be guessed, indicates that most health care professionals have a worldview that is ethnocentric and based on their own cultural perspective. An ethnocentric health care professional cannot provide culturally sensitive patient care. Therefore, training health care professionals is imperative.

Intercultural competence development is a complex life-long learning process that includes not only knowledge but also the acquisition of skills, learning to manage emotions in the face of ambiguity and developing ethnorelative attitudes. To accomplish this, lecturing is insufficient. Experiential learning activities within a safe learning environment are essential for intercultural learning. In addition, conducting an in-depth student analysis, relationship building, creating a sense of community, sequencing intercultural content and process, and tailoring educational interventions based on the DMIS are just a few ideas to assist with the development of intercultural competence. Ideally intercultural competence development should be integrated into the curriculum. Educators play a pivotal role, but they are currently inadequately prepared. Institutions should focus on staff development and provision of adequate resources for the training of faculty. A summary of the final implications derived from the previous discussion is presented below.

Implications for educators and institutions:

- Educators need to be adequately prepared to facilitate intercultural development. The intercultural educator profile is foundational for the competences required providing a focus for development in relation to knowledge, skills, values and attitudes that are required to facilitate intercultural competence. An essential requirement is that the educator is ethnorelative.

- Institutional commitment focuses on all students and the integration of intercultural competence development in the curriculum. The initial step is to support faculty on their path to become intercultural educators in addition to their usual topics.

Implications for clinical practice

- Health care practitioners need to focus on their personal and professional development, the first two dimensions of the intercultural educator profile. The focus lies on becoming ethnorelative to ensure patient care that is culturally sensitive. This will also reduce health care costs and suffering.

Implication for research

- Future research should focus on assessing training utilizing experiential learning activities that focus not only on knowledge but attitudes, values and skills as well. These activities should take a developmental approach and include methods to reduce anxiety and threat.

- Research studies should use multiple assessment methods – for example intercultural competence value rubric, critical incidents, student self-reports etc. in addition to assessment instruments that ensure nonsignificant associations with social desirability.

References

Adler, P. S. (1975). The transitional experience: An alternative view of culture shock. *Journal of Humanistic Psychology, 15*(4), 13-23.

Arvanitis, E., Bauer, M., Covarrugias Vengas, B., Crameri, A., D'Amato, G., Davione, E., Farrar, J., Glaveanu, V., Grünenfelder, R., Hassi, A., Lambelet, A.-C., Lezou Koffi, A.-D., Ogay, T., Pechr, J., Saudelli, M. G., Schärli-Lim, S., Shaules, J., Spencer-Oatey, H., Stalder, P., ... Zittoun, T. (2021). *Futures of education: Learning to become: How should what we learn, how we learn, and where we learn change in the future?* UNESCO/SIETAR Switzerland. https://en.unesco.org/futuresofeducation/sites/default/files/2021-04/UNESCO%20Report%20_SIETAR%20Switzerland%20Focus%20Group%20-%2012.4.21.pdf

Baghdadi, N. A., & Ismaile, S. (2018). Cultural competency of nursing faculty teaching in baccalaureate nursing programs in the United States. *Australasian Medical Journal, 11*(2), 126–134. https://doi.org/10.21767/AMJ.2018.3335

Beach, M. C., Price, E. G., Gary, T. L., Robinson, K. A., Gozu, A., Palacio, A., & Powe, N. R. (2005). Cultural competency: A systematic review of health care provider educational interventions. *Medical care, 43*(4), 356-373.

Bennett, J. M. (2013). *The intercultural context of training. [MAIR 260 Course Packet].* January 2013. The Intercultural Communication Institute & University of the Pacific.

Bennett, M.J. (2013). *Basic concepts of intercultural Communication: Paradigms, principles and practices* (2nd. Ed.). Intercultural Press.

Bennett, J. M., & Bennett, M. J. (2013). Training content challenges. In J. M. Bennett (Ed.), *The intercultural context of training. [MAIR 260 Course Packet]* (53). The Intercultural Communication Institute & University of the Pacific.

Bennett, M. J. (2021). *The developmental model of intercultural sensitivity.* IDRInstitute. https://www.idrinstitute.org/dmis/

Burns, S. (2020). California State University (CSU) System nursing faculty: Are you culturally competent to teach in a multicultural state? *Journal of Professional Nursing, 36*(6), 635–648. https://doi.org/10.1016/j.profnurs.2020.09.001

College of Nurses of Ontario (2022) *Patient-centred care*.https://www.cno.org/en/learn-about-standards-guidelines/educational-tools/ask-practice/patient-centred-care/

Cuellar, N. G., Brennan, A. M. W., Vito, K., & de Leon Siantz, M. L. (2008). Cultural competence in the undergraduate nursing curriculum. *Journal of Professional Nursing, 24*(3), 143-149.

Deardorff, D. K. (2006). Identification and assessment of intercultural competence as a student outcome of internationalization. *Journal of Studies in International Education, 10*(3), 241–266.

de Lorenzo, E. (2018). La inmersión en una cultura sanitaria distinta como estrategia de desarrollo de la competencia cultural en estudiantes de enfermería: Un estudio del proceso de aculturación y de los efectos inmediatos y mediatos. Universidad del País Vasco/Euskal Herriko Unibertsitatea. https://addi.ehu.es/handle/10810/36067

DiBiasio, P. A., Vallabhajosula, S., & Eigsti, H. J. (2022). Assessing cultural competence: a comparison of two measures and their utility in global learning experiences within health care education. *Physiotherapy (United Kingdom)*. https://doi.org/10.1016/j.physio.2022.09.007

Dimitrov, N., & Haque, A. (2016). Intercultural teaching competence in the disciplines: Teaching strategies for intercultural learning. In N. Dimitrov, A. Haque, G. M. G. Pérez, & C. Rojas-Primus (Eds.), *Promoting intercultural communication competencies in higher education* (pp. 89–119). IGI Global.

Duffy, M. E., Farmer, S., Ravert, P., & Huittinen, L. (2005). International community health networking project: Two-year follow-up of graduates. *International Nursing Review, 52*(1), 24-31.

Farber, J. E. (2019). Cultural competence of baccalaureate nurse faculty: Relationship to cultural experiences. *Journal of Professional Nursing, 35*(2), 81-88. https://10.1016/j.profnurs.2018.09.005

Florczak, K. L. (2013). Culture: Fluid and complex. *Nursing Science Quarterly, 26*(1), 12-13. doi:10.1177/0894318412466741

Horvat, L., Horey, D., Romios, P., & Kis-Rigo, J. (2014). Cultural competence education for health professionals. *Cochrane Database of Systematic Reviews, 2014*(5). https://doi.org/10.1002/14651858.CD009405.pub2

Houge Mackenzie, S., Son, J. S., & Hollenhorst, S. (2014). Unifying psychology and experiential education: toward an integrated understanding of why it works. *Journal of Experiential Education, 37*(1), 75-88. doi:10.1177/1053825913518894

Huckabee, M., & Matkin, G. (2012). Examining intercultural sensitivity and competency of physician assistant students. *Journal of Allied Health, 41*(3), 55E-61E.

Jankowski, P. J. (2019). A construct validation argument for the Intercultural Development Inventory. *Measurement and Evaluation in Counseling and Development, 52*(2), 75-89.

Kirby, K. F., Earle, M., Calahan, C. A., & Karagory, P. (2021). Preparing nursing students for diverse populations. *Nurse Education in Practice*, 55, 103140.

Kruse, J. A., Didion, J., & Perzynski, K. (2014). Utilizing the Intercultural Development Inventory® to develop intercultural competence. *SpringerPlus, 3*(1), 1-8. https://doi.org/10.1186/2193-1801-3-334

Laveist, T., Gaskin, D., & Richard, P. (2011). Estimating the economic burden of racial health inequalities in the United States. *International Journal of Health Services, 41*(2), 231–238. https://doi.org/10.2190/HS.41.2.c

Liaw, S.-T., Hasan, I., Wade, V., Canalese, R., Kelaher, M., Lau, P., Harris, M., (2015). Improving cultural respect to improve aboriginal health in general practice: a multi-methods and multi-perspective pragmatic study. *Aust. Fam. Physician, 46*, 387–392.

Majumdar, B., Browne, G., Roberts, J., & Carpio, B. (2004). Effects of cultural sensitivity training on health care provider attitudes and patient outcomes. *Journal of Nursing Scholarship, 36*(2), 161–166. https://doi.org/10.1111/j.1547-5069.2004.04029.x

Marzilli, C. (2016). Assessment of cultural competence in Texas nursing faculty. *Nurse Education Today, 45*, 225–229. https://doi.org/10.1016/j.nedt.2016.08.021

Napier, A. D., Ancamo, C., Butler, B., Calabrese, J., Chater, A, Chatterjee, H.,...Woolf, K. (2014). Culture and health. *The Lancet, 348*, 1607-1639. doi: 10.1016/S0140-6736(14)61603-2

OECD. (2020). *PISA 2018 Results (Volume VI): Are students ready to thrive in an interconnected world?* OECD Publishing. https://doi.org/10.1787/d5f68679-en

Paige, R. M., & Martin, J. N. (1996). Ethics in intercultural training. In D. Landis & R. Bath (Eds.), *Handbook of intercultural training* (pp. 35–60). Sage Publications.

Paige, R. M., & Vande Berg, M. (2012). Why students are and are not learning abroad. In M. Vande Berg, R. M. Paige, & K. H. Lou (Eds.), *Student learning abroad: What our students are learning, what they're not, and what we can do about it* (1st ed., Vol. 2012, pp. 29–58). Stylus Publishing, LLC.

Patel, M. R., Song, P. X., Bruzzese, J. M., Hao, W., Evans, D., Thomas, L. J., & Brown, R. W. (2019). Does cross-cultural communication training for physicians improve pediatric asthma outcomes? A randomized trial. *Journal of asthma, 56*(3), 273-284.

Pettigrew, T. F., Tropp, L. R., Wagner, U., & Christ, O. (2011). Recent advances in intergroup contact theory. *International Journal of Intercultural Relations, 35*, 271-280. doi:10.1016/j.ijintrel.2011.03.001

Poitras, M. E., Maltais, M. E., Bestard-Denommé, L., Stewart, M., & Fortin, M. (2018). What are the effective elements in patient-centered and multimorbidity care? A scoping review. *BMC Health Services Research, 18*(1). https://doi.org/10.1186/s12913-018-3213-8

Schärli, S. (2017). *Development and feasibility of the European Nursing Module to improve intercultural competence for nursing students.* (Unpublished master's thesis). University of the Pacific, Stockton.

Schärli-Lim, S. (2020). Introduction: The importance of transcultural (intercultural) competence in health care. In S. van den Bergh, S. Schärli-Lim & S. S.Wong (Eds.), *Intercultural interactions for health professions: a critical incident approach* (pp. 9-11). hep Verlag.

Schärli-Lim, S., de Lorenzo, E., Bønløkke, M., Bourkia, P., Filov, I., Gradellini, C., Händler-Schuster, D., Mecugni, D., Bennet, M., Mijatovic, M., Pretorious, M., Vanceulebroeck, V., Vermeiren, S., Weber, U., Zarandona, J. (2020). *The profile of an intercultural dompetence educator for health care and other professions*. World Council on Intercultural and Global Competence https://iccglobal.org/2020/09/30/the-profile-of-an-intercultural-competence-educator-for-healthcare-and-other-professions/?fbclid=IwAR0Q1aVh5ms5ELKTWErRWz_ci2Qj67emD4rbw71zF8F03Y4xe0T9JCKm6f4

Schellhase, E., Hasan, I., Hendricks, S., & Miller, M. L. (2021). Integration of intercultural learning into an international advanced pharmacy practice experience in London, England. *Pharmacy*, *9*(1), 37. https://doi.org/10.3390/pharmacy9010037

Schroeder, P. (2012). *The influence of cultural immersion on transcultural self-efficacy for nursing students at private faith-based baccalaureate nursing programs*. (Unpublished doctoral dissertation). University of South Dakota, Vermillion, SD.

Smallwood, R. (2018, April 25). *High cost of poor cultural competency in health care*. https://www.relias.com/blog/high-costs-of-poor-cultural-competency-in-health care

Taras, V., Steel, P. & Kirkman, B. L. (2016). Does country equate with culture? Beyond geography in the search for cultural boundaries. *Management International Review*. *56*, 455–487.

TraINErS projects outcomes – Trainers. (n.d.). Retrieved 20 November 2023, from https://trainers.ap.be/the-trainers-projects-outcomes/

Truong, M., Paradies, Y., & Priest, N. (2014). Interventions to improve cultural competency in health care: A systematic review of reviews. *BMC Health Services Research*, *14*(1), 99. https://doi.org/10.1186/1472-6963-14-99

Vande Berg, M., Quinn, M., & Menyhart, C. (2012). An experiment in developmental teaching and learning. In M. Vande Berg, R. M. Paige, & K. Hemming Lou (Eds.), *Student learning abroad: what our students are learning, what they're not, and what we can do about it* (pp. 383-407). Stylus Publishing.

Vella, E., White, V. M., & Livingston, P. (2022). Does cultural competence training for health professionals impact culturally and linguistically diverse patient outcomes? A systematic review of the literature. *Nurse Education Today*, *118*, 105500. https://10.1016/j.nedt.2022.105500

Zazzi, E. (2020). Contributors to the development of intercultural competence in nursing students. *Nurse Education Today, 90.* https://doi.org/10.1016/j.nedt.2020.104424

Bios

Schärli-Lim, BSc-Nursing - RN, Dipl. Ed, MA Intercultural Relations. She is Head of International Relations at the Institute of Nursing, Zurich University of Applied Sciences. Her focus for the last 15 years has been on intercultural competence development of staff and students. She is author of the book "Intercultural Interactions for Health Professions", Coordinator of the Health care group in the World Council on Intercultural and Global Competence and Board Member of SIETAR Switzerland.

Mette Bønløkke is Coordinator of Academic Studies, International Coordinator and Lector at the VIA University Nursing Programme and has worked with intercultural competence development competence for many years. My professional background is intensive care nursing. I have a Master of Public Health and a diploma in Pedagogic.

Elena de Lorenzo Urien, (RN, Master in Public Health, MSc in Health Research, PhD) is a professor of the School of Nursing of Vitoria-Gasteiz (Spain) for more than 30 years involve in community nursing and the development of intercultural competence, in fact, this interest was the aim of her PhD and further research. She is member of the World Council on Intercultural and Global Competence.

Editors' Afterword

The contributors of this volume have provided snapshots of perspectives on intercultural and global competence - from different cultural and disciplinary perspectives, from emerging perspectives and from practitioners' and researchers' perspectives. There are countless other perspectives to explore further and this then, is the work of the World Council and of all of us. Through the perspectives shared in this volume, several overarching themes emerge. First, intercultural and global competence remains a complex construct that continues to yield more questions than answers. Second, despite the complexity of this construct, there are practical tools and applications in a variety of contexts that can be used to develop and assess intercultural competence and in the end, it is this practicality that will build a better world, not ongoing academic debates and discussions. Third, intercultural and global competence are about human connection and relationship, coming back to the question of what is necessary for us to learn to live together on and with this planet we all share.

Appendix 1: Global Intercultural Circle

A Process, a Pedagogy, and a Way of Life

Christa Olson
The College of New Jersey, United States of America

Katharine Krebs
Binghamton University, United States of America

ABSTRACT:

Why are so many people at a loss in engaging effectively with those who are culturally different from themselves? The Global Intercultural Circle (GIC) is a community-based group dedicated to probing this question, processing intercultural dynamics, and practicing skills needed to engage constructively. After framing comments, this piece presents GIC's practices and aspirations. These practices include regular group gatherings, listening and storytelling, reading for context and reflective narrative writing. GIC also experiments with culinary and creative arts as tools for being present with people of other cultures. Because intercultural dynamics include conflict, our aspiration is to enhance our capacity to work through dissonance. We appreciate that we change the world one encounter, one family, one community at a time.

KEYWORDS: community-based; intercultural dynamics; storytelling; reading for context; reflective narratives; culinary & creative arts; dissonance

Editors' Preface: Circles have been used in indigenous cultures for centuries and have come into mainstream societies to be used for many different purposes including reading circles, support circles, healing circles and talking circles. This appendix contains an example of how circles can be used in what is called Global Intercultural Circles. In addition, the World Council on Intercultural and Global Competence is committed to furthering UNESCO Story Circles, a structured yet adaptable intercultural methodology used for the purpose of practicing and developing key intercultural competencies such as listening for understanding (rather than listening for response which is more typical). Within the World Council, there is a special group for facilitators of UNESCO Story Circles. In addition, the UNESCO Chair on Intercultural Competence at Stellenbosch University is engaged in capacity building with UNESCO Story Circles across the African continent and beyond. To learn more about UNESCO Story Circles, which is available as an open-access manual in 7+ languages, go to www.iccglobal.org.

The three women had fled war-torn Sudan, secured refugee status to come to the United States, and resettled in Des Moines, Iowa. They had lived productively here for eight years. During that time no U.S. citizen had ever invited them into their home. Then they received an invitation for dinner and an evening of sharing life-experiences from a group of women, known as the *Global Intercultural Circle (GIC)*.

Throughout our lives, most of us have many intercultural experiences, interacting with family members and individuals in our community, work places, or travels. But do we reflect on how our intercultural connections bring meaning into our lives or cause misunderstandings or missed opportunities? Given the state of affairs in the world, the work of bridging cultural divides does not seem to be reaching a broad audience. Why are so many people at a loss in talking about global intercultural relations and engaging effectively with those who are culturally different from themselves?

The GIC was formed by adult women from across the US who value experiences with cultures different from their own. In crafting our Circle, we created a support system for probing the above questions. Over the years, GIC has spawned in-person local community groups and virtual international groups. Whether marrying into a family from another culture, hosting someone from another country, working in global intercultural education, or living, studying or traveling in other countries, we each bring different perspectives to our gatherings.

During monthly gatherings, we share our intercultural experiences, reflect together upon our efforts, decipher particular interchanges, and examine challenges and discoveries. Together we process the various intercultural dynamics in our lives and practice the skills needed to engage with difference constructively.

Our Mission, Framework and Process

The mission of Global Intercultural Circle is to share our intercultural journeys, to advance our well-being and creative expression, and to support each other in facilitating intercultural engagement across generations in our families and communities.

Our framework defines global as both a local and international phenomena. Many people in our local communities have deep international connections. Global interchange is not new, but it is complicated by how compressed and accelerated our interactions are in modern times. If we want our interactions to go well, they are likely to require more time and determination, as well as new awareness, communication and behavioral skills.

Our process raises consciousness of the ways in which each of us are intercultural people. We aim to stimulate personal discovery and development and to invite others to share this journey. A broad awareness that everyone is on a global, intercultural journey is often absent, especially among those who are members of a dominant cultural or linguistic group. The process of recognizing and accepting the personal, professional, and spiritual implications of this reality is the centerpiece of GIC work.

Our Practice

GIC has experimented with different techniques to stimulate discovery, build skill sets, and deepen connections with each other. Now captured on the website, these practices include the following:

Regular Gatherings Consistency and regularity of gathering is critical to our success. We either meet in person (for those in the same locale) or on Zoom (for those more dispersed) on a fixed day of every month for 1 to 1 ½ hours. Members take turns co-facilitating each gathering. Agendas include a short opening activity, one or two themes for discussion, and a closing poem/song to end our time together. Discussion themes alternate between organizational and skill-building topics and include: vision and future directions, inclusiveness in extending our work, asking great intercultural questions, chants across cultures, gratitude and generosity across cultures, and UNESCO Story Circles for Intercultural Competence.

Starting a Global Intercultural Circle Facilitators of an emerging Global Intercultural Circle group will want to be sensitive to the reality that each member will be in a different place on their journey of self discovery. For some, the process of identifying themselves as global intercultural people may come easily. For most, identifying oneself as such is a journey of self discovery that takes time to internalize, as well as courage to share.

When creating a new group or when inviting a new member into an existing group, it is helpful to think about how to welcome people into the Circle experience. One exercise for introducing new members is "What's In a Name." The facilitator invites each member to share their full name, the cultural origins of each part of their name, and how their name is personally meaningful to them. The purpose is to offer a simple way to introduce oneself and foster insight into the cultural values represented in one's name. The simple act of asking people to discuss how their names are meaningful to them presents an opportunity to share in ways we do not typically do with new acquaintances.

The Practice of Listening Listening to stories and hearing another person talk about an intercultural interaction is foundational. Through actively listening, we can step into another's story, be present with their emotions, and be changed through the experience. If we *listen deeply*, the individual sharing their story feels heard and not judged. We have experienced how challenging it can be to lean in and *really listen to* stories without interrupting, expressing judgment (positive or negative), or launching into our own stories. But when we manage to listen deeply, we find the telling and listening process sparks deep connections.

To listen and to be heard are fundamental to authentic communication and human connection. Yet, in our daily lives, it is rare that we stop and focus fully on what others are saying to us. This is increasingly true with all of the communication devices available. Too frequently our smart phones distract us from being fully present. Even when we set aside devices, we still have internal distractions. We bring our preconceptions, emotional impressions, and physical reactions to the individual before us. That person brings the same. So much is happening.

Often our activities involve meeting with people with different linguistic and/or national origins, cultural backgrounds, class, race and gender identities. Becoming comfortable with the accents or slower communication of non-English speakers, listening for the meaning of what the other person is trying to say, and listening for the nuances of expression that comes from different backgrounds are key and require practice.

Narrating our Global Intercultural Journeys Having shared intercultural experiences during our monthly gatherings, we determined to probe these experiences more deeply through reflective writing. Inspired by Baldwin's (2005) "Storycatcher" prompts and questions, Circle members developed questions to prompt reflection so each member could begin to write their own narrative about becoming the intercultural person they are today. We began to share extracts from our writing at meetings. Prompts are included on the site under practices. One sample prompt:

- What are your earliest memories of engaging with another person who was notably different from you? Perhaps they were from another community or country far from your home. Perhaps they have lived in your community for a long time. Tell a story about one of your experiences together and how it impacted the two of you.

Meals as a Centerpiece to Intercultural Engagement   There are powerful intercultural dimensions to the art of cooking and sharing food. Preparing meals is a centerpiece of our in-person gatherings. Members volunteer to prepare the meal. We select menus from our cultures of origin or a culture in which we have immersed ourselves. When we chop vegetables, shape potstickers, roll sushi, or cook in the hot-pot, we are learning. As the meal begins, our host tells us why this menu is meaningful to her. She talks about what kinds of ingredients are common in this cuisine and shares the customs for serving and eating the food.

We practice how to gracefully navigate dietary constraints and personal tastes in food. In the comfort of our Circle, we can name our constraints without offending others, but considering how this might be perceived in a different intercultural context. It can be awkward the first time you explain to someone that you are not going to try something they have carefully prepared for you. This provides insight into how we could navigate constraints in other contexts. Examples of meal-centered events can be found on under practices

Creative Expression   Art, music, and drama are another cornerstone of GIC work. In addition to personal expression, the Arts are powerful mediums for connection and discovery, especially when language and socio-economic barriers render expression and engagement more difficult.

Our members who are musicians gather music from diverse cultures and lead us in song. Feeling new rhythms that vary from those we are familiar with or pronouncing words from other languages is a form of intercultural work. Our visual artists lead us in creating meaningful art works that express cultural elements of the places we explore. We act out folk tales and read plays from a variety of cultures. Dramatists give voice to a cultural group's experience and the intercultural dynamics that emerge as people from diverse cultures interact. Theatre includes climactic moments of dissonance and resolution. Through actively playing a role, we can deepen our sensitivity to another person's narrative.

Global Intercultural Circle Retreats

Gathering for several days at an annual retreat has allowed our Circle to delve deeply into intercultural exploration and strengthen bonds among members. We plan a combination of interactive workshops, spiritual/emotional nourishment practices, meals of place, outdoor activities, art and music projects, and local intercultural engagement. At a retreat, a workshop can last an entire morning, allowing time to prepare, engage, and debrief afterwards. Our spiritual/emotional practices include morning yoga or woodland, beach, and urban walks.

Selecting Themes and Grounding Ourselves in Place Retreat destinations are usually in the community of one of our members. Each GIC retreat has an overarching theme. Our 2016 retreat in Washington, focused on "Expressing our Intercultural Journeys" and featured workshops on creating a journal to illustrate our intercultural journeys.

Beginning with our 2018 retreat in Iowa, we embraced a recurring sub-theme of "global intercultural dynamics." The goal was to understand historical and recent cultural influences shaping the intercultural dynamics of a given location. In Des Moines, one dynamic is the multiple waves of immigration. To understand that dynamic, we invited Japanese, Bulgarian, Chinese, Indians, and Sudanese to be our guests. To prepare, we practiced a conversation protocol by pairing up and taking turns with one telling a meaningful experience (Story Telling) and the other actively listening (Story Catching). In debriefing we asked ourselves: *What was it like to actively listen for this extended period of time? What was it like to be heard? What discoveries occurred to you as you were sharing?* Following dinner with our guests, we drew upon this protocol, inviting our new friends to share part of their global intercultural journeys with us. Each of us was moved to hear the immigration stories of struggle, sacrifice, and joy.

Reading for Context and Perspective In preparation for retreats, we select readings that contextualize our planned engagement with community members. Memoirs, travel narratives, and historical novels are valuable for fostering intercultural mindfulness. As we read narratives different from our own, we step into another's perspective. This **perspective taking** can inform our interactions with people from the cultures depicted in these works.

Our Aspiration: Perfect the Practice of Working Through Dissonance

Intercultural dynamics inherently include conflict and dissonance. Without intentional practice in working through dissonance, conflict all too frequently erupts in subtle micro or overt macro violence. Over the years, our monthly sessions have evolved to include reflections on power dynamics, class privilege, hate crimes, racism, and genocide. We have drawn upon resources to navigate these challenging topics and work through conflict and guilt towards authenticity in our intercultural relationships. In our retreats, we grapple directly with cultural dissonance.

In the Northwest, this dissonance is manifest in how European settlers impacted the Native peoples. Our preparatory reading of Dunbar-Ortiz's *An Indigenous Peoples' History of the United States* opened us to alternate historical narratives. Also in preparation, we examined attitudes and beliefs about Native American cultures developed during our individual growing-up experiences.

Our hearts opened when we visited local Suquamish sites. A docent at the Suquamish Museum and Cultural Center presented his people's narrative in careful detail. Later, we met with Shawn, a young Makah, who told his experience of being born into one indigenous culture (Makah); being adopted by a woman of another indigenous tradition (Yakima); attending school with children of yet another indigenous culture; and now studying indigenous traditions as a student at Evergreen College. His testimony highlighted the commonalities and dissonance of the Puget Sound indigenous experience.

Our 2022 retreat in New Jersey featured the fundamental contribution of immigration to the intercultural dynamics of that region. We prepared by reading immigrant narratives and visiting Ellis Island and the New York City Tenement Museum. We met with an immigration lawyer and an immigration advocate. Recent immigrant guests shared their personal reasons for immigrating, their journey, and gradual settling into a new society. These experiences challenged the meta historical narratives of the US and our constructs of immigration. We felt the dissonance of our complacency in the face of our new friends' heart-wrenching stories.

In Conclusion: Our Vision for a Way of Life

We aspire with each gathering to move beyond our self conception and experience as intercultural people towards the adoption of global intercultural behaviors as *a way of life.* We recognize this global intercultural work as a continuous journey of discovery which involves addressing barriers to adopting such a way of life. We are committed to facilitating global intercultural learning in our families, neighborhoods, and broader communities. We have experienced how consciousness raising and intercultural bridge-building can radiate out through connections to others locally and around the world. As we explore further and practice working through dissonance, we appreciate that we can only change the world one encounter, one relationship, one family, one community at a time. We invite other kindred spirits to create their own Global Intercultural Circle and join us on this aspirational journey.

References

Baldwin, C. (2005). *Storycatcher: Making sense of our lives through the power and practice of story.* New World Library.

Carrier, J. (2017). *Ten ways to fight hate: A community resource guide.* 5th edition updated by Wendy Via and Lecia Brooks. Poverty Law Center. Retrieved from https://www.splcenter.org/20170814/ten-ways-fight-hate-community-respons e-guide

Deardorff, D. K. (2020). *Manual for developing intercultural competencies: Story circles.* United Nations Scientific and Cultural Organization (UNESCO) and Routledge.

Dunbar-Ortiz, R. (2015). *An indigenous people's history of the United States.* Beacon Press.

Global Intercultural Circle Website. https://global-in-circle.org/

Lambach, R. (1996). What's in a name? In Seelye, H. N. (Ed.), *Experiential activities for intercultural learning, volume 1,* (p. 53). Intercultural Press.

Bios

In addition to being co-creators of the GIC, Christa Olson (christaleeolson@gmail.com) and Katharine Krebs (kkrebs@binghamton.edu) are both international education professionals.

Christa Olson, currently the Executive Director for Global Engagement at The College of New Jersey, develops global intercultural learning opportunities for faculty and students through international partnerships.

Katharine Krebs, retired from her position as Vice Provost for International Affairs at Binghamton University, currently researches intercultural communicative competence among recent college graduates.

Appendix 2: Intercultural Competence and Interculturality in Internationalization of Higher Education

A Brazilian Higher Education Institutional Perspective

Lourdes Evangelina Zilberberg Oviedo
Fundação Armando Alvares Penteado-FAAP, Brazil

ABSTRACT

This chapter presents the results of a study carried out in the Brazilian higher education system and aimed to analyze the contributions of the internationalization of higher education to the development of intercultural competence in students from the member institutions of FAUBAI- Associação Brasileira de Educação Internacional. The methodology used is the Mixed Methods Explanatory Sequential Study with qualitative predominance, which allowed combining initial questionnaires with semi-structured interviews. In both instances we worked with international office administrators and with students. The most relevant contribution of this project is its unprecedented approach to the study of intercultural competence, analyzed as an outcome of the process of internationalization of higher education. The main takeaways to the theory are the first local definitions of Intercultural Competence and of Interculturality, which were the result of a collective construction emerging from the feedback of the research participants.

Keywords: intercultural competence, interculturality, internationalization

INTRODUCTION

In the context of the internationalization of higher education, intercultural competence (IC) is presented as necessary. We inhabit a globalized, interdependent, and multicultural world whose challenges can be faced more efficiently by individuals who, in addition to technical skills, acquire a determined type of knowledge that allows for the production of creative solutions, as well as for the promotion of intercultural dialogue and international cooperation.

In an effort of conceptualization, Darla Deardorff carried out a Delphi study with specialists on the subject and administrators of Higher Education Institutions (HEIs) in the United States. For its relevance and originality, this work constitutes an important advance in the theory of internationalization of higher education and is the principal theoretical referent in this work (Deardorff, 2004).

In the Brazilian higher education system, scientific production has been centered on the analysis of the process of internationalization and its advances. One example is the survey undertaken by the Ministry of Education's *Coordenação de Aperfeiçoamento de Pessoal de Nível Superior* (Coordination for the Improvement of Higher Education Personnel – CAPES), which mapped the development of the internationalization of participating HEIs. This study concluded that the process of internationalization in these institutions is passive, since it is based on the sending of students and teachers abroad without promoting, to the same extent, the attraction of foreign students and professors to their respective campuses (CAPES, 2015).

Based on this reality and keeping prior research in mind, with the objective of contributing to the development of knowledge on the subject from a local perspective, this study is concerned with the contributions of the internationalization of higher education to the development of IC in students of the Brazilian higher education system.

The study population consists of member institutions of FAUBAI and covers the period between 2011 and 2017. Along with this general objective, the following specific objectives are addressed: determining the meaning and reach of IC in the processes of internationalization according to the representations of the international offices administrators and the students of participating HEIs; identifying the convergent and divergent points of these representations; and identifying and justifying the dimensions of the internationalization process that contribute on a wider scale to the development of IC, according to these same representations.

LITERATURE REVIEW

The literature analysis carried out in the initial stages of this research revealed that the concept of IC is generally presented as an outcome of internationalization of higher education (Deardorff, 2004). Moreover, there are also studies indicating that the set of these competences constitutes one of the reasons for internationalization. In both views there is a recursive relationship between internationalization and IC that was corroborated in this study (Knight, 2012).

Further to the proven correlation between both concepts, it is also relevant to mention that it has been laborious to come to a consensus about what terminology to use since Tewksbury introduced the concept of "intercultural person" in 1957. While some refer to competence in communication or intercultural communication, others refer to global competence or global mentality, global learning, cultural learning, intercultural effectiveness, education for democracy, cosmopolitan citizenship, globalizing knowledge, competence in global leadership, interculturality, and IC (Bennett, 2009; Schmidmeier & Takahashi, 2018).

In Latin America various researchers prefer to work with the concept of interculturality (Unesco, 2006; Guerrero Arias, 1999; De la Torre, 2006; Fornet-Bentancourt, 2009).

In an effort of conceptualization, Darla Deardorff carried out a Delphi study with specialists on the subject and administrators of HEIs in the US. For its relevance and originality, this work constitutes an important advance in the theory of internationalization of higher education and is the main theoretical reference in its area.

The most significant conclusion of the study was to determine the first consensual definition of IC, which came to be understood as "the ability to communicate efficiently and appropriately in intercultural situations based on one's intercultural knowledge, skills, and attitudes" (Deardorff, 2008 p. 33). According to the same study IC implies in a set of components categorized in 3 dimensions: knowledge, attitudes and abilities presented in the Table 1.

Table 1

IC Dimensions and Subdimensions framework

	Knowledge	Attitudes	Abilities (skills)
	About other countries and cultures	Openness Awareness	Practice of the Profession (experience)
	About the world	Identity	Organizational abilities
	About our own culture	Diversity	Technical skills
	About the globalized world	Acceptance	Effective interaction with
	Other language, effective communication	Tolerance Empathy	others (ethnorelative view) Teamwork skills
Intercultural Competence	Understanding the cultural concept	Respect Sensitivity	Creative thinking Observe
	Understanding diversity	Interaction	Analyze
	Understanding diverse perspectives		Question Critical judgment
	Understanding cultural patterns		Interact Adapt

Note. Based on Deardorff, 2004, 2008.

All aspects presented about IC were raised in the field research stage and served as a theoretical basis for the elaboration of the questionnaire and interviews.

RESEARCH METHOD

The research methodology used is the Mixed Methods Explanatory Sequential Study with qualitative predominance (Johnson, Onwuegbuzie & Turner, 2007, p. 124). The analysis of literature of the internationalization of higher education served as a base for the field study, in which quantitative techniques (initial questionnaires 1a and 1b sent to international office administrators and students recommended by them) were combined with qualitative techniques (semi-structured interviews conducted with international office administrators and students who participated voluntarily).

The research focused on the member institutions of FAUBAI (The Brazilian Association for International Education) during the period between 2011 and 2017. FAUBAI comprises 207 member institutions, showcasing a heterogeneous organization. Of the HEIs participating in the questionnaire, 44.07% are private (community or philanthropic and private), followed by federal public institutions (40.68%) and state public institutions (15.25%), with 74.58% being universities.

Within this framework, 59 international office administrators from Brazilian HEIs, representing 21 states and 43 cities, answered the initial questionnaire 1a, while 30 students from 11 states and 16 cities answered questionnaire 1b.

In the second part of the field study, semi-structured interviews were conducted with 20 international office administrators and 12 students. Subsequently, the preliminary results obtained from the field study were validated by 30 international office administrators who made a significant contribution to the research.

RESULTS

Among the main findings of the study what stands out is the fact that the process of internationalization, in most of the analyzed cases and, according to the research subjects themselves (77.59% of international office administrators and 82.76% of students), is established in a strategy included in the institutional plan.

One of the specific objectives of the research was to determine the meaning and the scope of IC in the internationalization processes. In this regard, it was observed that the international office administrators preferred to use the concept of IC (47%) and Interculturality (28.81%), while the students felt more familiar with Interculturality (31.3%) whereas IC came second with 20.69% of support. Given this result, we took the decision of working with both concepts, IC and Interculturality.

In addition, the concept of IC implies a set of knowledge, skills, and attitudes. In the Brazilian context of higher education, respect for other cultures, understanding cultural diversity, others' worldviews and disposition to intercultural learning are considered to be the most important competences for the development of IC.

Likewise, it was observed that internationalization contributes to the development of IC in students. HEIs, on implementing their processes of internationalization, establish their objectives and strategies and develop a vast range of activities. In this way, by including global, international, and intercultural dimensions in their functions, these HEIs create situations of initial connection, dialogue, and meaningful exchanges between cultures, which allows the development of IC.

On the other hand, certain dimensions of internationalization (understood as activities) contribute more than others to the development of IC. Dimensions that promote experiences of direct contact with other cultures generate more possibilities of acquiring IC. For example, student mobility, professional internships abroad, and the presence of foreign students on campus. These dimensions promote proximity, dialogue, and intercultural interaction.

To illustrate the weight of the different dimensions in the development of IC, we turn to Table 2 that shows the dimensions of internationalization, classified by the research subjects, according to the following criteria: does not contribute, contributes or contributes a lot. On a scale from 0 to 3, the table shows us the weighted averages of the responses of the international office administrators and students.

Table 2

Dimensions of internationalization according to their contribution to the development of IC

Dimensions	International relations administrators	Students	Results combination
Student Mobility (semester or year abroad)	2.9	2.8	2.85
Internships abroad	2.79	2.76	2.78
International students on campus	2.74	2.6	2.67
Curriculum internationalization (undergraduate and graduate courses)	2.58	2.67	2.63
Professors Mobility (field trips, research works and sabbaticals)	2.56	2.31	2.44
Academic Staff training in IC	2.54	2.6	2.57
Administrative staff training in IC	2.54	2.41	2.48
Program of visiting scholars on campus	2.53	2.37	2.45
Joint research projects with foreign institutions	2.49	2.72	2.61
Student mobility (short courses, up to six months)	2.46	2.34	2.40
Joint COIL-Collaborative Online International Learning programs with foreign institutions	2.39	2.38	2.39
Seminars, presentations, disciplines on campus and online about culture and IC	2.37	2.37	2.37
Contact with local communities based on cultural/ ethnics groups	2.37	2.63	2.50
Credit transfer and recognition	2.22	2.67	2.45

Note. Source the author based on Knight, 2012.

The relevant contribution of this project is its unprecedented approach to studying IC, analyzed as an outcome of the process of internationalization of higher education in Brazil. The main takeaways to the theory are the first local definitions of IC and of interculturality, which were the result of a collective construction emerging from the research subjects' feedback.

According to these research subjects, IC is "the set of skills and knowledge that the subject acquires or amplifies to be able to relate with people of different cultures, keeping respect, acceptance, and coexistence based on collaboration in mind." Definition approved by 67.65% of international relation administrators. Similarly, interculturality is "the relation between cultures who, in a process of rapprochement, based on respect and equality, look to construct spaces of coexistence and dialogue that permit the exchange of meanings and identities" (approved by 60% of international relation administrators).

DISCUSSION AND CONCLUSIONS

In an unprecedented approach to the study of IC, analyzed as an outcome of internationalization of higher education in Brazil, it was found that HEIs, by implementing these processes, establish their strategies and develop a wide range of activities. In this extent, by including the global, international and intercultural dimensions in their functions, they create situations of dialogue and exchange of meanings between cultures, facilitating the development of IC.

In addition, the research demonstrates that the concept of IC implies a set of knowledge, skills, and attitudes. In the Brazilian context of higher education, respect for other cultures and understanding cultural diversity are the competences considered to be the most important for the development of IC.

Conversely, there are particular dimensions of internationalization that have a more substantial impact on the development of intercultural competence (IC) than others. Dimensions that actively promote direct contact and interaction with diverse cultures create enhanced possibilities for skill acquisition.

These dimensions promote proximity, dialogue, and intercultural interaction. However, it is necessary to emphasize that dimensions that generate situations of experience or indirect contact with other cultures also contribute to the development of IC and should not be underestimated in the processes of internationalization.

Finally, it is pertinent to highlight that the results and conclusions of this study are limited to participating Brazilian HEIs. Thus, these results should not be analyzed as representative of the Brazilian higher education system or HEIs members of FAUBAI, given that the sample was not based on quantitative parameters. However, it should be noted that the exploratory nature of this study reveals the voice and vision of Brazilian HEIs that look to develop internationalization in higher education. Further studies must be undertaken to continue and strengthen the findings of this project.

REFERENCES

Bennett, J. M. (2009). Cultivating intercultural competence. A process perspective. In D. K. Deardorff (Ed.), *The SAGE handbook of intercultural competence* (pp. 121-140). Sage Publications.

CAPES. (2015). A internacionalização na universidade brasileira: Resultados do questionário aplicado pela CAPES. Retrieved from http://www.capes.gov.br/images/stories/download/diversos/A-internacionalizacao-nas-IES-brasileiras.pdf.

Deardorff, D. K. (2004). The identification and assessment of intercultural competence as a student outcome of internationalization at institutions of higher education in the United States [Doctoral dissertation, North Carolina State University]. Retrieved from https://repository.lib.ncsu.edu/ bitstream/handle/1840.16/5733/etd.pdf?sequence=1&isAllowed=y

Deardorff, D. K. (2008). Intercultural competence. In V. Savicki (Ed.), *Developing intercultural competence and transformation* (pp. 32-52). Stylus Publishing.

De la Torre, L. (2006). La interculturalidad desde la perspectiva del desarrollo socialy cultural. *Revista Sarance, 25*, 62-67. https://revistasarance.ioaotavalo. com.ec/index.php/revistasarance/article/view/308

Fornet-Bentancourt, R. (2009). De la importancia de la filosofía intercultural para la concepción y el desarrollo de nuevas políticas educativas en América Latina. In J. Viaña, L. Claros, J. Estermann, R. Fornet-Bentancourt, F. Garcés, V. H. Quintanilla & E. Ticona (Eds.), *Interculturalidad crítica y descolonización. Fundamentos para el debate* (pp. 171-181). IIII-CAB. Retrieved from http://www.ceapedi.com.ar/imagenes/biblioteca/libreria/309.pdf

Guerrero Arias, P. (1999). La interculturalidad solo será posible desde la insurgencia de la ternura. In C. Fernández- Salvador (Ed.), *Reflexiones sobre interculturalidad* (pp. 7-31). Abya-Yala.

Johnson, B. R., Onwuegbuzie, A. J. & Turner, L. A. (2007). Toward a definition of mixed methods research. *Journal of Mixed Methods Research. 1*(2), 112-133.

Knight, J. (2012). Concepts, rationales and interpretive frameworks in the internationalization of higher education. In D. K. Deardorff, H. De Wit, J. D. Heyl & T. Adams (Eds.). *The SAGE handbook of international higher education* (pp. 27-42). Sage Publications.

Schmidmeier, J. & Takahashi, A. R. W. (2018). Competência intercultural grupal: uma proposição de conceito. In *Cadernos EBAPE.BR 16*(1), 135-151. http://dx.doi.org/10.1590/1679-395159430

Tewksbury, D. G. (1957) The American Student and the Non-Western World. Harvard University Press.

UNESCO (2006). *UNESCO guidelines on intercultural education.* United Nations Educational, Scientific and Cultural Organization. Retrieved from https://unesdoc.unesco.org/ark:/48223/pf0000147878.

Bio

LOURDES EVANGELINA ZILBERBERG OVIEDO, PhD, Director of International Office and Local Director of the Business Confucius Institute at *Fundação Armando Alvares Penteado* (FAAP), Brazil. Lecturer of Global and Intercultural Competence. Her major research interests lie in the field of Internationalization of Higher Education, Policy and Management of Higher Education and Intercultural and Global Competence. E-mail: lourdes.oviedo.zilberberg@gmail.com

Appendix 3: The Quest for Globally Competent Human Resources in Japan

Ana Sofia Hofmeyr
Kansai University, Japan

ABSTRACT

In Japan, the concept of intercultural competence (IC) has been intimately linked to that of global human resources (GHR), a workforce capable of working across borders and cultures. In this context, IC is perceived as a tool to reach economic goals, and higher education (HE) as the primary means to foster interculturally and globally competent graduates. This chapter will first discuss how the role of IC has evolved parallel to Japan's historical relationships with other countries and cultures, culminating in the current notion of GHR. Second, the author will explore the central role of internationalization policies at the higher education level in the development of IC, particularly through foreign language education, study abroad programs, and virtual exchange. Finally, the author will discuss the challenges posed to the intentional and meaningful development of IC in Japan, namely conceptual limitations, a disconnect between policy and practice, and inadequate faculty training.

Keywords: global competence, global human resources, higher education, intercultural competence, internationalization, Japan

INTRODUCTION

The concept of global *jinzai*, commonly translated as "global human resources" (GHR), has become ubiquitous in policy documents at both governmental and educational levels in Japan. Officially defined in broad terms as those who possess "rich linguistic and communication skills and intercultural experiences, and thrive internationally" (CPHRGD, 2011, p.3), GHR has emerged from a growing demand for graduates who can deal with an interconnected world and who can strengthen the political and economic presence of Japan internationally (Chapple, 2014). Further expanded by the Japan Business Federation as "Japanese or foreign talent who are able to take on the burden of globalising Japanese companies' business activities and take an active part in global business" (Keidanren, 2011, as cited in Burgess, 2014, p.494), the concept of GHR emphasizes many of the components associated with intercultural competence (IC) in Japan (Hofmeyr, 2021).

Originally emerging from the changing needs of Japanese corporations (Yoshida, 2017), the GHR concept has permeated policy at the tertiary level, and universities are tasked with fostering interculturally competent graduates with foreign language skills who can be the driving force behind Japan's economic growth. As Japan faces a declining birthrate, a shortage of skilled labour, and growing global competition, IC as a key component of GHR is approached by the Japanese Ministry of Education, Culture, Sports, Science and Technology (MEXT) as a practical tool to reach economic goals.

This chapter will begin by exploring the changing role of IC in Japan, leading to the current notion of GHR. Second, we will discuss the role of internationalization strategies at the tertiary level in fostering GHR, particularly as regards foreign language education, study abroad, and virtual exchange. Finally, we will consider three major obstacles to the meaningful development of IC in the Japanese context – conceptual limitations, a disconnect between theory and practice, and inadequate faculty training.

THE CHANGING ROLE OF INTERCULTURAL COMPETENCE IN JAPAN

In very broad terms, the international relationships between Japan and other countries have historically been brought on by Japan's desire to boost economic growth and characterized by an interest in borrowing from foreign cultures rather than in intercultural interaction (Inuzuka, 2017). In fact, Japan's first contact with Western nations in the 16th century was guided by a desire to trade. However, fears that Western countries were also attempting to exert a strong cultural influence on Japanese society led the government to close the borders and to restrict international contact (the Sakoku period).

When Japan was forced to reopen its doors to the United States in 1868, it began a large-scale modernization process known as Westernization (Inuzuka, 2017), leading to increased demand for foreign language education to access Western knowledge and technology (Kariya, 2018). The grammar-translation method, historically adopted by Japan, encouraged language learning with limited intercultural interaction beyond what was deemed necessary for economic and political purposes.

With intensified globalization from the 1970s and a period of large economic growth in the 1980s and 1990s, Japan witnessed an increase in the number of foreign nationals and in the need to internationalize education. Nevertheless, internationalization in Japan has remained a patriotic endeavour, designed to build up Japan as a nation (Inuzuka, 2017).

The term "global *jinzai*", or GHR, first emerged in the business context. Yoshida (2017) explains that the term was originally used to denote "a new type of employee who is hired by a Japanese company as its business expands overseas, and an employee who is different from traditional types of employees" (p.84). Due to the role of Japanese universities in preparing graduates for the job market, higher education institutions (HEIs) became central to the development of GHR.

In 2011, an interim report published by The Council on Promotion of Human Resource for Globalization Development (p.7) defined GHR as workers with:

Factor I: Linguistic and communication skills;

Factor II: Self-direction and positiveness, a spirit for challenge, cooperativeness and flexibility, asense of responsibility and mission;

Factor III: Understanding of other cultures and a sense of identity as a Japanese.

This definition, which included not only language skills but also the ability to understand other cultures, would become central to large internationalization projects developed and funded by the government (Yoshida, 2017). However, later attempts to assess the outcomes of these projects were made difficult by the broadness of the term, leading both the government and HEIs to misguidedly focus on numerical indicators as a proxy for successful internationalization (Shimmi & Yonezawa, 2015). Recent studies aiming to define GHR more concretely have found that stakeholders often emphasize a wide range of elements, including openness to other cultures, foreign language skills, cultural awareness, and critical thinking (Hofmeyr, 2021; Sakamoto, 2022).

IC THROUGH INTERNATIONALIZATION POLICIES

Internationalization policies began being implemented in Japan from the mid-19th century, but it was only from the late 2000s that system reform was deemed necessary to cultivate GHR, leading to the funding and implementation of internationalization strategies top-down through projects such as the Global 30 (2009–2014), the Go Global Japan (2012–2017), and the Top Global University Project (2014–2023).

Even though GHR remains one of the most significant products of internationalization strategies in Japan, IC does not generally appear as a primary goal of these efforts in HEIs (Whitsed & Volet, 2011). Nevertheless, government-funded programs have emphasized the need to cultivate GHR with an international outlook, particularly through the expansion of English language education and the increase in the number of Japanese students who go abroad. In recent years, with the drop in student mobility aggravated by a global pandemic, virtual exchange also emerged as a viable alternative to outbound mobility programs.

Foreign Language Education

Seeing that the concept of GHR has emerged from Japan's perceived necessity to increase its economic competitiveness in the global arena, improved foreign language ability, particularly English as the de facto language of international communication, has become central to MEXT's policies (Aspinall, 2013). Having become a required subject in elementary school from 2020, most Japanese students will have spent eight to ten years learning English by the time they graduate from university.

Historically, foreign languages have been taught through the grammar-translation process, thus allowing Japanese scholars to access vast amounts of written knowledge despite limited intercultural contact. However, as companies aim to recruit employees with practical English abilities, the shift has moved from a reading-centric to a communication-centric curriculum (Horie, 2019). Efforts have also been made to expose Japanese students to people from other cultures, notably through the Japan Exchange and Teaching (JET) Program. Nevertheless, concerns remain that linguistic skills are perceived as the primary solution for global communication (Sakamoto, 2022), that intercultural content is addressed only superficially in foreign language classrooms (Hofmeyr, 2022), and that languages other than English are excluded from the national curriculum (Chapple, 2014).

Study Abroad Programs and Virtual Exchange

The relationship between internationalization, study abroad programs and IC has been thoroughly researched. In general, studies have shown that study abroad programs can be effective in developing intercultural and global competence, particularly when lasting longer than six months and when students become more deeply involved with the host culture (Dwyer, 2004; Hanada, 2019).

In Japan, internationalization projects such as the Global 30 and the Top Global University Project have strongly encouraged outbound student mobility as the principal means to foster an intercultural mindset. Chapple (2014, p.216) explains that "[there] seems to be an overwhelming feeling that by sending students abroad such talent can be fostered; it is not something that can be easily nurtured domestically. This most likely stems from the fact that multiculturalism is seen as something that exists in other settings (rarely in Japan) and therefore the required special skills can only be fostered overseas."

The reliance on mobility to foster intercultural understanding has been hindered, however, by a drop in the number of Japanese students going abroad since the early 2000s (Yonezawa, 2014). To address this issue, the government has started to promote very short study abroad programs, lasting anything from two weeks to three months, though researchers question whether these can be effective in fostering an intercultural mindset (Hanada, 2019; Yoshida, 2017).

With the global pandemic that assailed the world in 2020, there was a sudden shift to virtual exchange as the means to encounter and communicate with other cultures. While virtual exchange initiatives, and the positive effects of intentional intercultural collaborative projects, had been advocated prior to 2020, the pandemic provided Japanese universities with the first major opportunity to explore virtual programs. Overall, research studies suggest that virtual exchange has the potential to increase students' confidence on their ability to interact interculturally (Chu et al., 2022), and global mindedness (Deacon & Miles, 2022), and it may prove to be an attractive alternative for those students who are unable to study abroad.

CHALLENGES TO MEANINGFUL IC DEVELOPMENT

While the Japanese government is to some extent attempting to cultivate interculturally competent GHR, the strategies under implementation face serious challenges. First, the concept of GHR is broad and conflicting, intensifying difficulties reaching specific outcomes. Second, there is a strong disconnect between policy and the implementation of programs that aim to foster

GHR at the ground level. Finally, though HE is perceived as the main means to foster GHR in preparation for the job market, there is very little to no faculty training to support the students.

Conceptual limitations

One of the main challenges to the development of interculturally competent GHR are limitations to the attitudes, knowledge, and skills associated with GHR. First, at the policy level, English communicative ability remains at the core of GHR (Horie; 2019), while other foreign languages and elements are repeatedly downplayed. Admittedly, from the three factors of GHR proposed by the government (CPHRGD, 2011), foreign language ability is the easiest to assess quantitatively. However, researchers warn of the danger of seeing English communication as a goal rather than as the means to understanding culture (Horie, 2019) and to discuss global issues with people from other cultures (Yoshida, 2017).

Moreover, English language education in Japan is still very much associated with images of European-looking native speakers of English (Simmons & Chen, 2017). As a result, communication differences are often downplayed in Japan in favour of a "Western" approach that requires students to be outspoken and assertive. Sakamoto (2022, p.222) warns that "Global competence is about respecting and navigating diversity, not minimizing or eliminating it, and that means appreciating and accommodating different communication styles too".

Finally, although the Japanese government proposed GHR as a seemingly outward-looking concept (Chapple, 2014), the Interim report on GHR (CPHRGD, 2011), asks not only for an "understanding of other cultures", but also "a sense of identity as a Japanese". Hashimoto (2000) argues that internationalization in Japan is actually "Japanisation". Inuzuka (2017) explains that from a governmental perspective, "Presumably, students who are well-grounded in their own culture are less likely to be influenced by foreign cultures" (p.216), mirroring the historical tendency of Japan to understand other cultures as something to explore from the outside. Consequently, while the concept of GHR aims, on the surface, to encourage graduates to embrace intercultural interaction, the debate to accept greater diversity within is overshadowed, effectively hindering the development of an interculturally competent workforce.

Disconnect between theory and practice

A second obstacle to the development of interculturally competent graduates is the gap between the theoretical framework supporting GHR and the implementation of relevant and effective strategies at the tertiary level. One of the reasons for this gap is the focus on quantitative targets as a proxy for internationalization, which have repeatedly been subject to criticism and identified as a cause for concern (Shimmi & Yonezawa, 2015). By contrast, there is a general lack of agreement regarding the attitudes, knowledge, and skills associated with GHR other than foreign language skills (Hofmeyr, 2021), creating further obstacles to the fostering of GHR through internationalization.

Another reason for this gap is the contradictory emphasis placed on both a national identity, to be firmly retained, and a global identity, to be pursued for economic purposes. In fact, while the Japanese government and universities have made efforts to internationalize on the surface, these are not necessarily fuelled by an appreciation of cultural diversity (Inuzuka, 2017) or by an interest in cosmopolitanism (Aspinall, 2013). English is perceived as both necessary to economic growth and as a threat to national identity (Simmons & Chen, 2017), with high proficiency marking the speaker as someone who no longer is "authentically" Japanese (Aspinall, 2013). Similarly, though study abroad programs are considered to be a gateway to intercultural experiences, these are increasingly shorter in duration. Universities that genuinely aim to cultivate interculturally competent GHR will likely need to bypass the emphasis placed on numerical targets and rather focus on the quality of intercultural contact.

Inadequate faculty training

One final major challenge to the development of interculturally competent GHR is the shortage of adequately trained faculty to support students. This problem has been pointed out by researchers who discuss the resistance among many teachers educated in Japan to develop more global awareness and experience (Chapple, 2014). In addition, while intercultural and global competence education is often perceived as the responsibility of foreign faculty, courses often focus on foreign language proficiency, which is not sufficient for the cultivation of GHR (Sakamoto, 2022).

CONCLUSIONS AND IMPLICATIONS

To conclude, Japan's historical attempts to successfully navigate complex political, economic, and social relations with other countries has culminated in the current notion of GHR – graduates with the ability to work and interact across cultures. With this goal in mind, the Japanese government has tasked HEIs with fostering interculturally competent graduates, mainly through the implementation and development of foreign language education and study abroad programs.

Despite continuous efforts, however, internationalization as the means to cultivate GHR is still closely linked to quantitative targets. The emphasis placed on numbers and scores rather than on the depth of intercultural experiences appears to serve a purpose – that of protecting Japanese national identity while increasing Japan's economic power globally. In this sense, Japan's historical approach to intercultural relations has changed very little in the past 400 years. For Japan to move forward in its quest for an interculturally and globally competent workforce, intentional and meaningful change must occur at both policy and implementation levels.

REFERENCES

Aspinall, R. W. (2013). *International education policy in Japan in an age of globalisation and risk*. Global Oriental.

Burgess, C. (2014). To globalise or not to globalise? 'Inward-looking youth' as scapegoats for Japan's failure to secure and cultivate 'global human resources.' *Globalisation, Societies and Education, 13*(4), 487–507. https://doi.org/10.1080/14767724.2014.966805

Chapple, J. (2014). "Global Jinzai," Japanese higher education, and the path to multiculturalism: Imperative, imposter, or immature? In K. Shimizu & W. S. Brady (Eds.), *Multiculturalism and conflict reconciliation in the Asia-Pacific* (pp. 213–228). Palgrave Macmillan.

Chu, C. S. S., Hooper, T., Takahashi, M., & Michael, H. (2022). Would participating in asynchronous virtual exchange affect intercultural communicative competence among undergraduate students? *2022 International Conference on Open and Innovative Education*. Hong Kong.

Deacon, B., & Miles, R. (2022). Assessing the impact of a virtual short-term study-abroad program on Japanese university students' global-mindedness. *Journal of Virtual Exchange, 5*, 155–175. https://doi.org/10.21827/jve.5.38652

Dwyer, M. M. (2004). More is better: The impact of study abroad program duration. *Frontiers: The Interdisciplinary Journal of Study Abroad, 10*(1), 151–164. https://doi.org/10.36366/frontiers.v10i1.139

CPHRGD [The Council on Promotion of Human Resource for Globalization Development]. (2011). *An interim report of the council on promotion of human resource for globalization development.*

Hanada, S. (2019). A quantitative assessment of Japanese students' intercultural competence developed through study abroad programs. *Journal of International Students, 9*(4), 1015–1037. https://doi.org/10.32674/jis.v9i4.391

Hashimoto, K. (2000). 'Internationalisation' is 'Japanisation': Japan's foreign language education and national identity. *Journal of Intercultural Studies, 21*(1), 39–51. https://doi.org/10.1080/07256860050000786

Hofmeyr, A. S. (2021). Rethinking the concept of global human resources in the Japanese higher education context. *Asia Pacific Journal of Education*, 1–17. https://doi.org/10.1080/02188791.2021.1889970

Hofmeyr, A. S. (2022). Japanese university student responses to intercultural scenarios: Contact strategies and perceptions of otherness. *International Journal of Intercultural Relations, 90*, 73–85. https://doi.org/10.1016/j.ijintrel.2022.07.008

Horie, K. (2019). Building intracultural knowledge through English education: An essential quality for global human resources. *The Studies in Economics and Trade (Kanagawa University Annual Bulletin), 45*, 29–36.

Inuzuka, A. (2017). A dialectic between nationalism and multiculturalism: An analysis of the internationalization discourse in Japan. In S. Toyosaki & S. Eguchi (Eds.), *Intercultural communication in Japan: Theorizing homogenizing discourse* (pp. 207–223). Routledge.

Kariya, T. (2018). Meritocracy, modernity, and the completion of catch-up: Problems and paradoxes. In A. Yonezawa, Y. Kitamura, B. Yamamoto, & T. Tokunaga (Eds.), *Japanese education in a global age: sociological reflections and future directions* (pp. 287–306). Springer.

Sakamoto, F. (2022). Global competence in Japan: What do students really need? *International Journal of Intercultural Relations, 91*, 216–228. https://doi.org/10.1016/j.ijintrel.2022.10.006

Shimmi, Y., & Yonezawa, A. (2015). Japan's "top global university" project. *International Higher Education, 81*, 27–28. https://doi.org/10.6017/ihe.2015.81.8742

Simmons, N., & Chen, Y.-W. (2017). "I never wanted to be famous": pushes and pulls of Whiteness through the eyes of foreign English language teachers in Japan. In S. Toyosaki & S. Eguchi (Eds.), *Intercultural communication in Japan: Theorizing homogenizing discourse* (pp. 224–237). Routledge.

Whitsed, C., & Volet, S. (2011). Fostering the intercultural dimensions of internationalisation in higher education: Metaphors and challenges in the Japanese context. *Journal of Studies in International Education, 15*(2), 146–170. https://doi.org/10.1177/1028315309357941

Yonezawa, A. (2014). Japan's challenge of fostering "global human resources": Policy debates and practices. *Japan Labor Review, 14*(2), 37–52.

Yoshida, A. (2017). 'Global human resource development' and Japanese university education: 'Localism' in actor discussions. *Educational Studies in Japan, 11*, 83–99. https://doi.org/10.7571/esjkyoiku.11.83

Bio

ANA SOFIA HOFMEYR, PhD, is an Associate Professor at the Faculty of Foreign Language Studies, Kansai University, Japan. Her major research interests lie conceptualizations of intercultural competence and the development of intercultural competence through internationalization-at-home strategies. Email: hofmeyr@kansai-u.ac.jp

Also supported by

Humane Letters Grant

KEEP FREE THINKING ALIVE

ChatGPT and Global Higher Education

Using Artificial Intelligence in Teaching and Learning

Xi Lin, Roy Y. Chan, Shyam Sharma, Krishna Bista

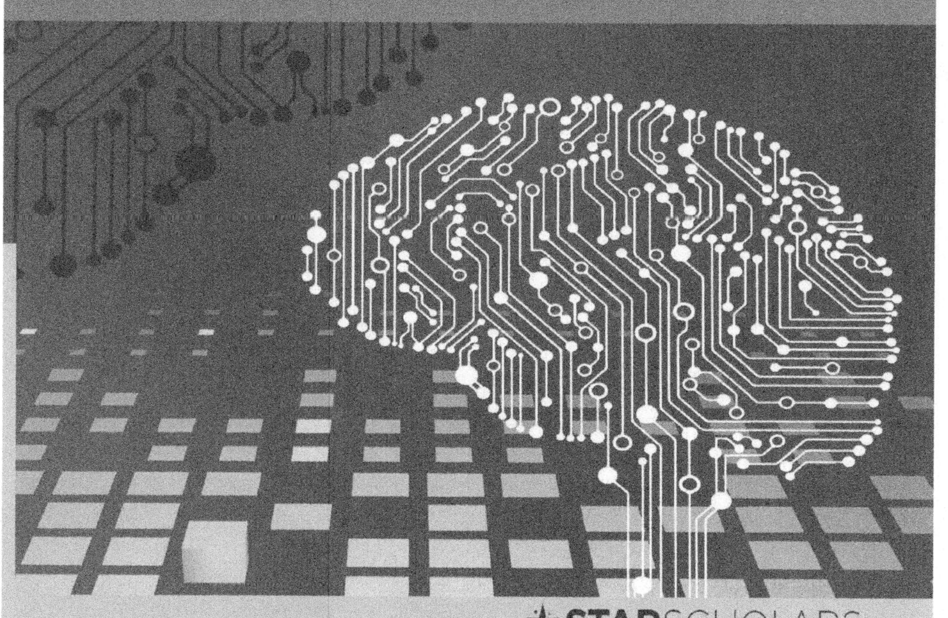

The International Handbook of

French Education

Editors

Jerry L. Parker and Amany Saleh

Made in the USA
Coppell, TX
10 June 2024

33348701R00118